F1 Get the Most out of Excel Formulas & Functions

The Ultimate Excel Formulas & Functions Help Guide

F1 Get the Most out of Excel Formulas & Functions

The Ultimate Excel Formulas & Functions Help Guide

Written by: Joseph Rubin, CPA

Published by: Limelight Media Inc.
               3402 Motor Ave.
               Los Angeles, CA USA 90034
               sales@limelightmediainc.com
               www.limelightmediainc.com

Distributed by: Limelight Media Inc.

First printing: November 2005,

Second printing: May 2006, Printed in the state of India

Library of Congress Control Number (LCCN): 2005905906

ISBN: 9780974636856

Trademarks:
All brand names and product names used in this book are trade names, service marks, trademarks, or registered trade marks of their respective owners. Limelight Media Inc. is not associated with any product or vendor mentioned in this book.

About The Author

Joseph Rubin, CPA, principal of **www.exceltip.com** (a leading Excel Web site) is the author of the very successful books:

- *F1 Get the Most out of Excel!*

  The Ultimate Excel Tip Help Guide

- *Financial Statements.xls*

  A Step by Step Guide on Creating Financial Statements

  Using Microsoft Excel

- *Mr Excel On Excel*

Joseph Rubin has over 27 years of financial experience in the accounting industry. He has served as CFO, Controller and has run his own CPA practice for many years. Joseph Rubin, CPA, is an independent consultant specializing in the development of applications using Microsoft Excel for the financial industry and has instructed thousands of professionals on Microsoft Excel.

Contact the author - jrubin@exceltip.com

This book is dedicated to my family, my wife, and my three children.

Thanks to

Yael Schneebaum

Chris Tobin

Sara Amihud

Without them this book would never have been born.

Thanks to Excel Gurus

Iki Sapoznik

Ido Ben-Horin

Joseph Rubin, CPA

How to Use this Resource Effectively

In the Book

Use the Table of Contents at the front of the book and the Index at the back to find the topic you are looking for.

Each topic (Q&A) in the book contains the following parts:

- Title

- Problem

- Solution

- Screenshot

- Explanation

In Excel workbooks on the CD-ROM

- All the formula solutions presented in the book are included in Excel workbook files.

On the Internet

- All the formula solutions presented in the book have been entered into the www.exceltip.com database. To discuss a specific formula, visit www.exceltip.com/fx- & the page number in the book. For example, if you want to discuss a formula from page 100, type the following URL into your browser: www.exceltip.com/fx-100.

Contents at a Glance

Table of Contents

Chapter 7   Summing... 289

Chapter 1

Working With Formulas

About This Chapter

This chapter contains fundamentals, shortcuts, tips, and techniques that are essential when working with Formulas & Functions. It includes the following sections:

☞ **Inserting, Editing, & Copying Formulas, page 2:** This section covers easy techniques on inserting, editing, and copying formulas, understanding the correct use of relative/absolute references, and creating power formulas.

☞ **Selecting, Displaying, Printing & Pasting Formulas, page 7:** In this section you will find techniques on displaying formula syntax, displaying formulas and values, selecting cells containing formulas, pasting values, adding comments to formulas, and printing formula syntax.

☞ **Array Formulas, page 12:** This section provides an explanation of the concept of an *Array* and how Excel uses *Arrays* in formulas, You will also learn how to create an *Array* formula.

☞ **Using Range Names in Formulas, page 13**: In this section, learn about range name rules, how to define range names, and how to use range Names in formulas.

☞ **Auditing Formulas, page 16**: In this section, find essential shortcuts and techniques on tracing and moving between precedent and dependent cells, stepping into formulas, and tracing errors in a formula.

☞ **Protecting Formulas, page 22:** In this section, you will learn how to protect formulas in both protected and unprotected sheets.

Inserting, Editing, & Copying Formulas

Inserting/Editing Formulas

➢ **To open the Insert Function dialog box:**

Select an empty cell and press <**Shift+F3**>.

➢ **To open a Function Arguments dialog box:**

Select a cell containing a formula and press <**Shift+F3**>.

➢ **To insert a new Formula into a cell using the Function Arguments dialog box:**

1. Select an empty cell, and then type the = sign.

2. Type the formula name and press <**Ctrl+A**>.

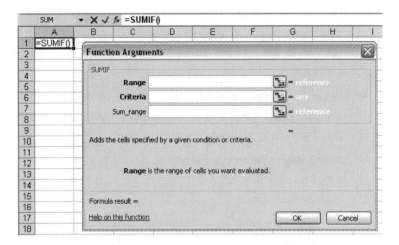

➢ **To insert a formula by typing it while being guided by the formula syntax tooltip:**

1. Select an empty cell, and then type the = sign followed by the formula name and a left parenthesis, i.e. (.

2. Press <**Ctrl+Shift+A**> (in Excel version 2003 the syntax appears immediately after step 1 above).

SUM	▾ ✕ ✓ *fx* =sumif(			
	A	B	SUMIF(**range**, criteria, [sum_range])	F
1	=sumif(			
2				
3				

Nesting Formulas

A formula can be copied and pasted into the appropriate place within another formula in the *Formula Bar* by using the <**Ctrl+C**> and <**Ctrl+V**> keyboard shortcuts.

➢ **To combine Formulas into one long nested power Formula:**

1. Insert the following formula into a cell:
   =SUMIF(TB_DB_Level3,A12,G12)

2. Insert the following formula into an adjacent cell:
   =OFFSET(TB_DB_Level3,0,MonthSelectionNumber+2)

3. In the *Formula Bar* of the second formula, select the formula without the = sign, and then press <**Ctrl+C**>.

4. Click **Cancel** or **Enter** (the two buttons between the *Name Box* and the formula in the *Formula Bar*) to exit edit mode.

5. Select the cell containing the first formula, and in the *Formula Bar*, select the reference G12, and then press <**Ctrl+V**>.

	A	B	C	D	E	F
	File Edit View Insert Format Tools Data Window Help					
	C12 ▼ *fx* =SUMIF(TB_DB_Level3,A12,OFFSET(TB_DB_Level3,0,MonthSelectionNumber+2))					
1						
2	December 31, 2003 ▼					
3						
4	XYZ Corporation Inc.					
5	BALANCE SHEET					
6						
7			December 31			
8		Notes	2003	2002		
9	ASSETS					
10						
11	Current Assets					
12	Cash	5	301,124	318,697		
13	Accounts Receivable	7	1,653,558	1,538,494		
14	Inventories	8	546,173	520,133		
15	Prepaid Expenses	9	13,552	23,659		
16	Total Current Assets		2,514,407	2,400,982		

Changing an Absolute Reference to a Relative Reference or Vice Versa

☞ **Relative Reference**

When a formula is copied, a *Relative* reference is used. A *Relative* reference is the distance, in rows and columns, between the reference and the cell containing the formula.

Example:

In cell A1, type the number 100, and in cell B1, type the formula =A1. Cell B1 is one column to the right of cell A1. When the formula is copied from cell B1 to cell B10, the distance between the reference and the cell containing the formula remains one column, and the formula in cell B10 is =A10.

☞ **Absolute Reference**

Select cell B1 from the previous example. In the *Formula Bar*, select A1, and then press <**F4**>. The result is =$A$1.

Copy the contents of cell B1 to cell B10. Notice that the formula does not change — the formula reference remains constant as =$A$1.

☞ **The <F4> Key**

The <**F4**> keyboard shortcut has four states:

State 1: *Absolute* reference to the column and row, =$A$1

State 2: *Relative* reference (column) and *Absolute* reference (row), =A$1

State 3: *Absolute* reference (column) and *Relative* reference (row), =$A1

State 4: *Relative* reference to the column and row, =A1

Copying a Formula from a Cell While Keeping the Absolute Reference or Relative Reference

Avoid the nightmare of pressing <**F4**> multiple times when coping and pasting formulas.

➢ **To copy/paste a Formula without changing the Absolute or Relative references:**

Option 1: Select a cell under the cell containing a formula and press <**Ctrl+ '**>.

Option 2: Copy and paste the formula from the *Formula Bar* to a cell, instead of from *a cell to another cell*.

Example, cell **C12** contains a formula:

1. Select the formula string in the *Formula Bar* and press <**Ctrl+C**> to copy it.

2. Leave the *Formula Bar* by clicking the **Enter** or **Cancel** icons to the left of the *fx* on the *Formula Bar*.

3. Select another cell and press <**Ctrl+V**>.

		A	B	C	D	E	F
	File Edit View Insert Format Tools Data Window Help						
	SUM ▾ ✗ ✓ *fx* =SUMIF(TB_DB_Level3,A12,OFFSET(TB_DB_Level3,0,MonthSelectionNumber+2))						
1							
2	December 31, 2003 ▼						
3							
4		XYZ Corporation Inc.					
5		BALANCE SHEET					
6							
7				December 31			
8			Notes	2003	2002		
9	ASSETS						
10							
11	Current Assets						
12	Cash		5	tionNumber+2))	318,697		
13	Accounts Receivable		7	1,653,558	1,538,494		
14	Inventories		8	546,173	520,133		
15	Prepaid Expenses		9	13,552	23,659		
16	Total Current Assets			2,514,407	2,400,982		

Copying Formulas from a Range of Cells without Changing the Absolute or Relative References

➤ To copy/paste Formulas from a range of cells without changing the Absolute or Relative references:

1. Select the range of cells containing the formulas and press <**Ctrl+H**>.

2. In the *Find what* box, type the = sign.

3. In the *Replace with* box, type the # symbol (to change the formulas to text).

4. Click *Replace All,* and then click **Close**.

5. Copy and paste the cells to a new location.

6. Repeat steps 1 through 3, reversing the # and = signs (to change the text to formulas).

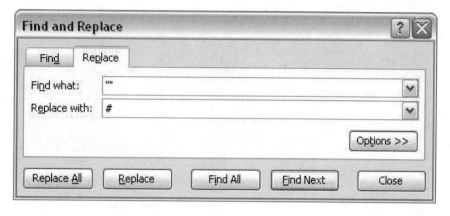

Selecting, Displaying, Printing, & Pasting Formulas

Displaying Formula Syntax

➢ **To display the syntax of all formulas in a sheet:**

❖ Press <**Ctrl+'**> (the ' symbol is located to the left of the number 1 on the keyboard).

OR

From the *Tools* menu, select *Options*, the *View* tab, *Formulas*, and then click **OK**.

❖ To return to the normal display, press <**Ctrl+'**> again (this keyboard shortcut is a toggle).

Regular display:

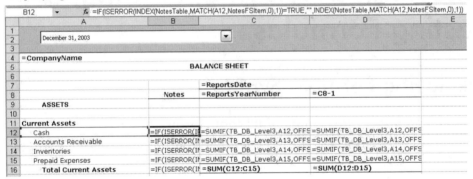

Displaying Formulas:

Displaying Both Formulas and Values for Cells

➤ **To display both formulas and values for cells:**

1. From the *Window* menu, select *New Window*.

2. From the *Window* menu, select *Arrange*.

3. Select the *Horizontal* option button and click **OK**.

4. Select one of the two windows and press **<Ctrl+'>** (the key to the left of the number 1).

To move between windows, press **<Ctrl+Tab>** or **<Ctrl+F6>**.

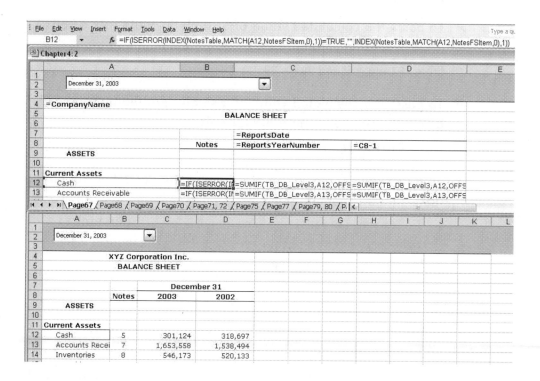

Selecting Cells That Contain Formulas

➢ To select cells containing Formulas in order to color, delete, or protect, use the Go To dialog box:

1. Press **<F5>**.

   OR

   From the *Edit* menu, select *Go To*.

2. In the *Go To* dialog box, click *Special*.

3. Select *Formulas*, and then click **OK**.

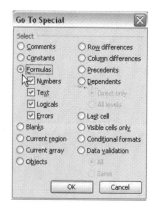

Pasting Values

➢ **To paste the calculated value of a single formula into a cell (thus overwriting the formula):**

Press <**F2**> to edit and then <**F9**> to calculate.

➢ **To paste the calculated value of a single formula into the cell below the cell containing the formula:**

Press <**Ctrl+Shift+"**>.

➢ **To paste values in a range of cells, use the Paste Special dialog box:**

1. Copy a range of cells containing formulas, press <**Shift+F10**> or right-click, and then select *Paste Special* from the shortcut menu.

2. Select *Values* and click **OK**.

➢ **Use the Paste Values Icon:**

Add the *Paste Values* icon from the *Edit* category in the *Customize* dialog box.

➢ **New in Excel 2002 and Excel 2003**

The *Paste* icon has been expanded, enabling some options from the *Paste Special* dialog box to be quickly accessed.

Adding a Comment to a Formula

> ## To add a Comment to a formula:

1. At the end of the formula, add a + (plus) sign.

2. Type the letter N, and, in parentheses, type your Comment in quotation marks.

Example:

=CurrentAssets / CurrentLiabilities+ N("The formula returns Current Ratio")

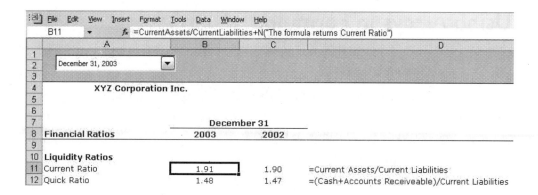

Printing Formula Syntax

> ## To print the formula syntax for a range of cells:

1. Display the formula syntax by pressing **<Ctrl+'>** (the key to the left of the number 1).

2. Print the desired area.

Array Formulas

Understanding Arrays

For those who do not have a background in programming or mathematics, the expression *Array* may not be familiar.

So what exactly is an *Array?*

For our purposes, an *Array* is simply a set of values which can be stored in a formula, a range of cells, or the computer's memory.

The size of an *Array* can range from two to thousands of values.

Using Arrays in Formulas

There are several different types of *Arrays* used by Excel when working with formulas:

☞ An *Array* stored in a Worksheet in a range of cells: For example, when the **SUM** function sums the values stored in range of cells, it is treating those values as an *Array.*

☞ An *Array* stored in a formula:

Instead of entering cell addresses to enable a formula to operate on the values stored in those locations, you may enter an *Array* of values into the **SUM** function arguments: =SUM(1,2,3,4,5).

OR

Enter an *Array* enclosed in brackets into the formula argument. For example, use the **MATCH** function to return the position of the number 10 in an *Array* of values: =MATCH(10,{3,7,10,15,20}). The result = 3

☞ Excel formulas create *Arrays* to store values:

Formulas such as **SUMPRODUCT** utilize computer memory to store values temporarily while calculating complicated math problems. These values are stored in an *Array.*

Example:

To add the total sales amount of 3 items when the quantities sold are 10, 20, and 30 and the sale prices are $3, $4, and $5 respectively, the **SUMPRODUCT** formula stores each multiplication product in an *Array* (*Array* size is 3) and then adds the three values from the *Array*.

The **SUMPRODUCT** formula: =SUMPRODUCT(A1:A3,B1:B3), Result - total sales=$260.

☞ Let Excel create an *Array formula*:

As explained in the previous section, many formulas create *Arrays* when they need to store values during calculations. However, an Excel user may create a formula that deliberately enforces the program to open an *Array/Arrays* to store values.

Example:

Use the **SUM** function to return total sales (see previous example). The formula will now look like this: {=SUM(A1:A3*B1:B3)}, Result- total sales=$260.

To apply an *Array formula*:

Enter the formula, select the cell, press <**F2**>, and then simultaneously press <**Ctrl+Shift+Enter**>.

Using Range Names in Formulas

Range Name Syntax

Name syntax rules:

☞ The *Name* string must begin with a text character, not a number, and consists of adjacent characters.

☞ Two words can be joined with an underscore (_). For example, to enter the Name "Excel Book", you should type Excel_Book.

☞ You cannot use a *Name* that could otherwise be used as a cell reference. For example, A1 or IS2002.

Notes:

☞ There is no limit on the number of *Names* you can define.

☞ Be sure to define unique *Names* for a specific workbook. Defining *Names* that resemble *Names* in other sheets will only complicate your work.

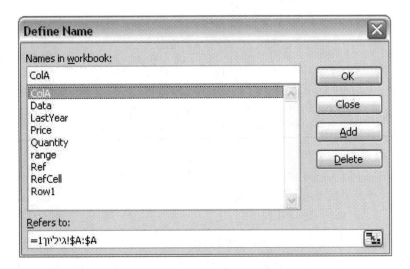

Defining a Range Name

➢ **To define a range Name, use one of the following two techniques:**

☞ **Type the text directly into the Name box**

1. Select cell A1.

2. In the *Name* box, type the text, and then press <**Enter**>.

☞ **Define a Name using the Define Name dialog box**

1. Select cell B1.

2. Press <**Ctrl+F3**>.

   OR

   From the *Insert* menu, select *Name* and then *Define*.

3. Type the text in the *Names in workbook* box, and then click **OK**.

Deleting a Range Name

Why it is highly recommended to delete unnecessary range Names:

☞ Large numbers of range *Names* makes it more difficult to locate a specific *Name*.

☞ Range *Names* create references and unwanted links.

➢ **To find unnecessary/unwanted range Names:**

1. Select a cell in a new sheet.

2. Press **<F3>** and click *Paste List*. A full list of range names and their references is pasted into the new sheet; delete each unwanted *Name*.

➢ **To delete a range Name:**

Press **<Ctrl+F3>**, select the *Name*, and then click **Delete**.

Using a Range Name in a Formula

➢ **To use a range Name in a formula:**

1. Define the following range *Names* for ranges B2:B11, C2:C11, and D2:D11 respectively: Jan_2004, Feb_2004, and Mar_2004 (see the screenshot below).

2. Select a cell and type the formula =SUM.

3. Press **<Ctrl+A>**.

4. Select the first argument box and press **<F3>**.

5. Select the *Name* Jan_2004, and then click **OK**.

6. Paste the *Names* Febr_2004 and Mar_2004 in the next two argument boxes, and then click **OK**. The following formula has now been inserted into the cell:

=SUM(Jan_2004, Feb_2004, Mar_2004)

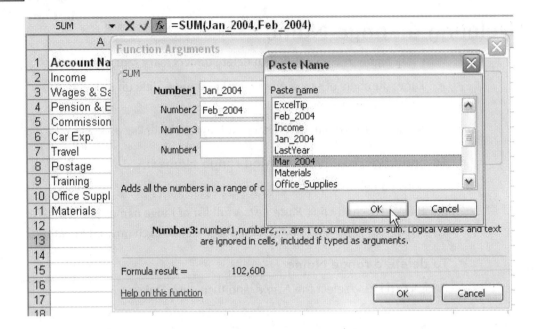

Auditing Formulas

Moving Between Precedent and Dependent Cells

➢ **To move to a precedent cell(s):**

Select a cell containing a formula and press **<Ctrl+[>**.

❖ The **<Ctrl+[>** shortcut is one of the most important keyboard shortcuts, and is highly recommended.

It can trace a precedent cell(s) in the active sheet, in another sheet in the workbook, in a sheet in another open workbook, and it can even open a closed workbook and select the precedent cell(s) after opening.

➤ **To Add three icons to the Standard toolbar**

❖ Trace Precedents

❖ Trace Dependents

❖ Remove All Arrows

➤ **To add an icon to the toolbar:**

1. Right-click a toolbar and then select **Customize** from the shortcut menu.

2. Select the **Commands** tab, and from **Categories**, select **Tools**.

3. Drag the three icons from the **Commands** area to the **Standard** toolbar and close the **Customize** dialog box.

➤ **To use the Trace Precedents or Trace Dependents icons to move between linked cells in the same sheet:**

1. Type a number into cell A1 and then type the formula =A1 into cell D1.

2. Select cell D1 and click *Trace Precedents*. Double-click the blue arrow between the cells to move between the precedent cell and the dependent cell.

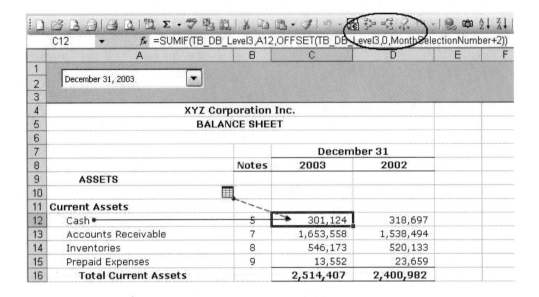

> ➤ **To use the Trace Precedents and Trace Dependents icons to move between linked cells outside the sheet:**

1. Insert a link formula =[Book1.xls]Sheet1!$A$1 into cell A1 in an open workbook.

2. Select cell A1 in the new workbook and click *Trace Precedents*. Double-click the dotted-line arrow to open the *Go To* dialog box, select the address, and then click **OK**.

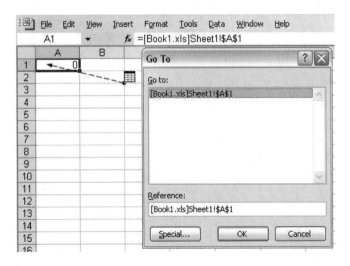

➤ **To move to a precedent cell:**

1. From the Tools menu, select *Options*.

2. Select the *Edit* tab, and deselect the *Edit directly in cell* checkbox.

3. Select a cell with a linked formula and double-click it to move to a precedent cell.

➤ **To return to the last four selected addresses:**

The *Go To* dialog box holds the last four references moved to via *Go To*.

Press <**F5**> to open the *Go To* dialog box (the last step is shown in the *Reference* box). Check the address and click **OK**.

Stepping into a Formula
(For Excel Versions 2002 & 2003)

The time spent evaluating complicated nested formulas can be enormous. This excellent new technique will save time.

❖ From the *Tools* menu, select *Formula Auditing*, and then *Evaluate Formula*.

OR

From the *Formula Auditing* toolbar, click *Evaluate Formula*.

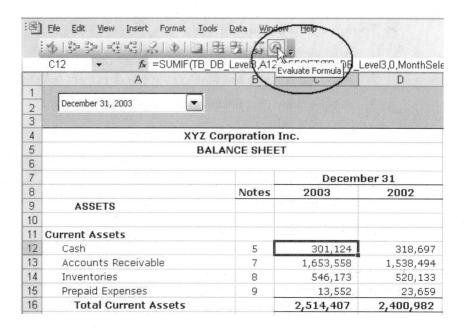

The *Evaluate Formula* dialog box allows moving between the arguments in a formula and checking the calculation result step-by-step.

Click *Step In* to move between arguments.

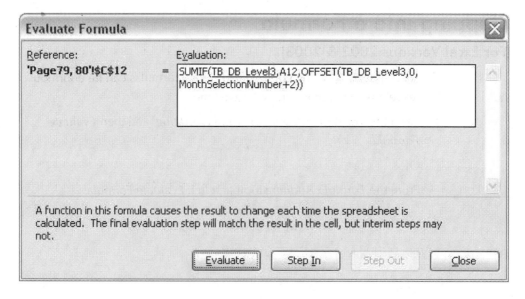

Tracing Errors in Formula Results

(For Excel Versions 2002 & 2003)

➢ **To trace an error:**

1. Select cell B1 (a cell containing an error), and click *Error Checking* (the first icon on the left of the *Auditing Formulas* toolbar).

   OR

   Use the *Smart Tag* to open the *Error Checking* dialog box.

2. Click **Options**.

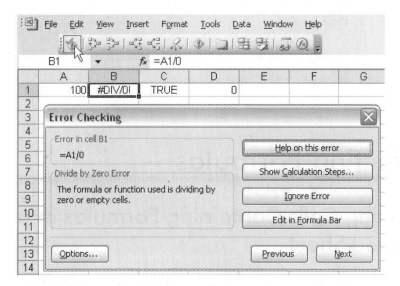

Protecting Formulas

Protecting Cells Containing Formulas in a Protected Sheet

> ➢ **To protect cells containing Formulas, two conditions must be met:**
>
> ❖ **The cell must be locked:**
>
> Select a cell in the sheet and press **<Ctrl+1>**.
>
> In the *Format Cells* dialog box, select the *Protection* tab.
>
> Select the *Locked* option.
>
> ❖ **The sheet must be protected:**
>
> From the *Tools* menu, select *Protection* and then *Protect Sheet*.
>
> Click **OK**.

Protecting cells containing Formulas, requires isolating the cells containing the Formulas from the rest of the cells in the sheet, locking them, and then protecting the sheet.

☞ **Step 1: Cancel the locked format of all the cells in the sheet:**

1. Select all cells in the sheet by pressing **<Ctrl+A>**.

2. Press **<Ctrl+1>**.

3. Select the *Protection* tab, and deselect the *Locked* option.

4. Click **OK**.

☞ **Step 2: Selecting cells containing Formulas:**

1. Press **<F5>**.

2. Click *Special*, and then select the *Formulas* option.

3. Click **OK**.

☞ **Step 3: Locking cells containing Formulas:**

1. Press **<Ctrl+1>**.

2. Select the *Protection* tab, and then select the Locked option.

3. Click **OK**.

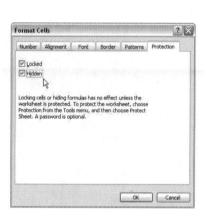

☞ **Step 4: Protecting the sheet:**

1. From the *Tools* menu, select *Protection*, and then *Protect Sheet*.

2. Click **OK** (a password is optional).

Protecting Cells Containing Formulas in an Unprotected Sheet

➢ **To protect cells containing Formulas in an unprotected sheet, use Validation:**

☞ **Step 1: Selecting cells containing formulas:**

1. Press **<F5>**.

2. Click *Special*, and then select the *Formulas* option.

3. Click **OK**.

☞ **Step 2: Validation:**

1. From the *Data* menu, select *Validation*.

2. Select the *Settings* tab, and select *Custom* from the *Allow* dropdown list.

3. In the *Formula* box, type =""", and then click **OK**.

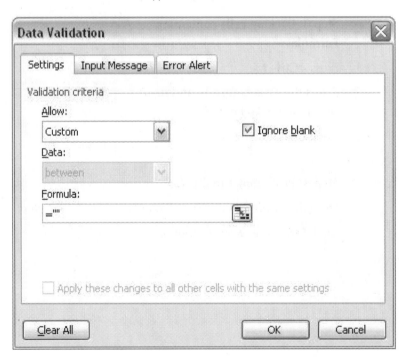

Chapter 2

Text

About This Chapter

This chapter provides a wide range of information on the many issues and problems involved with the use of Text formulas. It includes the following sections:

☞ **Entering Text, page 27:** This section covers techniques on restricting the entry of text into a cell, restricting the number of characters that may be entered, and preventing the entry of duplicate text.

☞ **Combining Text, Date, & Numbers, page 30:** This section deals with formulas that combine text from different cells into one single text value, that combine text with date values (while formatting the date) or leading zeros, that combine every Nth cell into one single cell, and that create new coded text.

☞ **Text Formatting - Troubleshooting, page 36:** This section contains formulas dealing with redundant characters, hidden apostrophes, and blank cells. Also covered are formulas erroneously appearing as text and ways to avoid having numeric values appear as text.

☞ **Subdividing Text, page 45:** The formulas in this section deal with mixed string & number techniques, splitting first and last names, splitting a full address, and extracting a given number of words from a string.

☞ **Replacing Characters, page 50:** This section covers formulas that replace substrings with numbers while creating new strings such as a new IP address.

☞ **Searching a String, page 55:** This section contains formulas that search strings for a matching word, find the alphabetically lowest letter, and search for specific substring, of the desired value.

☞ **Rearranging & Sorting Text, page 64:** This section contains formulas that reverse the words within a string and rearrange strings in alphabetic order.

☞ **Retrieving Cell Address, Row Number, page 66:** This section deals with formulas that find a cell address and row number.

Entering Text

Restricting Cell Entries to Text Only

➢ **Problem:**

We want to ensure that only text may be entered into the cells of column A.

➢ **Solution:**

Use *Data Validation*:

1. Select Column A.

2. *Data → Data Validation → Settings → Custom*

3. Enter the following formula in the *Formula* box:

   =ISTEXT(A1)

4. Click OK.

Thus, if an entry is not text, an error message will pop up, forcing the user to try again.

	A	B	C
1	a		**Data Validation Formula in Column A**
2	****		=ISTEXT(A1)
3	George		
4	X		
5			
6	20/50		
7	<7		
8			

Explanation:

The **ISTEXT** function returns TRUE if the value in cell A1 is text and FALSE otherwise.

The use of *Data Validation* prevents the user from entering values for which the **ISTEXT** function returns FALSE.

Restricting the Number of Characters Entered into a Cell

➢ **Problem:**

Restricting the length of entries in column A to a maximum of 5 characters.

➢ **Solution:**

Use *Data Validation*:

1. Select Column A.

2. *Data → Data Validation → Settings → Custom*

3. Enter the following formula in the *Formula* box:

    =LEN(A2)<6

4. Click OK.

If an entry is longer than 5 characters, an error message will pop up, forcing the user to try again.

	A	B	C
1	**List1**		**Data Validation Formula**
2	abcde		=LEN(A2)<6
3			
4	12a b		
5	-2345		
6	$20,000		
7	X Y Z		
8	A		
9	**&**		
10			

Explanation:

The **LEN** function returns the number of characters stored in cell A2.

The use of *Data Validation* prevents the user from entering values for which the **LEN** function returns a number larger than 5.

Preventing Duplicates When Entering Data

> ➢ **Problem:**

We want to make it impossible to enter duplicate values in List1 (cells A2:A10).

> ➢ **Solution:**

Use *Data Validation* as follows:

1. Select the range to validate (cells A2:A10)
2. *Data → Data Validation → Settings*
3. From the *Allow* dropdown list, select *Custom*.
4. Enter the following **COUNTIF** formula in the *Formula* box:

    =COUNTIF($A$2:$A$10,A2)=1

5. Select the *Error Alert* tab.
6. In the *Title* box, enter "Duplicate Entry".
7. In the *Error* Message box, enter "The value you entered already appears in the list above."
8. Click OK.

After following this procedure, any duplicate entry will cause the error message to pop up, forcing the user to enter a different value.

	A	B	C
1	List1		Data Validation Formula in A2:A10
2	1		=COUNTIF($A$2:$A$10,A2)=1
3	2		
4	3		
5	4		
6	5		
7	6		
8	7		
9	8		
10			

Explanation:

The **COUNTIF** function returns the number of values in List1 (cells A2:A10) that are equal to the one currently being entered.

Data Validation prevents the acceptance of a value for which the result of the **COUNTIF** function is greater than 1 (i.e. that value already exists in List1).

Combining Text, Date, & Number

Combining Text and Formatted Numbers into a Single Entity

➢ **Problem:**

Combining the data from cells A2:C2 into a single cell and ensuring that the number in B2 is formatted as currency.

➢ **Solution:**

Use the **TEXT** function as shown in the following formula:

=A2&" "&TEXT(B2,"$#,##0")&" "&C2

To display the dollar amount in thousands, modify the second argument in the **TEXT** function as follows:

=A2&" "&TEXT(B2,"$ #, K")&" "&C2

	A	B	C
1	**Text1**	**Number**	**Text2**
2	IBM owe Limelight Media Inc.	4222	for services supplied in March 2005.
3			
4	**Result**		
5	IBM owe Limelight Media Inc. $4,222 for services supplied in March 2005.		
6	IBM owe Limelight Media Inc. $ 4 K for services supplied in March 2005.		
7			
8	**Formula Syntax in cell A5:**		
9	=A2&" "&TEXT(B2,"$#,##0")&" "&C2		
10			
11	**Formula Syntax in cell A6:**		
12	=A2&" "&TEXT(B2,"$ #, K")&" "&C2		
13			

Explanation:

The **TEXT** function formats the number stored in cell B2 as a dollar amount ("$#,##0") and converts it to text.

That text is then joined with the contents of cells A2 and C2 to create a single string.

Combining Text and a Formatted Date into a Single Entity

➤ **Problem:**

Combining the text in cell A2 with the date in cell B2 to form a single text value in cell C2.

➤ **Solution:**

Use the **TEXT** function as shown in the following formula:

=A2&" "&TEXT(B2,"mm/dd/yyyy")

	A	B	C
1	**Text**	**Date**	**Result**
2	Expiration Date is	06/19/2005	Expiration Date is 06/19/2005
3			
4	**Formula Syntax in cell C2:**		
5	=A2&" "&TEXT(B2,"mm/dd/yyyy")		
6			

Explanation:

The **TEXT** function formats the date in cell B2 as "mm/dd/yyyy" and converts it to text.

That text is then joined with the contents of cell A2 to create a single string.

Combining Numbers that Have Leading Zeros

➤ **Problem:**

Column A (List1) is formatted to display a leading zero before each number. That is, "1" is displayed as "01", "2" as "02", and so on.

The following formula was created to concatenate the numbers from List1 into one string:

=A2&A3&A4&A5

However, an incorrect result of "1234" is returned.

How can we modify the formula to honor the leading zeros?

➤ **Solution:**

Use the **TEXT** function as shown in the following formula:

=TEXT(A2,"00")&TEXT(A3,"00")&TEXT(A4,"00")&TEXT(A5,"00")

	A	B	C	D	E	F
1	**List1**		**Result**			
2	01		01020304			
3	02					
4	03					
5	04					
6						
7	**Formula Syntax in cell C2:**					
8	=TEXT(A2,"00")&TEXT(A3,"00")&TEXT(A4,"00")&TEXT(A5,"00")					
9						

Explanation:

The **TEXT** function formats each of the numbers in List1 as "00" and converts them to text.

The values returned by each of the **TEXT** functions are then joined into a single string.

Combining the Contents of Every N Number of Cells into One Value

> ➤ **Problem:**

Column A contains an imported list of addresses; however, each address has been distributed over 4 cells.

Therefore, we want to combine the contents of each block of four cells so that the addresses will appear as complete entities.

> ➤ **Solution:**

Use the **IF**, **MOD**, and **ROW** functions as shown in the following formula:

=IF(MOD(ROW()-ROW($A$2),4)=0, A2&" "&A3&" "&A4&" "&A5," ")

Enter the formula in cell B2 and then copy it down the column until all the addresses in column A are recombined.

	A	B
	Imported Addresses	**Result**
1		
2	John Smith,	John Smith, 123 Xyz St, Chicago, IL 12345, USA
3	123 Xyz St,	
4	Chicago, IL 12345,	
5	USA	
6	Jane Doe,	Jane Doe, 6789 Abc St, LA, CA 45678, USA
7	6789 Abc St,	
8	LA, CA 45678,	
9	USA	
10	Adam Kane,	Adam Kane, 3456 Bcd St, San Francisco, CA 23456, USA
11	3456 Bcd St,	
12	San Francisco, CA 23456,	
13	USA	
14		
15	**Formula Syntax in column B:**	
16	=IF(MOD(ROW()-ROW($A$2),4)=0, A2&" "&A3&" "&A4&" "&A5,"")	
17		

Explanation:

The **ROW** functions are used to calculate the row number of each cell within the address list.

The **MOD** function divides that row number by 4 and returns the remainder.

If the remainder is 0, the value in column A is the first line of one of the addresses and the **IF** function returns a string consisting of the text stored in that cell and the three cells below it.

If the remainder is not 0, the formula returns a blank cell.

Encoding a Sequence of Letters

➢ **Problem:**

Column A contains a series of letters, column B contains matching codes for each letter.

We want to create new strings composed of the codes matching each of the letter strings shown in column D.

➢ **Solution:**

Use the **VLOOKUP** and **MID** functions as shown in the following formula:

=VLOOKUP(MID(D2,1,1),$A$2:$B$7,2,FALSE)&"
"&VLOOKUP(MID(D2,2,1),$A$2:$B$7,2,FALSE)&"
"&VLOOKUP(MID(D2,3,1),$A$2:$B$7,2,FALSE)

	A	B	C	D	E
1	Letter	Code		String	Coded String
2	A	10		BED	40 15 30
3	B	40		CAB	25 10 40
4	C	25		FEE	80 15 15
5	D	30			
6	E	15			
7	F	80			
8					
9	Formula Syntax in cell E2:				
10	=VLOOKUP(MID(D2,1,1),$A$2:$B$7,2,FALSE)&" "&VLOOKUP(MID(D2,2,1),$A$2:$B$7,2,FALSE)&" "&VLOOKUP(MID(D2,3,1),$A$2:$B$7,2,FALSE)				
11					

Explanation:

The **MID** function used in the first **VLOOKUP** function extracts the first character in cell D2.

The **VLOOKUP** function looks for that character in the first column of range A2:B7, and returns the corresponding value from the second column. Thus, the code matching the first character in cell D2 is returned.

Similarly, the second and third **VLOOKUP** functions return the codes matching the second and third characters in cell D2.

The results of all three **VLOOKUP** functions are joined into a single string with spaces separating them.

Combining Text and Numerically Calculated Results into One Output String

➤ **Problem:**

We want to calculate the reduced price corresponding to each full price in column A.

The result is to be included in the following output string: "Reduced price is $XX.XX".

Price reductions are calculated as follows:

80% of full price for prices over $80.

90% of full price for all other prices.

➤ **Solution:**

Use the **CONCATENATE**, **TEXT**, and **IF** functions as shown in the following formula:

= CONCATENATE("Reduced price is",
    TEXT(IF(A2>80,80%*A2,90%*A2),"$00.00"))

	A	B	C	D	E	F
1	**Full Price**	**Result**				
2	$100.00	Reduced price is $80.00				
3	$50.00	Reduced price is $45.00				
4						
5	**Formula Syntax in cell B2:**					
6	=CONCATENATE("Reduced price is ",TEXT(IF(A2>80,80%*A2,90%*A2),"$00.00"))					
7						

Explanation:

The **IF** function determines whether or not the full price in cell A2 is greater than $80.

If so, it returns 80% of that price. Otherwise, it returns 90 %.

The **TEXT** function formats the number returned by the **IF** function as currency ("$00.00") and converts it to text.

Finally, the **CONCATENATE** function joins the text "Reduced price is" with the result of the **TEXT** function.

Thus, a string is returned displaying the reduced price that matches the full price in cell A2.

Text Formatting – Troubleshooting

Formulas Erroneously Appearing as Text

➤ **Problem:**

Column B displays the text of the entered formulas, rather than their results.

➤ **Solution:**

Column B was probably formatted as text prior to the formulas being entered.

In order for the formulas to return their correct results do the following:

1. Select all the formulas.

2. Set the format of their cells to "General" or "Number".

3. Select the formulas again.

4. Press <Ctrl+Shift+~>

5. Press **<F2>** and then Enter for each of the selected formulas.

	A	B
1	**Results**	**Formulas Appear as text in column A**
2	0.165410825	=RAND()
3	4	=SQRT(16)
4	2	=MOD(5,3)
5	5	=ROW()
6		

Avoiding Problems when Numeric Values are used as Text

> ➤ **Problem:**

The following formula in column B was designed to return "5" for all the numbers in List1 (column A) that are greater than or equal to 5, and "2" for all the numbers that are less than 5.

=IF(A2>=5,"5","2")

This appears successful, however, when the following **SUM** formula is used to provide a total of the results in column B, an incorrect result of "0" is returned:

=SUM(B2:B8)

> ➤ **Solution:**

The numbers "5" and "2", returned by the **IF** function in column B, are actually text values because they are entered within double quotes.

Hence, column B contains text values, not numbers.

As the **SUM** function operates on numeric values only, there are no numbers in column B to add up, and therefore, it returns 0.

To solve the problem, we must convert the text values in column B to numbers in one of the following ways:

1. Modify the **IF** function in column B to return numbers by removing the double quotes from "5" and "2", as follows:

   =IF(A2>=5,5,2)

2. Use the **SUM** and **VALUE** functions to convert the text values in column B to numbers, using one the following *Array formulas*:

   {=SUM(--B2:B8)}

   {=SUM(VALUE(B2:B8))}

☞ To apply *Array formula*:

   Select the cell, press <**F2**> and simultaneously press <**Ctrl+Shift+Enter**>.

	A	B	C	D	E
1	List1	Original IF Formula Result	Formula Syntax Column B	Corrected IF Formula Result	Formula Syntax Column D
2	5	5	=IF(A2>=5,"5","2")	5	=IF(A2>=5,5,2)
3	10	5		5	
4	2	2		2	
5	7	5		5	
6	3	2		2	
7	20	5		5	
8	6	5		5	
9	SUM	0	=SUM(B2:B8)	29	=SUM(D2:D8)
10					
11					
12		Corrected SUM Formula Result	Array Formula Syntax		
13		29	{=SUM(VALUE(B2:B8))}		
14		29	{=SUM(--B2:B8)}		
15					

Adjusting a Formula to Return a Blank, Rather than a Zero, When Operating on Empty Cells

➢ **Problem:**

List1 (column A) includes numbers as well as blank cells.

When using the following formula to multiply each number in List1 by 3:

=IF(ISBLANK(A2),,A2*3)

Zeros are returned for all empty cells.

We want to adjust the formula so that blanks are returned for all empty cells in List1.

➢ **Solution:**

Use two quote marks (""), as shown in the adjusted formula below, to indicate that a blank should be returned:

=IF(ISBLANK(A2),"",A2*3)

	A	B	C
1	List1	Result	
2	2	6	
3	3	9	
4			
5	5	15	
6			
7	4	12	
8			
9	Formula Syntax in cell B2:		
10	=IF(ISBLANK(A2),"",A2*3)		
11			

Explanation:

The **ISBLANK** function determines whether or not the value in cell A2 is blank and returns TRUE/FALSE accordingly.

If TRUE is returned, the **IF** function returns a blank (""). Otherwise, it returns the value stored in A2 multiplied by 3.

Checking Whether Cells in a Range are Blank, and Counting the Blank Cells

➢ **Problem:**

Checking whether or not each of the cells in List1 (column A) is blank, and Counting the Blank Cells.

➢ **Solution:**

Use either of the following formulas in column B:

=IF(ISBLANK(A2),"",A2)

=IF(A2="","",A2)

Either formula will return the corresponding value from column A only if the cell is not blank.

Use the **COUNTBLANK** function, as shown in the following formula, to count the number of blank cells in List1:

=COUNTBLANK(A2:A7)

	A	B	C	D
1	List1	ISBLANK Formula	Number of Blank Cells	
2	10	10	2	
3				
4	Excel	Excel		
5	5	5		
6				
7	0	0		
8				
9	ISBLANK Formula Syntax in cell B2:			
10	=IF(ISBLANK(A2),"",A2)			
11				
12	Number of Blank Cells Formula Syntax in cell C2:			
13	=COUNTBLANK(A2:A7)			
14				

Explanation:

☞ **ISBLANK Formula:**

The **ISBLANK** function determines whether or not the value in cell A2 is blank and returns TRUE/FALSE accordingly.

If TRUE is returned, the **IF** function returns a blank (""). Otherwise, it returns the value stored in cell A2.

☞ **COUNTBLANK Formula:**

The **COUNTBLANK** function counts the number of blank cells within the range A2:A7.

Creating Formulas that Only Return Results from Non-Blank Cells

➢ **Problem:**

We want to create a formula that only returns a result from the non-blank cells in List1.

➢ **Solution:**

Use the **ISBLANK** function as shown in the following formula:

=IF(ISBLANK(A2)=FALSE,A2,"")

To return text values only, use the **ISTEXT** function as shown in the following formula:

=IF(ISTEXT(A2),A2,"")

To return numeric values only, use the **ISNUMBER** function as shown in the following formula:

=IF(ISNUMBER(A2),A2,"")

	A	B	C	D
		ISBLANK	ISTEXT	ISNUMBER
1	List1	function	function	function
2	22	22		22
3				
4	12/04/2005	12/04/2005	12/04/2005	
5	Excel	Excel	Excel	
6				
7	Formula Syntax in cell B2:		Formula Syntax in cell C2:	
8	=IF(ISBLANK(A2)=FALSE,A2,"")		=IF(ISTEXT(A2),A2,"")	
9				
10			Formula Syntax in cell D2:	
11			=IF(ISNUMBER(A2),A2,"")	
12				

Explanation:

☞ **ISBLANK Formula**:

The **ISBLANK** function determines whether or not the value in cell A2 is blank and returns TRUE/FALSE accordingly.

If the result of the **ISBLANK** function is FALSE, the **IF** function returns the value stored in cell A2. Otherwise, it returns a blank.

Thus, the corresponding value in cell A2 is returned only if it's not blank.

☞ **ISTEXT Formula:**

The **ISTEXT** function determines whether or not the value in cell A2 is text and returns TRUE/FALSE accordingly.

If TRUE is returned, the **IF** function returns the value stored in cell A2. Otherwise, it returns a blank.

Thus, the corresponding value in cell A2 is returned only if it's a text value.

☞ **ISNUMBER Formula:**

The **ISNUMBER** function determines whether or not the value in cell A2 is numeric and returns TRUE/FALSE accordingly.

If TRUE is returned, the **IF** function returns the value stored in cell A2. Otherwise, it returns a blank.

Thus, the corresponding value in cell A2 is returned only if it's a number.

Removing Redundant Characters from a Range of Cells and Resetting the Format

➢ **Problem:**

The text values in the range A2:A5 contain redundant parentheses.

We want to create a formula that will remove the parentheses and set the format of the cells to "general".

➢ **Solution:**

Use the **TEXT**, **TRIM**, and **SUBSTITUTE** functions as shown in the following formula:

=TEXT(TRIM(SUBSTITUTE(SUBSTITUTE(A2,")",""),"(","")),"General").

	A	B	C	D	E	F
1	**Originial Text**	**Result**				
2	(Excel)	Excel				
3	Power point)	Power point				
4	(Access)	Access				
5	(Outlook)	Outlook				
6						
7	**Formula Syntax in cell B2:**					
8	=TEXT(TRIM(SUBSTITUTE(SUBSTITUTE(A2,")",""),"(","")),"General")					
9						

Explanation:

The nested **SUBSTITUTE** function returns the text in cell A2 after having replaced the parentheses with nothing.

The **TRIM** function removes any redundant spaces from the text returned by the **SUBSTITUTE** function.

The **TEXT** function sets the format of the string returned by the **TRIM** function to "General".

Removing Hidden Apostrophes from Imported Numbers

➢ **Problem:**

Column B contains an imported list of numbers.

All the numbers include a leading apostrophe.

Excel interprets such values as text. They are unable to be formatted as currency, nor can they be used in calculations such as **SUM** and **AVERAGE**.

We, therefore, want to remove the apostrophe from each of the values in column B and convert them to normal numbers.

➢ **Solution:**

Use the **VALUE** function as shown in the following formula:
=VALUE(B2)

	A	B	C	D
1		**Imported List**	**Result**	
2		20	$20.00	
3		50	$50.00	
4		45	$45.00	
5		80	$80.00	
6		100	$100.00	
7		35	$35.00	
8		120	$120.00	
9		90	$90.00	
10		55	$55.00	
11	Sum	0	$595.00	
12				
13	Formula Syntax in B11:C11			
14		=SUM(B2:B10)	=SUM(C2:C10)	
15				
16	Formula Syntax in cell C2:			
17	=VALUE(B2)			
18				

Explanation:

The **VALUE** function converts the contents of cell B2 to a number.

Thus removing the apostrophe from the original value.

Subdividing Text

Subdividing a Mixed String into Separate Cells Containing only Numbers or Characters

> ➤ **Problem:**

The strings in column A can be composed of both numbers and characters; however, the numbers may only appear at the beginning of the string and the characters at the end.

We want to separate the strings into two columns, one containing only numbers and the other containing characters.

> ➤ **Solution:**

Use the **LEFT**, **MAX**, **IF**, **ISNUMBER**, **MID**, **INDIRECT**, and **ROW** functions as shown in the following *Array formula* entered in column B:

{=LEFT(A2,MAX(IF(ISNUMBER(--MID(A2,ROW(INDIRECT("1:1024")),1)),ROW(INDIRECT("1:1024")))))}

Then use the **SUBSTITUTE** function as shown in the following formula entered in column C:

=SUBSTITUTE(A2,B2,"")

> ☞ To apply *Array formula*:

Select the cell, press **<F2>** and simultaneously press **<Ctrl+Shift+Enter>**.

	A	B	C	D	E
1	**Numbers & Text**	**Numbers**	**Text**		
2	1A	1	A		
3	22ABCD	22	ABCD		
4	35	35			
5	34567C	34567	C		
6	X		X		
7	55mm	55	mm		
8					
9	**Array Formula Syntax in cell B2:**				
10	{=LEFT(A2,MAX(IF(ISNUMBER(-- MID(A2,ROW(INDIRECT("1:1024")),1)),ROW(INDIRECT("1:1024")))))}				
11					
12	**Formula Syntax in cell C2:**				
13	=SUBSTITUTE(A2,B2,"")				
14					

Explanation:

☞ **Extracting Numbers:**

The **ROW**, **INDIRECT**, and **MID** functions are used to create an Array consisting of each of the characters in the string stored in cell A2.

The **IF** function returns an Array containing the position of each numeric character in the above Array (using the **ISNUMBER** function).

The **MAX** function returns the maximal value in that Array (i.e. the position of the last number in the string).

The **LEFT** function extracts the leftmost characters from cell A2 up to the position returned by the **MAX** function, i.e. the numeric portion of the string.

☞ **Extracting Text:**

The **SUBSTITUTE** function searches cell A2 for the text stored in cell B2 (the numeric part of cell A2 returned by the first formula), and replaces it with nothing.

Thus, only the character portion of the original string is returned.

Splitting a Full Address into Three Separate Cells

> ➢ **Problem:**

Separating the addresses shown in column A into three columns, one each for City, State, and Zip Code.

> ➢ **Solution:**

Use the **LEFT**, **MID**, **RIGHT**, and **FIND** functions as shown in the following formulas:

To extract the City: =LEFT(A2,FIND(",",A2)-1)

To extract the State: =MID(A2,FIND(",",A2)+2,2)

To extract the Zip code: =RIGHT(A2,5)

	A	B	C	D	E
1	City State Zip		City	State	Zip
2	New York, NY 10164		New York	NY	10164
3	Chicago, IL 60616		Chicago	IL	60616
4	Los Angeles, CA 90099		Los Angeles	CA	90099
5					
6	City Formula in cell C2:		=LEFT(A2,FIND(",",A2)-1)		
7	State Formula in cell D2:		=MID(A2,FIND(",",A2)+2,2)		
8	Zip Formula in cell E2:		=RIGHT(A2,5)		
9					

Explanation:

☞ **City Formula:**

The **FIND** function returns the position of the comma within the string stored in cell A2.

The **LEFT** function extracts the leftmost characters up to the character to the left of the comma (the position returned by the **FIND** function minus 1), i.e. the City part of the address.

☞ **State Formula:**

The **FIND** function returns the position of the comma within the string stored in cell A2.

The **MID** function returns the two characters to the right the comma (the position returned by the **FIND** function plus 2), i.e. the State part of the address.

☞ **Zip Code Formula:**

The **RIGHT** function extracts the 5 rightmost characters of the string stored in cell A2, i.e. the Zip Code.

Separating First and Last Names

➤ **Problem:**

Separating the full names in column A into first and last names in columns B and C.

➤ **Solution:**

To retrieve the first name use the **LEFT** and **FIND** functions as shown in the following formula:

=LEFT(A2,FIND(" ",A2))

To retrieve the last name use the **RIGHT**, **LEN**, and **FIND** functions as shown in the following formula:

=RIGHT(A2,LEN(A2)-FIND(" ",A2))

	A	B	C
1	Full Name	First Name	Last Name
2	John Doe	John	Doe
3	George Bush	George	Bush
4	Jerry Seinfeld	Jerry	Seinfeld
5			
6	First Name Formula Syntax in cell B2:		
7	=LEFT(A2,FIND(" ",A2))		
8			
9	Last Name Formula Syntax in cell C2:		
10	=RIGHT(A2,LEN(A2)-FIND(" ",A2))		
11			

Explanation:

☞ **First Name Formula:**

The **FIND** function returns the position of the space within the full name stored in cell A2.

The **LEFT** function extracts the leftmost characters up to the position returned by the **FIND** function, i.e. the first name.

☞ **Last Name Formula:**

The **FIND** function returns the position of the space within the full name stored in cell A2.

The **LEN** function returns the number of characters in the full name.

The number of characters to the right of the space (i.e. the number of characters in the last name) is calculated by subtracting the number that represents the position of the space (returned by the **FIND** function) from the length of the name (returned by the **LEN** function).

The **RIGHT** function extracts as many characters as calculated above, starting at the rightmost character, i.e. the last name.

Extracting the First N Number of Words from a String

➤ **Problem:**

Extracting the first three words from each of the strings in column A.

➤ **Solution:**

Use the **TRIM**, **LEFT**, **FIND**, and **SUBSTITUTE** functions as shown in the following formula:

=TRIM(LEFT(A2,FIND("^",SUBSTITUTE(TRIM(A2)&" "," ","^",3))-1))

	A	B	C	D
1	**Full String**	**First 3 Words**		
2	One two three four five	One two three		
3	Ab cdefg H ij kl	Ab cdefg H		
4				
5	**Formula Syntax in cell B2:**			
6	=TRIM(LEFT(A2,FIND("^",SUBSTITUTE(TRIM(A2)&" "," ","^",3))-1))			
7				

Explanation:

The following expression removes any redundant spaces from the text in cell A2, and adds a space at the end of it: TRIM(A2)&" "

The **SUBSTITUTE** function returns the string created above after having its 3rd space replaced by the "^" symbol.

The **FIND** function returns the position of the "^" sign within that string.

The **LEFT** function extracts the leftmost characters in the string up to the "^" sign (the position returned by the **FIND** function minus 1), i.e. the first three words.

The **TRIM** function removes any redundant spaces from the text returned by the **LEFT** function.

Replacing Characters

Creating New IP Addresses

➤ **Problem:**

Creating new IP addresses composed of the first three original segments coupled with the last original segment multiplied by two.

➤ **Solution:**

Use the **LEFT**, **FIND**, and **MID** functions as shown in the following formula:

=(LEFT(A2,FIND(".",A2,FIND(".",A2,FIND(".",A2)+1)+1)))&(MID(A2,
FIND(".",A2,FIND(".",A2,FIND(".",A2)+1)+1)+1,99)*2)

	A	B	C	D	E
1	Original IP's	New IP's			
2	123.45.678.90	123.45.678.180			
3	123.456.789.61	123.456.789.122			
4	123.456.78.222	123.456.78.444			
5	123.456.78.43	123.456.78.86			
6					
7	Formula Syntax in cell B2:				
8	=(LEFT(A2,FIND(".",A2,FIND(".",A2,FIND(".",A2)+1)+1)))&(MID(A2,FIND(".",A2,FIND(".",A2,FIND(".",A2)+1)+1)+1,99)*2)				
9					

Explanation:

The nested **FIND** functions are used to calculate the position of the last "." in the IP address stored in cell A2.

The **LEFT** function extracts all the characters to the left of that position (i.e. the first three segments of the address).

The **MID** function extracts 99 characters starting with the position calculated by the **FIND** function plus 1 (i.e. the last segment in the address).

Finally, the last segment is multiplied by 2 and joined with the first three segments of the original address.

Converting Numbers with Trailing Minus Signs to Normal Negative Numbers

➢ **Problem:**

Column A contains an imported list of positive and negative numbers.

For negative numbers, the minus sign appears to the right, rather than to the left.

We want to convert all the numbers with trailing minus signs to normally-signed negative numbers.

➤ **Solution:**

1. Use the **RIGHT** and **SUBSTITUTE** functions as shown in the following formula in column B:

    =IF(RIGHT(A2,1)="-",SUBSTITUTE(A2,"-","")*-1,A2)

2. Use the **VALUE, IF, RIGHT, LEFT**, and **LEN** functions as shown in the following formula in column C:

    =VALUE(IF(RIGHT(A2,1)="-",RIGHT(A2,1)&LEFT(A2,LEN(A2)-1),A2))

	A	B	C
1	Imported List	Corrected List (Formula 1)	Corrected List (Formula 2)
2	12-	-12	-12
3	10	10	10
4	123	123	123
5	5-	-5	-5
6			
7	Formula Syntax in cell B2:		
8	=IF(RIGHT(A2,1)="-",SUBSTITUTE(A2,"-","")*-1,A2)		
9			
10	Formula Syntax in cell C2:		
11	=VALUE(IF(RIGHT(A2,1)="-",RIGHT(A2,1)&LEFT(A2,LEN(A2)-1),A2))		
12			

Explanation:

☞ **First Formula:**

The **RIGHT** function extracts the rightmost character of the value in cell A2.

If that character is a minus sign, the **IF** function returns the result of the following expression:

SUBSTITUTE(A2,"-","")*-1

The **SUBSTITUTE** function replaces the minus sign in cell A2 with nothing. The value is then multiplied by -1, to create the proper negative number.

If the rightmost character from cell A2 is not a minus sign, the **IF** function returns the original value.

☞ **Second Formula:**

The **RIGHT** function extracts the rightmost character from cell A2.

If that character is a minus sign, the **IF** function returns a string composed of that minus sign and the rest of the characters in cell A2, extracted by the **LEFT** function (based on the string's length, calculated by the **LEN** function).

If the rightmost character from cell A2 is not a minus sign, the **IF** function returns the original value.

The **VALUE** function converts the text returned by the **IF** function to a number.

Replacing Substrings with Numbers from Adjacent Cells

➢ **Problem:**

Replacing the "XX" substring in each of the strings in column A with the corresponding number from column B.

➢ **Solution:**

Use the **LEFT**, **FIND**, and **MID** functions as shown in the following formula:

=LEFT(A2,FIND("XX",A2)-1)&B2&MID(A2,FIND("XX",A2)+2,255)

	A	B	C	D	E	F
1	**Strings**	**Numbers**	**Result**			
2	12/XX/50	10	12/10/50			
3	3/XX	11	3/11			
4	XX	12	12			
5	XX/4	13	13/4			
6	5/60/XX	14	5/60/14			
7						
8	**Formula Syntax in cell C2:**					
9	=LEFT(A2,FIND("XX",A2)-1)&B2&MID(A2,FIND("XX",A2)+2,255)					
10						

Explanation:

The **LEFT** function extracts the leftmost characters in cell A2 up to the "XX" substring (based on its position within cell A2 calculated by the **FIND** function).

The **MID** function extracts 255 characters from cell A2, starting one character after the "XX" substring (the position calculated by the **FIND** function plus 2).

The text returned by the **LEFT** and **MID** functions is concatenated on either side of the number in cell B2, thus creating a new string in which "XX" has been replaced.

Performing Numeric Operations on Substrings

➢ **Problem:**

Column A contains a list of strings that are composed of two numbers separated by a "/" symbol.

We want to add 10 to the left number of each string.

➢ **Solution:**

Use the **LEFT**, **FIND**, and **MID** functions as shown in the following formula:

=LEFT(A2,FIND("/",A2)-1)+10&MID(A2,FIND("/",A2),255)

	A	B	C	D	E
1	**Strings**	**Result**			
2	20/40	30/40			
3	100/50	110/50			
4	45/300	55/300			
5	700/700	710/700			
6	80/20	90/20			
7					
8	**Formula Syntax in cell B2:**				
9	=LEFT(A2,FIND("/",A2)-1)+10&MID(A2,FIND("/",A2),255)				
10					

Explanation:

The **FIND** function returns the position of the "/" symbol within the string in cell A2.

The **LEFT** function extracts the leftmost characters up to the calculated position minus 1 (i.e. the first number).

The **MID** function, in combination with the **FIND** function, extracts the remaining characters of the string in cell A2 (i.e. the "/" symbol and the right number).

Finally, the left number has 10 added to it and is then joined with the rest of the original string.

Searching a String

Searching a String for a Matching Word from another String

➢ **Problem:**

Determining whether the first word from each string in column A appears within the corresponding string in the same row of column B.

➢ **Solution:**

Use the **IF**, **ISNUMBER**, **FIND**, and **LEFT** functions as shown in the following formula:

=IF(ISNUMBER(FIND(LEFT(A2,FIND(" ",A2)-1),B2)),"1st Word Found","1st Word Not Found")

	A	B	C	D
1	**String1**	**String2**	**Result**	
2	One Two	Three Two One	1st Word Found	
3	Bush George W	George W Bush	1st Word Found	
4	Excel Tip	Microsoft Excel	1st Word Found	
5	Michael Jordan	Chicago Bulls	1st Word Not Found	
6				
7	**Formula Syntax in cell C2:**			
8	=IF(ISNUMBER(FIND(LEFT(A2,FIND(" ",A2)-1),B2)),"1st Word Found","1st Word Not Found")			
9				

Explanation:

The second **FIND** function returns the position of the first space in the string stored in cell A2.

The **LEFT** function extracts the leftmost characters in that string up to the calculated position minus 1 (i.e. the first word from cell A2).

The first **FIND** function returns the position of that first word within the string stored in cell B2.

If the word is not found within that string, the function returns an error.

The **ISNUMBER** function determines whether or not the result of the **FIND** function is a number (i.e. whether or not the word was found).

If the **ISNUMBER** function returns TRUE, the **IF** function returns the string "1st Word Found". Otherwise, it returns the string "1st Word Not Found".

Find the Alphabetically Lowest Letter in a List

➤ **Problem:**

When the following formula is used to find the alphabetically lowest letter in List1 (column A):

=CHAR(SMALL(CODE(A2:A6),1))

An incorrect result of "z" is returned.

➤ **Solution:**

Use the **CHAR**, **SMALL**, and **CODE** functions as shown in the following *Array formula*:

{=CHAR(SMALL(CODE(A2:A6),1))}

☞ To apply *Array formula*:

Select the cell, press **<F2>** and simultaneously press **<Ctrl+Shift+Enter>**.

	A	B	C	D
1	**List1**		**Result**	
2	g		b	
3	z			
4	c			
5	m			
6	b			
7				
8	**Array Formula Syntax in cell C2:**			
9	{=CHAR(SMALL(CODE(A2:A6),1))}			
10				

Explanation:

The **CODE** function returns an Array containing the numeric code (ASCII) for each letter in column A.

The **SMALL** function returns the smallest number in that Array, which is the ASCII code of the alphabetically lowest letter in List1.

The **CHAR** function returns the character specified by that particular ASCII code.

Identifying Numeric Values within a Range Formatted as Text

➢ **Problem:**

Column A contains both numeric and text values, however, all values are formatted as text.

We want to determine which of the values are actually text (i.e. consist of alphabetic characters) and which are only formatted as text, but are in fact numeric.

➢ **Solution:**

Use the **IF** and **ISERROR** functions as shown in the following formula:

=IF(ISERROR(A2+0),"Text","Number")

	A	B	C	D
1		**Result**		
2	20	Number		
3	abc	Text		
4	G	Text		
5	5	Number		
6				
7	**Formula Syntax in cell B2:**			
8	=IF(ISERROR(A2+0),"Text","Number")			
9				

Explanation:

The above formula is based on the assumption that performing a calculation on a text value would result in an error.

Therefore, the value stored in A2 has a 0 added to it.

The **ISERROR** function determines whether or not the calculation results in an error and returns TRUE/FALSE accordingly.

If TRUE is returned, the **IF** function returns the string "Text". Otherwise, it returns the string "Number".

Identifying the Case of Letters within Strings

> ## ➤ Problem:

Determining whether each of the names in List1 (column A) are exclusively upper case, exclusively lower case, or a combination of both.

> ## ➤ Solution:

Use the **IF**, **EXACT**, **UPPER**, and **LOWER** functions as shown in the following formula:

=IF(EXACT(A2,UPPER(A2)),"Upper Case",IF(EXACT(A2,LOWER(A2)),"Lower Case","Upper and Lower Case"))

	A	B	C	D
1	**List1**	**Result**		
2	Doe, John	Upper and Lower Case		
3	BUSH, GEORGE	Upper Case		
4	seinfeld, jerry	Lower Case		
5	JORDAN, Michael	Upper and Lower Case		
6				
7	**Formula Syntax in cell B2:**			
8	=IF(EXACT(A2,UPPER(A2)),"Upper Case",IF(EXACT(A2,LOWER(A2)),"Lower Case","Upper and Lower Case"))			
9				

Explanation:

The **UPPER** function converts the name in cell A2 to uppercase.

The **EXACT** function determines whether or not the original name in cell A2 and the name returned by the **UPPER** function are identical, and returns TRUE/FALSE accordingly.

If TRUE is returned, the **IF** function returns the string "Upper Case".

Otherwise, it returns the result of the second **IF** function:

The **LOWER** function converts the name in cell A2 to lowercase.

The **EXACT** function determines whether or not the original name in cell A2 and the name returned by the **LOWER** function are identical, and returns TRUE/FALSE accordingly.

If TRUE is returned, the **IF** function returns the string "Lower Case". Otherwise, it returns the string "Upper and Lower Case".

Finding the Relative Position of Numbers within a String

➢ **Problem:**

List1 (column A) consists of strings composed of numbers and characters.

Numbers may appear at the beginning or the end of the string, but not in the middle.

For each of the strings, we want to determine whether the numbers appear at the beginning or the end.

➢ **Solution:**

Use the **ISNUMBER**, **RIGHT**, and **LEFT** functions as shown in the following formula:

=IF(ISNUMBER(-RIGHT(A2,1)),"End",IF(ISNUMBER(-LEFT(A2,1)),"Beginning"))

	A	B	C	D
1	**List1**	**Result**		
2	D33	End		
3	1A	Beginning		
4	23G	Beginning		
5	AB12	End		
6	C2	End		
7				
8	**Formula Syntax in cell B2:**			
9	=IF(ISNUMBER(-RIGHT(A2,1)),"End",IF(ISNUMBER(-LEFT(A2,1)),"Beginning"))			
10				

Explanation:

The **RIGHT** function extracts the rightmost character of the string stored in cell A2.

The "-" sign then converts that character, if representing a number, to a negative number.

If that character does not represent a number, that conversion will result in an error.

The **ISNUMBER** function determines whether or not the result of the above conversion is a number (whether or not the rightmost character of cell A2 represents a number).

If it does, the **IF** function returns the string "End".

Otherwise, the leftmost character of the string (extracted by the **LEFT** function) is checked to see if it is a number (using the "-" sign to convert it to a negative number and the **ISNUMBER** function determine whether or not the result of that conversion is numeric). If so, the **IF** function returns the string "Beginning".

Searching a String for a Specific Substring

> **Problem:**

Checking whether each of the substrings in column A exist in the corresponding strings from the same row of column B.

> **Solution:**

For case sensitive results: Use the **ISNUMBER** and **FIND** functions as shown in the following formula:

=ISNUMBER(FIND(A2,B2))

For case insensitive results: use the **SEARCH** and **LEN** functions as shown in the following formula:

=SEARCH(A2,B2&A2)<LEN(B2)

	A	B	C	D
1	**String to Find**	**Strings**	**Case Sensitive Results**	**Case Insensitive Results**
2	BC	ABC	TRUE	TRUE
3	cd	acd	TRUE	TRUE
4	eg	efg	FALSE	FALSE
5				
6	**Case Sensitive Formula Syntax in cell C2:**			
7	=ISNUMBER(FIND(A2,B2))			
8				
9	**Case Insensitive Formula Syntax in cell D2:**			
10	=SEARCH(A2,B2&A2)<LEN(B2)			
11				

Explanation:

☞ **Case Sensitive Formula:**

The **FIND** function retrieves the position of the string to find (cell A2) within the corresponding string in cell B2.

If the string is not found within cell B2, the formula returns an error.

The **ISNUMBER** function determines whether or not the result of the **FIND** function is a number (i.e. whether or not the string was found), and returns TRUE/FALSE accordingly.

As the **FIND** function is case sensitive, this formula returns case sensitive results.

☞ **Case Insensitive Formula:**

The **SEARCH** function retrieves the position of the string to find (cell A2) within a string combining cells B2 and A2.

If that number is smaller than the length of the string in B2 (calculated by the **LEN** function), the formula returns TRUE. Otherwise, it returns FALSE.

As the **SEARCH** function is case insensitive, this formula returns case insensitive results.

Determining Long Distance Phone Calls, Based on the Number Dialed

➢ **Problem:**

Column A lists the numbers dialed for all phone calls made on a particular day.

All numbers starting with "1", except for those starting with "1800", are for long distance calls

We want to analyze each number in column A and determine whether or not it was used for a long distance call.

➢ **Solution:**

Use the **IF**, **AND**, **LEFT**, and **MID** functions as shown in the following formula:

=IF(AND(LEFT(A2,1)="1", MID(A2,2,3)<>"800"),"Long Distance", "Not Long Distance")

	A	B	C	D	E	F
1	**Dialed Phone Numbers**	**Result**				
2	18001111111	Not Long Distance				
3	13059999999	Long Distance				
4	5678912	Not Long Distance				
5	18001234567	Not Long Distance				
6	12345678901	Long Distance				
7	9876543	Not Long Distance				
8						
9	**Formula Syntax in cell B2:**					
10	=IF(AND(LEFT(A2,1)="1", MID(A2,2,3)<>"800"),"Long Distance", "Not Long Distance")					
11						

Explanation:

The **LEFT** function extracts the leftmost character in cell A2 (i.e. the first digit of the dialed number).

The **MID** function extracts the three characters starting in the second character in cell A2.

If the first digit extracted is equal to "1" and the next three digits extracted are not equal to "800", the **AND** function returns TRUE. Else, it returns FALSE.

The **IF** function returns "Long Distance" for TRUE or "Not Long Distance" for FALSE.

Rearranging & Sorting Text

Rearranging a String in Alphabetic Order

➢ **Problem:**

The cells in column A contain 3-letter strings.

We want to rearrange each string so that its characters are sorted in alphabetic order.

➢ **Solution:**

Use the **CHAR**, **SMALL**, **CODE**, and **MID** functions as shown in the following formula:

=CHAR(SMALL(CODE(MID(A2,{1,2,3},1)),1))&CHAR(SMALL(CODE(MID(A2,{1,2,3},2)),2))&CHAR(SMALL(CODE(MID(A2,{1,2,3},3)),3))

	A	B	C	D	E
1	**Strings**	**Sorted Strings**			
2	CAB	ABC			
3	XZY	XYZ			
4	HGF	FGH			
5					
6	**Array Formula Syntax in cell B2:**				
7	=CHAR(SMALL(CODE(MID(A2,{1,2,3},1)),1))&CHAR(SMALL(CODE (MID(A2,{1,2,3},2)),2))&CHAR(SMALL(CODE(MID(A2,{1,2,3},3)),3))				
8					

Explanation:

The **MID** function in the first **CHAR** function returns an Array consisting of each of the three characters in cell A2.

The **CODE** function returns an Array containing a numeric code (ASCII) for each of those characters.

The **SMALL** function returns the smallest code in that Array (i.e. the ASCII code corresponding with the alphabetically lowest letter).

The **CHAR** function returns the character specified by that particular code, which, in this case, is alphabetically the lowest letter in cell A2.

Similarly, the second and third **CHAR** functions return the second and the third lowest letters in cell A2.

Finally, the letters returned by all the **CHAR** functions are joined into a single sorted string.

Reversing the Word Order within a String

➢ **Problem:**

Reversing the order of words in each of the two-word strings in column A.

➢ **Solution:**

Use the **RIGHT**, **LEN**, **FIND**, and **LEFT** functions as shown in the following formula:

=RIGHT(A2,LEN(A2)-FIND(" ",A2))&" "&LEFT(A2,FIND(" ",A2)-1)

	A	B	C	D	E
1	**Strings**	**Result**			
2	John Lennon	Lennon John			
3	A B	B A			
4	Excel Tip	Tip Excel			
5	$$ *	* $$			
6					
7	**Formula Syntax in cell B2:**				
8	=RIGHT(A2,LEN(A2)-FIND(" ",A2))&" "&LEFT(A2,FIND(" ",A2)-1)				
9					

Explanation:

In order to calculate how many characters are contained in the second word, the position of the space is calculated by the **FIND** function and this is subtracted from the string's length (returned by the **LEN** function).

To extract the second word, the **RIGHT** function extracts as many characters as was calculated above from the right end of the string.

Based on the position calculated by the **FIND** function, the **LEFT** function extracts all characters to the left of the space, i.e. the first word in the string.

Finally, the second word and the first word are joined together and separated with a space.

Retrieving Cell Address, Row Number

Retrieving the Cell Address of the Largest Value in a Range

➢ **Problem:**

Retrieving the address of the cell that contains the largest value within Range1 (A2:D7).

➢ **Solution:**

Use the **ADDRESS, SUM, IF, MAX, ROW**, and **COLUMN** functions as shown in the following *Array formula*:

{=ADDRESS(SUM(IF(A2:D7=MAX(A2:D7),ROW(A2:D7))),SUM(IF(A2:D7
=MAX(A2:D7),COLUMN(A2:D7)))))}

☞ To apply *Array formula*:

Select the cell, press **<F2>** and simultaneously press **<Ctrl+Shift+Enter>**.

	A	B	C	D	E	F
1		Range1				Cell containing Max Value
2	5	3	32	11		$C$5
3	1	23	6	2		
4	8	30	28	16		
5	12	15	40	9		
6	17	4	2	25		
7	22	34	14	7		
8						
9	Array Formula Syntax in cell F2:					
10	{=ADDRESS(SUM(IF(A2:D7=MAX(A2:D7),ROW(A2:D7))),SUM(IF(A2:D7=MAX (A2:D7),COLUMN(A2:D7)))))}					
11						

Explanation:

The first **IF** function determines whether or not a given value in Range1 is equal to the maximum for that range (calculated by the **MAX** function).

It returns an Array containing the row number (calculated by the **ROW** function) of the value in Range1 that matches the maximum value, and a "FALSE" for every other value in Range1.

The first **SUM** function adds the values in that Array, thus returning the row number of the maximum value in Range1.

Similarly, the second **SUM** function returns the column number (calculated by the **IF** and **COLUMN** functions) of the maximum value in Range1.

Finally, the **ADDRESS** function returns a text value, representing the cell reference indicated by the row and column numbers returned by the two **SUM** functions.

Retrieving Each Row Number that Corresponds with Successful Matches in a Look Up

> ### Problem:

We want to search List1 (column A) for the value stored in cell B2 and retrieve the row numbers that correspond with every successful match.

> ### Solution:

Use the **SMALL**, **IF**, and **ROW** functions as shown in the following *Array formula*:

{=SMALL(IF($A$2:$A$8=$B$2,ROW($A$2:$A$8),99999),ROW()-ROW($B$2)+1)}

Copy the formula down column C until 99999 is returned, which indicates that no further matches were found.

☞ To apply *Array formula*:

Select the cell, press **<F2>** and simultaneously press **<Ctrl+Shift+Enter>**.

	A	B	C	D
1	**List1**	**Lookup Value**	**Match's Row #**	
2	1	3	4	
3	2		6	
4	3		8	
5	2		99999	
6	3			
7	1			
8	3			
9				
10	**Array Formula Syntax in cell C2:**			
11	{=SMALL(IF($A$2:$A$8=$B$2,ROW($A$2:$A$8),99999),ROW()-ROW($B$2)+1)}			
12				

Explanation:

The **IF** function determines whether or not a given value in column A matches the lookup value in cell B2.

It returns an Array consisting of the row number (calculated by the **ROW** function) of every matching value and the number "99999" for every non-matching value.

The **ROW** functions, used as the Kth argument of the **SMALL** function, return the position of the current cell within the result column (C).

The **SMALL** function returns the Kth smallest number in the Array returned by the **IF** function.

Thus, the smallest number in the Array (the row number of the first match) is returned into cell C2, the second smallest number in the Array (the row number of the second match) into cell C3, and so on.

Retrieving the Row Number that Corresponds with a Matched Value in a Look Up

➤ **Problem:**

We want to search List1 (column A) for each of the letters in column C and retrieve the corresponding row number.

> ➢ **Solution:**

Use the **MAX**, **IF**, and **ROW** functions as shown in the following *Array formula*:

{=MAX(IF($A$2:$A$15=C2,ROW($A$2:$A$15)))}

> ☞ To apply *Array formula*:

Select the cell, press **<F2>** and simultaneously press **<Ctrl+Shift+Enter>**.

	A	B	C	D	E
1	List1		Letter	# Row	
2	C		M	7	
3	A		Z	15	
4	S		V	10	
5	G		A	3	
6	K		G	5	
7	M				
8	B				
9	R				
10	V				
11	E				
12	H				
13	X				
14	P				
15	Z				
16					
17	Array Formula Syntax in cell D2:				
18	{=MAX(IF($A$2:$A$15=C2,ROW($A$2:$A$15)))}				
19					

Explanation:

The **IF** function determines whether or not a given value in column A matches the letter in cell C2.

It returns an Array containing the row number (calculated by the **ROW** function) of the successful match, and a "FALSE" for each of the other values in column A.

The **MAX** function returns the largest number in that Array, i.e. the row number of the matching letter from column A.

Chapter 3

Date & Time

About This Chapter

This chapter deals with many of the issues and problems that may be encountered when using Date & Time formulas. It includes the following sections:

☞ **Date, page 72:** This section covers techniques on entering dates quickly into a cell and calculating the difference between dates by day, month, quarter, and year. You will also learn how to calculate the last day of a given month, a project end, a payment due date, and more.

☞ **Time, page 102:** This section deals with techniques on entering time values quickly, adding and subtracting times, converting times to decimal values, calculating military time, calculating by time zone, rounding time values, and more.

☞ **Date & Time, page 125:** This section contains formulas dealing with dates & time, such as date & time stamps, converting date & time from GMT to CST, separating date & time, and more.

☞ **Wages, Shifts & Time Worked, page 135**: This section covers formulas on date & time that are used to calculate time sheets, employee hours worked, shifts, sick leave, pay days, and more.

Date

Entering Dates Quickly

> ➤ **Problem:**

Entering dates quickly, without having to use delimiters to separate month, day, and year.

> ➤ **Solution 1:**

Enter only the "day" part of the date and complete it by using the **DATE, YEAR, TODAY,** and **MONTH** functions in the following formula:

=DATE(YEAR(TODAY()),MONTH(TODAY()),A2)

Thus, on entering "5", the formula will automatically create a date representing the 5th of the current month in the current year.

> ➤ **Solution 2:**

Enter the entire date, without delimiters, and use the **DATEVALUE, LEFT, MID,** and **RIGHT** functions as shown in the following formula to convert it to a proper date:

=DATEVALUE(LEFT(D2,2)&"/"&MID(D2,3,2)&"/"&RIGHT(D2,2))

Thus, on entering "060705", the above formula will return "06/07/05".

	A	B	C	D	E
1	Entry	Date		Entry	Date
2	5	07/05/2005		060705	06/07/2005
3	20	07/20/2005		120804	12/08/2004
4					
5	Formula Syntax in cell B2:				
6	=DATE(YEAR(TODAY()),MONTH(TODAY()),A2)				
7					
8	Formula Syntax in cell E2:				
9	=DATEVALUE(LEFT(D2,2)&"/"&MID(D2,3,2)&"/"&RIGHT(D2,2))				
10					

Calculating Number of Days, Weeks, Months and Years between Dates

➢ **Problem:**

Calculating the difference between each pair of dates listed in columns A & B.

➢ **Solution:**

❖ To calculate the difference in days, use the **DATEDIF** function as shown in the following formula:

=DATEDIF(A2,B2,"d")

❖ To calculate the difference in weeks, use the **INT** function as shown in the following formula:

=INT((B2-A2)/7)

❖ To calculate the difference in months, use the **DATEDIF** function as shown in the following formula:

=DATEDIF(A2,B2,"m")

❖ To calculate the difference in years, use one of the following two solutions:

Use the **DATEDIF** function as shown in the following formula:
=DATEDIF(A2,B2,"y")

OR

Use the **YEAR, MONTH, AND**, and **DAY** functions as shown in the following formula:
=YEAR(B2)-YEAR(A2)-(MONTH(B2)<MONTH(A2))-
(AND(MONTH(B2)=MONTH(A2),DAY(B2)<DAY(A2)))

❖ To calculate the number of months over years, use the **DATEDIF** function as shown in the following formula:

=DATEDIF(A2,B2,"ym")

❖ To calculate the number of days over years, use the **DATEDIF** function as shown in the following formula:

=DATEDIF(A2,B2,"yd")

	A	B	C	D	E	F	G	H
1	Start Date	End Date	Difference (Days)	Difference (Weeks)	Difference (Months)	Difference (Years)	Difference (Months above Years)	Difference (Days above Years)
2	01/01/2005	06/20/2005	170	24	5	0	5	170
3	01/01/2005	12/31/2006	729	104	23	1	11	364
4	01/01/2004	01/31/2004	30	4	0	0	0	30
5								
6	Formula Syntax in cell C2:			Formula Syntax in cell D2:			Formula Syntax in cell E2:	
7	=DATEDIF(A2,B2,"d")			=INT((B2-A2)/7)			=DATEDIF(A2,B2,"m")	
8								
9	Alternative Formula for cell E2:							
10	=YEAR(B2)-YEAR(A2)-(MONTH(B2)<MONTH(A2))-(AND(MONTH(B2)=MONTH(A2),DAY(B2)<DAY(A2)))							
11								
12	Formula Syntax in cell F2:			Formula Syntax in cell G2:			Formula Syntax in cell H2:	
13	=DATEDIF(A2,B2,"y")			=DATEDIF(A2,B2,"ym")			=DATEDIF(A2,B2,"yd")	
14								

Calculating a Date Based on Year, Week Number and Day of the Week

➢ **Problem:**

Calculating a date using the relevant numbers for day of the week, week number, and year number.

➢ **Solution:**

Use the **DATE** and **WEEKDAY** functions as shown in the following formula:

=DATE(C2,1,3)-WEEKDAY(DATE(C2,1,3),1)+7*(B2-1)+A2

	A	B	C	D
1	Day of the Week	Week Number	Year	Result
2	1	10	2004	02/29/2004
3	4	25	2005	06/22/2005
4	7	50	2006	12/16/2006
5				
6				
7	Formula Syntax in cell D2:			
8	=DATE(C2,1,3)-WEEKDAY(DATE(C2,1,3),1)+7*(B2-1)+A2			
9				

Explanation:

The **DATE** function returns the date of January 3rd, for the year listed in cell C2.

The **WEEKDAY** function returns the day of the week (1-7) that corresponds with that date.

The number returned by the **WEEKDAY** function, representing a number of days, is subtracted from the date calculated by the **DATE** function.

To that date is added the number of days that result from the following calculation (based on the day of the week and week number listed in cells A2:B2):

7*(B2-1)+A2

The result is the date that corresponds to the year, week number, and day of the week listed in cells A2:C2.

Finding the Last Day of a Given Month

➢ **Problem:**

Calculating the date at the end of the current month, as well as the date at the end of each month (serial number) listed in column A.

➢ **Solution:**

❖ To calculate the date at the end of the current month, use the **EOMONTH** and **TODAY** functions as shown in the following formula:

=EOMONTH(TODAY(),0)

❖ To calculate the date at the end of next month, use the **EOMONTH** and **TODAY** functions as shown in the following formula:

=EOMONTH(TODAY(),1)

❖ To calculate the date at the end of each month listed in column A, use the **DATE** function as shown in the following formula:

=DATE(2005,A2+1,0)

	A	B	C	D
1	**Month**	**End of Month**		**Today's Date**
2	1	01/31/2005		07/13/2005
3	2	02/28/2005		
4	3	03/31/2005		**End of Current Month**
5	4	04/30/2005		07/31/2005
6	5	05/31/2005		
7	6	06/30/2005		**End of Next Month**
8	7	07/31/2005		08/31/2005
9	8	08/31/2005		
10	9	09/30/2005		
11	10	10/31/2005		
12	11	11/30/2005		**Formula Syntax in cell B2:**
13	12	12/31/2005		=DATE(2005,A2+1,0)
14				
15	**Formula Syntax in cell D5:**			**Formula Syntax in cell D8:**
16	=EOMONTH(TODAY(),0)			=EOMONTH(TODAY(),1)
17				

Explanation:

☞ **End of Current Month Formula (cell D5)**

The **TODAY**() function returns today's date.

The **EOMONTH** function calculates the date 0 months after the date returned by the **TODAY** function, and returns the last day of the month for that date.

Thus, it returns the last day of the current month.

☞ **End of Next Month Formula (cell D8)**

The **TODAY**() function returns today's date.

The **EOMONTH** function calculates the date 1 month after the date returned by the **TODAY** function, and returns the last day of the month for that date.

Thus, it returns the last day of the next month.

☞ **DATE Formula (column B)**

The **DATE** function calculates the date on day number 0 of the month following the month listed in cell A2 (A2+1), for the year 2005.

As day number 0 indicates the last day of the previous month, the **DATE** function returns the date of the last day of the month specified in cell A2.

Analysis ToolPak Add-In:

The **EOMONTH** function is included in the Analysis ToolPak Add-In. To install the Analysis ToolPak Add-in: Select *Tools → Add-Ins → Analysis ToolPak*, Click OK.

Calculating the Number of Business Days in a Specified Period

➢ **Problem:**

Calculating the number of business days between the dates entered in cells A2 & B2.

➢ **Solution:**

Use the **NETWORKDAYS** function as shown in the following formula:

=NETWORKDAYS(A2,B2)

	A	B	C
1	Date1	Date2	Business Days
2	04/01/2005	10/01/2005	131
3			
4	Formula Syntax in cell C2:		
5	=NETWORKDAYS(A2,B2)		
6			

Explanation:

The **NETWORKDAYS** function returns the number of whole workdays between the dates entered in cells A2 and B2.

Analysis ToolPak Add-In:

The **NETWORKDAYS** function is included in the Analysis ToolPak Add-In. To install the Analysis ToolPak Add-in: Select *Tools → Add-Ins → Analysis ToolPak*, Click OK.

Calculating a Project's End Date

> **Problem:**

Columns A & B contain the start date of various projects and the number of hours required for each project's completion.

We want to calculate each project's end date, based on the number of required hours, a specified number of daily working hours (cell C2), and the assumption that work is only done on weekdays.

> **Solution:**

Use the **WORKDAY** and **ROUNDUP** functions as shown in the following formula:

=WORKDAY(A2,ROUNDUP(B2/$C$2,0))

	A	B	C	D
1	Start Date	# Required Hours	Working Hours per Day	End Date
2	05/31/2005	50	8	06/09/2005
3	03/22/2005	150		04/18/2005
4	09/15/2004	800		02/02/2005
5	12/12/2003	1500		09/01/2004
6				
7	Formula Syntax in cell D2:			
8	=WORKDAY(A2,ROUNDUP(B2/$C$2,0))			
9				

Explanation:

The number of required hours (cell B2) is divided by the number of daily working hours (cell C2) and the **ROUNDUP** function rounds the result up to the nearest integer (0 decimal places). Thus, it returns the number of workdays required to complete the project.

The **WORKDAY** function calculates the date that is the number of workdays after the project's start date (cell A2) as was calculated by the **ROUNDUP** function.

Thus, it returns the end date for the project in cells A2:B2.

Analysis ToolPak Add-In:

The **WORKDAY** function is included in the Analysis ToolPak Add-In. To install the Analysis ToolPak Add-in: Select *Tools → Add-Ins → Analysis ToolPak*, Click OK.

Calculating a Required Date According to Two Criteria

➢ **Problem:**

Columns B & C contain test dates and paper deadlines for each of the subjects listed in column A.

A test requires 3 days of preparation and a paper requires 5 days.

For each subject, we want to calculate the earliest date required to start preparing for either a test or a paper.

➢ **Solution:**

Use the **MIN** and **IF** functions as shown in the following formula:

=MIN(IF(B2<>"",B2-3,C2-5),IF(C2<>"",C2-5,B2-3))

	A	B	C	D
1	**Subject**	**Test Date**	**Paper Deadline**	**Result**
2	A	05/15/2005	05/20/2005	05/12/2005
3	B		04/14/2005	04/09/2005
4	C	06/01/2005		05/29/2005
5	D	02/13/2005	02/11/2005	02/06/2005
6				
7				
8	**Formula Syntax in cell D2:**			
9	=MIN(IF(B2<>"",B2-3,C2-5),IF(C2<>"",C2-5,B2-3))			
10				

Explanation:

The first **IF** function determines whether or not cell B2 is blank. If it isn't, it subtracts 3 days from the test date stored in cell B2 and returns the result. Otherwise, it subtracts 5 days from the paper deadline stored in cell C2 and returns the result.

The second **IF** function determines whether or not cell C2 is blank. If it isn't, it subtracts 5 days from the paper deadline stored in cell C2 and returns the result. Otherwise, it subtracts 3 days from the test date stored in cell B2 and returns the result.

The **MIN** function returns the minimum date returned by the two **IF** functions.

Thus, it returns the earliest date required to start preparing for either a test or a paper.

Indicating Due Payments, Based on the Current Date

➤ **Problem:**

Column B contains the date of the last payment made by each of the clients listed in column A.

Payments are to be collected from each client every two weeks.

We want to indicate which clients have payments due today, based on the number of days since their last payment.

➤ **Solution:**

Use the **IF, MOD,** and **TODAY** functions as shown in the following formula:

=IF(MOD(TODAY()-B2,14)=0,"Pay Today","")

Thus, the string "Pay Today" will appear next to each client whose payment is due today.

	A	B	C
1	**Client**	**Last Paydate**	**Result**
2	A	08/29/2005	
3	B	08/30/2005	Pay Today
4	C	08/31/2005	
5	D	09/01/2005	
6	E	09/02/2005	
7			
8	**Formula Syntax in cell C2:**		
9	=IF(MOD(TODAY()-B2,14)=0,"Pay Today","")		
10			
11	**Today's Date:**	08/16/2005	
12			

Explanation:

The **TODAY()** function returns today's date.

The date stored in cell B2 (the last pay date) is then subtracted from today's date, returning the number of days since the last pay date.

The **MOD** function divides that number of days by 14 and returns the remainder.

If the remainder is 0 (the number of days since the last pay date is divisible by 14), the **IF** function returns the string "Pay Today". Otherwise, it returns a blank cell.

Thus, the formula indicates the clients who have payments due today.

Calculating the Date of the Nth Specific Day of the Month

➤ **Problem:**

Calculating the date of, for example, the first Saturday of each of the months listed in column A, for the year specified in cell B2.

➤ **Solution:**

Use the **WEEKDAY** and **DATE** functions as shown in the following formula:

=DATE($B$2,A2,1+((1-(6>=WEEKDAY(DATE($B$2,A2,1),2)))*7+(6-
WEEKDAY(DATE($B$2,A2,1),2))))

	A	B	C	D
1	**Months**	**Year**	**Date**	
2	1	2005	01/01/2005	
3	2		02/05/2005	
4	3		03/05/2005	
5	4		04/02/2005	
6	5		05/07/2005	
7	6		06/04/2005	
8	7		07/02/2005	
9	8		08/06/2005	
10	9		09/03/2005	
11	10		10/01/2005	
12	11		11/05/2005	
13	12		12/03/2005	
14				
15	**Formula Syntax in cell C2:**			
16	=DATE($B$2,A2,1+((1- (6>=WEEKDAY(DATE($B$2,A2,1),2)))*7+(6- WEEKDAY(DATE($B$2,A2,1),2))))			
17				

Explanation:

The **DATE** function in the following expression calculates the date on the first day of the month listed in cell A2 for the year specified in cell B2:

6>=WEEKDAY(DATE($B$2,A2,1),2)

The **WEEKDAY** function returns a serial number between 1 (Monday) & 7 (Sunday) that represents the day of the week matching that date.

Thus, it returns the day of the week on the first day of the month listed in cell A2.

If that day is smaller than or equal to 6 (represents Saturday), the above expression returns "1" (TRUE). Otherwise, it returns "0" (FALSE).

The value returned is subtracted from 1 and the result is multiplied by 7.

Then, 1 is added to the result, and the difference between 6 (Saturday) and the day of the week on the first day of the month (calculated by the **WEEKDAY** and **DATE** functions) is also added.

The number returned is the day number (1-31) of the first Saturday of the month shown in cell A2.

Finally, the **DATE** function returns the date that corresponds with that day number for the month listed in cell A2 and the year specified in cell B2.

Eliminating Negative Values from Date Subtractions

➢ **Problem:**

Creating a formula to return the number of days between each date in column A and the corresponding deadline in column B.

In cases where the date in column A is later than the deadline, the formula is to return zero rather than a negative number of days.

➢ **Solution:**

Use the **MAX** function as shown in the following formula:

=MAX(B2-A2,0)

	A	B	C
1	**Date**	**Deadline**	**Result**
2	09/17/2004	10/15/2004	28
3	04/02/2005	04/01/2005	0
4	05/05/2005	01/31/2006	271
5	01/03/2003	12/31/2002	0
6			
7	**Formula Syntax in cell C2:**		
8	=MAX(B2-A2,0)		
9			

Explanation:

The date in cell A2 is subtracted from the corresponding deadline in cell B2 and the number of days between them is returned.

If the date in cell A2 is later than the deadline, a negative number of days is returned.

The **MAX** function returns the maximum of the calculated number of days and 0.

Thus, if the date in cell A2 is later than the corresponding deadline, the formula returns zero, rather than a negative number of days.

Avoiding Negative Values when Calculating the Number of Days between Two Dates

➤ **Problem:**

We want to create a formula to calculate the number of days between each pair of dates in columns A & B, but the formula is never to return a negative value.

Empty cells in column A are to be considered the first day of the year, and empty cells in column B are to be considered the last day of the year.

➤ **Solution:**

Use the **MAX**, **MIN**, and **DATE** functions as shown in the following formula:

=MIN(B2,DATE(2005,12,31))-MAX(A2,DATE(2005,1,1))

	A	B	C	D
1	**Date1**	**Date2**	**Result**	
2	02/11/2005	09/23/2005	224	
3	05/04/2005		241	
4	07/20/2005	08/20/2005	31	
5		10/31/2005	303	
6				
7	**Formula Syntax in cell C2:**			
8	=MIN(B2,DATE(2005,12,31))-MAX(A2,DATE(2005,1,1))			
9				

Explanation:

The first **DATE** function returns the date of December 31st, 2005 (the last day of the year).

The **MIN** function returns the minimum of the date stored in cell B2 and that returned by the **DATE** function.

Thus, if cell B2 is empty, the **MIN** function returns the last day of the year.

The second **DATE** function returns the date of January 1st, 2005 (the first day of the month).

The **MAX** function returns the maximum of the date stored in cell A2 and that returned by the **DATE** function.

Thus, if cell A2 is empty, the **MAX** function returns the first day of the year.

Finally, the date returned by the **MAX** function is subtracted from the one returned by the **MIN** function.

The result is the number of days between the pair of dates in cells A2 & B2.

As the formula considers empty cells in column A as the first day of the year, and empty cells in column B as the last day of the year, negative results are never returned.

Avoiding False Results when Counting Dates Matching Specified Criteria

➢ **Problem:**

Column A contains dates formatted as "mm/dd/yyyy".

When using the following **COUNTIF** formula to count the number of dates after April 1st, 2005:

=COUNTIF(A2:A6,">"&--"04/01/05")

A false result of 4 was returned.

➢ **Solution 1:**

To avoid any format related problems, use the **COUNTIF** and **DATE** functions as shown in the following formula:

=COUNTIF(A2:A6,">"&DATE(2005,4,1))

➢ **Solution 2:**

Use the **COUNTIF** function as shown in the following formula:

=COUNTIF(A2:A6,">"&--"2005-04-01")

	A	B	C
1	Dates	Formula 1	Formula 2
2	02/12/2005	2	2
3	03/11/2005		
4	01/03/2005		
5	05/07/2005		
6	06/09/2005		
7			
8	Formula 1 Syntax in cell B2:		
9	=COUNTIF(A2:A6,">"&DATE(2005,4,1))		
10			
11	Formula 2 Syntax in cell C2:		
12	=COUNTIF(A2:A6,">"&--"2005-04-01")		
13			

Explanation:

The date entered in the above formula was considered by Excel to be January 4th, rather than April 1st.

The manner in which Excel reads dates is dependant of the date format set in the software's regional settings.

Other regional areas use different date formats to that used in the United States.

The two solutions provided above will return the proper results for any date format set in the software.

☞ **Solution 1:**

The **DATE** function returns the date of April 1st, 2005.

The **COUNTIF** function returns the number of dates in column A (cells A2:A6) that are greater than the date returned by the **DATE** function.

Thus, it returns the number of dates in column A after April 1st, 2005.

☞ **Solution 2:**

The string "2005-04-01" represents the date of April 1st, 2005.

The "--" sign converts that string to the date it represents.

The **COUNTIF** function returns the number of dates in column A (A2:A6) that are greater than that date.

Thus, it returns the number of dates in column A after April 1st, 2005.

Calculating the Week Number Corresponding with a Specific Date

➤ **Problem:**

Calculating the week number corresponding with each of the dates listed in column A.

➤ **Solution:**

Use the **WEEKNUM** function as shown in the following formula:

=WEEKNUM(A2,2)

	A	B
1	**Date**	**Week Number**
2	11/11/2003	46
3	04/21/2005	17
4	08/13/2006	33
5	03/06/2004	10
6		
7	**Formula Syntax in cell B2:**	
8	=WEEKNUM(A2,2)	
9		

Explanation:

The **WEEKNUM** function returns the week number corresponding with the date stored in cell A2.

The second argument of the **WEEKNUM** function represents week type: use "2" for a Monday-Sunday week, and "1" for a Sunday-Saturday week.

Analysis ToolPak Add-In:

The **WEEKNUM** function is included in the Analysis ToolPak Add-In. To install the Analysis ToolPak Add-in: Select *Tools → Add-Ins → Analysis ToolPak*, Click OK.

Determining whether Two Given Dates Occur within the Same Week

➢ **Problem:**

Determining whether each pair of corresponding dates in columns A & B occur within the same week.

➢ **Solution:**

Use the **WEEKNUM** and **IF** functions as shown in the following formula:

=IF(WEEKNUM(A2,2)=WEEKNUM(B2,2),"Same Week","Different Week")

	A	B	C	D	E
1	**Date1**	**Date2**	**Result**		
2	05/16/2005	05/21/2005	Same Week		
3	03/13/2004	03/15/2004	Different Week		
4	10/12/2006	10/13/2006	Same Week		
5	01/20/2005	01/26/2005	Different Week		
6					
7	**Formula Syntax in cell C2:**				
8	=IF(WEEKNUM(A2,2)=WEEKNUM(B2,2),"Same Week","Different Week")				
9					

Explanation:

The first **WEEKNUM** function returns the week number corresponding with the date stored in cell A2.

The second **WEEKNUM** function returns the week number corresponding with the date stored in cell B2.

If the two week numbers are equal, the **IF** function returns the string "Same Week". Otherwise, it returns "Different Week".

Note that the second argument of the **WEEKNUM** function represents week type:

Use "2" for a Monday-Sunday week, and "1" for a Sunday-Saturday week.

 Analysis ToolPak Add-In:

The **WEEKNUM** function is included in the Analysis ToolPak Add-In. To install the Analysis ToolPak Add-in: Select *Tools → Add-Ins → Analysis ToolPak*, Click OK.

Finding the Number of Days in a Given Month

➤ **Problem:**

Calculating the number of days in each of the months listed in column A, for the year specified in column B.

➤ **Solution:**

Use the **DAY** and **DATE** functions as shown in the following formula:

=DAY(DATE(B2,A2+1,0))

	A	B	C
1	**Month**	**Year**	**Result**
2	1	2005	31
3	2	2005	28
4	2	2004	29
5	7	2005	31
6	11	2005	30
7			
8			
9	**Formula Syntax in cell C2:**		
10	=DAY(DATE(B2,A2+1,0))		
11			

Explanation:

The **DATE** function calculates the date on day number 0 of the month following the month listed in cell A2 (A2+1) for the year specified in cell B2.

As day number 0 indicates the last day of the previous month, the **DATE** function returns the date of the last day of the month specified in cell A2.

The **DAY** function extracts the "day" part of the date calculated by the **DATE** function.

Thus, it returns the number of days in the month listed in cell A2 for the year specified in cell B2.

Finding the Serial Number of the Last Day of the Month

➢ **Problem:**

Finding the day of the week matching the last day of each month (serial number) listed in column A.

➢ **Solution:**

Use the **WEEKDAY** and **DATE** functions as shown in the following formula:

=WEEKDAY(DATE(2004,A2+1,0),2)

Thus, the formula will return a number between 1 & 7 for each month in column A, where 1 represents Monday, and 7 represents Sunday.

To return 1 for Sunday and 7 for Saturday, modify your formula as follows:

=WEEKDAY(DATE(2004,A2+1,0),1)

	A	B	C
1	Month	Day of the Week (Monday-Sunday)	Day of the Week (Sunday-Saturday)
2	1	6	7
3	2	7	1
4	3	3	4
5	4	5	6
6	5	1	2
7	6	3	4
8	7	6	7
9	8	2	3
10	9	4	5
11	10	7	1
12	11	2	3
13	12	5	6
14			
15	**Formula Syntax in cell B2:**		
16	=WEEKDAY(DATE(2004,A2+1,0),2)		
17			
18	**Formula Syntax in cell C2:**		
19	=WEEKDAY(DATE(2004,A2+1,0),1)		
20			

Explanation:

The **DATE** function calculates the date on day number 0 of the month following the month listed in cell A2 (A2+1) for the year 2004.

As day number 0 indicates the last day of the previous month, the **DATE** function returns the date of the last day of the month specified in cell A2.

The **WEEKDAY** function returns a number between 1 & 7 that represents the day of the week that corresponds with the date calculated by the **DATE** function. Thus, it returns the day of the week that corresponds with the last day of the month specified in cell A2.

The second argument of the **WEEKDAY** function represents week type:

Use "2" for a Monday-Sunday week, where 1 represents Monday and 7 represents Sunday.

Use "1" for a Sunday-Saturday week, where 1 represents Sunday and 7 represent Saturday.

Adding a Specified Number of Months to a Date

➢ **Problem:**

Column B contains numbers of months which are to be added to the corresponding dates shown in column A.

We want to calculate the appropriate cumulative dates.

➢ **Solution 1:**

Use the **DATE, YEAR, MONTH, MIN,** and **DAY** functions as shown in the following formula:

=DATE(YEAR(A2),MONTH(A2)+B2,MIN(DAY(A2),DAY(DATE(YEAR(A2), MONTH(A2)+B2+1,0))))

➢ **Solution 2:**

Use the **EDATE** function as shown in the following formula:

=EDATE(A2,B2)

	A	B	C	D	E
1	Date	Months to Add	DATE Formula	EDATE Formula	
2	05/16/2005	10	03/16/2006	03/16/2006	
3	03/11/2003	20	11/11/2004	11/11/2004	
4	07/31/2002	-4	03/31/2002	03/31/2002	
5	01/30/2004	1	02/29/2004	02/29/2004	
6					
7	DATE Formula Syntax in cell C2:				
8	=DATE(YEAR(A2),MONTH(A2)+B2,MIN(DAY(A2),DAY(DATE(YEAR(A2),MONTH(A2)+B2+1,0))))				
9					
10	EDATE Formula Syntax in cell D2:				
11	=EDATE(A2,B2)				
12					

Explanation:

☞ **DATE Formula**

The **DATE** function in the following expression, using the **YEAR** and **MONTH** functions, calculates the date of the last day in the month that corresponds with the cumulative date.

MIN(DAY(A2),DAY(DATE(YEAR(A2),MONTH(A2)+B2+1,0)))

The **DAY** function (the second one in the expression) returns the day part of that date, which is the number of days in the month of the cumulative date.

The first **DAY** function in the above expression returns the day part of the date in cell A2.

The **MIN** function returns the minimum of the numbers returned by the two **DAY** functions.

Thus, the result of the above expression is the number to be used as the day number of the cumulative date.

The **YEAR** function returns the year number of the date stored in cell A2.

The **MONTH** function returns the month number (1-12) of the date stored in cell A2.

The numbers of months specified in cell B2 is then added to that number. The result represents the month number of the cumulative date.

The **DATE** function returns the date that corresponds with the year number returned by the **YEAR** function, the cumulative month number, and the day number returned by the **MIN** function.

☞ **EDATE Formula**

The **EDATE** function returns the cumulative date for the date stored in cell A2 and the number of months specified in cell B2.

 Analysis ToolPak Add-In:

The **EDATE** function is included in the Analysis ToolPak Add-In. To install the Analysis ToolPak Add-in: Select *Tools → Add-Ins → Analysis ToolPak*, Click OK.

Converting a Month's Serial Number into Its Corresponding Name

➢ **Problem:**

Converting each month's serial number, as shown in column A, into its corresponding name.

➢ **Solution 1:**

To return a month's full name, use the **TEXT** function as shown in the following formula:

=TEXT(A2*29,"mmmm")

To return the first three letters of a month's name ("Jan", "Feb" etc.), use the **TEXT** function as shown in the following formula:

=TEXT(A2*29,"mmm")

➢ **Solution 2:**

Use the **CHOOSE** function as shown in the following formula:

=CHOOSE(A2,"Jan","Feb","Mar","Apr","May","Jun","Jul","Aug","Sep","Oct","Nov","Dec")

	A	B	C
1	**Month Number**	**TEXT Formula**	**CHOOSE Formula**
2	1	January	Jan
3	2	February	Feb
4	3	March	Mar
5	4	April	Apr
6	5	May	May
7	6	June	Jun
8	7	July	Jul
9	8	August	Aug
10	9	September	Sep
11	10	October	Oct
12	11	November	Nov
13	12	December	Dec
14			
15	**TEXT Formula Syntax in cell B2:**		
16	=TEXT(A2*29,"mmmm")		
17			
18	**CHOOSE Formula Syntax in cell C2:**		
19	=CHOOSE(A2,"Jan","Feb","Mar","Apr","May","Jun","Jul","Aug","Sep","Oct","Nov","Dec")		

Explanation:

☞ **TEXT Formula**

The month number in cell A2 is multiplied by 29.

The result is a number representing a date on that month.

The **TEXT** function formats that number as "mmmm" (a date format displaying the name of the month) and converts it to text.

Thus, the formula converts the month number in cell A2 into its corresponding name.

☞ **CHOOSE Formula**

The **CHOOSE** function returns the Nth value in the following list of month names (entered in the formula), where N is the month number stored in cell A2:

"Jan","Feb","Mar","Apr","May","Jun","Jul","Aug","Sep","Oct","Nov","Dec"

Thus, the formula converts the month number in cell A2 into its corresponding name.

Calculating the Quarter Number for Calendar and Fiscal Year

➤ **Problem:**

Calculating the quarter number corresponding with each of the dates listed in column A.

➤ **Solution:**

To calculate the quarter number based on a calendar year, use the **INT** and **MONTH** functions in the following formula:

=INT((MONTH(A2)-1)/3)+1

To calculate the quarter number based on a fiscal year (starting in September), use the **MOD**, **CEILING**, and **MONTH** functions as shown in the following formula:

=MOD(CEILING(22+MONTH(A2)-9-1,3)/3,4)+1

	A	B	C
1	Date	Quarter Number (Calendar Year)	Quarter Number (Fiscal Year First Month= September)
2	01/31/2005	1	2
3	02/28/2005	1	2
4	03/31/2005	1	2
5	04/30/2005	2	3
6	05/31/2005	2	3
7	06/30/2005	2	3
8	07/31/2005	3	4
9	08/31/2005	3	4
10	09/30/2005	3	4
11	10/31/2005	4	1
12	11/30/2005	4	1
13	12/31/2005	4	1
14			
15	Formula Syntax in cell B2:		
16	=INT((MONTH(A2)-1)/3)+1		
17			
18	Formula Syntax in cell C2:		
19	=MOD(CEILING(22+MONTH(A2)-9-1,3)/3,4)+1		
20			

Explanation:

☞ **Formula for Quarter Number in a Calendar Year:**

The **MONTH** function returns the month number (1-12) of the date stored in cell A2.

1 is then subtracted from that number and the result is divided by 3.

The **INT** function rounds the result of that calculation down to the nearest integer.

Finally, 1 is added to the number returned by the **INT** function.

The result is the quarter number matching the date stored in cell A2.

☞ **Formula for Quarter Number in a Fiscal Year:**

The **MONTH** function returns the month number (1-12) of the date stored in cell A2.

1 and 9 are then subtracted from that number and 22 is added to the result.

The **CEILING** function rounds up the result of that calculation to the nearest multiple of 3.

The number returned by the **CEILING** function is divided by 3 and the **MOD** function divides the result by 4 and returns the remainder.

Finally, 1 is added to that remainder.

The result is the quarter number matching the date stored in cell A2.

Converting a Date into a String, Indicating the Quarter Number and Year

➤ **Problem:**

Converting the dates listed in column A into strings indicating the relevant quarter number and year, using the following format:

"Quarter X, YYYY".

➤ **Solution:**

Use the **MONTH**, **INT**, and **YEAR** functions as shown in the following formula:

="Quarter " &INT((MONTH(A2)+2)/3)&", "&YEAR(A2)

	A	B	C	D
1	**Dates**	**Results**		
2	05/10/2005	Quarter 2, 2005		
3	08/02/2002	Quarter 3, 2002		
4	10/19/1998	Quarter 4, 1998		
5	02/08/2004	Quarter 1, 2004		
6				
7	**Formula Syntax in cell B2:**			
8	="Quarter " &INT((MONTH(A2)+2)/3)&", "&YEAR(A2)			
9				

Explanation:

The **MONTH** function returns the month number (1-12) of the date stored in cell A2.

2 is then added to that month number and the result is divided by 3.

The **INT** function rounds the result of that calculation down to the nearest integer.

Thus, it calculates the quarter number matching the date stored in cell A2.

The **YEAR** function returns the year number of the date stored in cell A2.

Finally, a single string is created by joining the text "Quarter ", the calculated quarter number (returned by the **INT** function), the text "," and the calculated year number (returned by the **YEAR** function).

Thus, the formula converts the date listed in cell A2 into a string indicating the quarter number and year.

Determining Which Quarter a Specified Date Corresponds With

➢ **Problem:**

Determining and indicating which quarter each of the dates listed in column A corresponds with.

➢ **Solution:**

Use the **CHOOSE, MATCH,** and **MONTH** functions as shown in the following formula:

=CHOOSE(MATCH(MONTH(A2),{1,4,7,10}),"Quarter1","Quarter2","Quarter3","Quarter4")

	A	B	C	D
1	**Dates**	**Result**		
2	01/11/2005	Quarter1		
3	12/26/2005	Quarter4		
4	03/18/2005	Quarter1		
5	06/14/2005	Quarter2		
6	08/11/2005	Quarter3		
7				
8	**Formula Syntax in cell B2:**			
9	=CHOOSE(MATCH(MONTH(A2),{1,4,7,10}),"Quarter1","Quarter2","Quarter3","Quarter4")			

Explanation:

The **MONTH** function returns the month number (1-12) of the date stored in cell A2.

The **MATCH** function returns the position of that number within the following Array, consisting of the first month of each quarter:

{1,4,7,10}

If the number returned by the **MONTH** function does not appear in the Array, the **MATCH** function returns the position of the closest smaller match.

Thus, the **MATCH** function returns a number between 1 & 4.

The **CHOOSE** function returns the Nth value in the list of the strings entered in the formula ("Quarter1","Quarter2","Quarter3","Quarter4"), where N is the number returned by the **MATCH** function.

Hence, the formula determines which quarter the date in cell A2 corresponds with and returns a string indicating the result.

Converting Older Dates to the Current Year

➤ **Problem:**

Converting the dates listed in column A into the corresponding day and month of the current year.

➤ **Solution:**

Use the **DATE, YEAR, TODAY, MONTH,** and **DAY** functions as shown in the following formula:

=DATE(YEAR(TODAY()),MONTH(A2),DAY(A2))

	A	B	C
1	**Dates**	**Result**	
2	02/11/1978	02/11/2005	
3	04/22/2002	04/22/2005	
4	09/13/1995	09/13/2005	
5	12/25/2004	12/25/2005	
6			
7	**Formula Syntax in cell B2:**		
8	=DATE(YEAR(TODAY()),MONTH(A2),DAY(A2))		
9			
10	**Today's Date:**	07/13/2005	
11			

Explanation:

The **TODAY** function returns today's date.

The **YEAR** function returns the year number of that date, which is the number of the current year.

The **DATE** function returns a date composed of the number of the current year (returned by the **YEAR** function), the month of the date stored in cell A2 (returned by the **MONTH** function), and the day of that date (returned by the **DAY** function).

Thus, the formula converts the date stored in cell A2 into the corresponding day and month of the current year.

Converting a Julian Date to a Calendar Date

➤ **Problem:**

Listed in column A are Julian dates in "YYJJJ" format.

"YY" represents a year between 1920 and 2020, and "JJJ" represents the serial number of the day within the year.

We want to convert each date in column A to its corresponding calendar date.

➤ Solution:

Use the **LEFT, IF,** and **MOD** functions as shown in the following formula and format the results as dates:

=("1/1/"&(IF(LEFT(A2,2)*1<20,2000,1900)+LEFT(A2,2)))+MOD(A2,1000)-1

	A	B	C
1	**Julian Dates**	**Calendar Dates**	
2	03171	06/20/2003	
3	89220	08/08/1989	
4	63002	01/02/1963	
5	05098	04/08/2005	
6	00360	12/25/2000	
7			
8	**Formula Syntax in cell B2:**		
9	=("1/1/"&(IF(LEFT(A2,2)*1<20,2000,1900)+LEFT(A2,2)))+MOD(A2,1000)-1		

Explanation:

The first **LEFT** function in the following expression extracts the two leftmost characters of the Julian date stored in cell A2:

("1/1/"&(IF(LEFT(A2,2)*1<20,2000,1900)+LEFT(A2,2)))

Those characters (the "YY" part of the date) are then multiplied by 1 to convert them to a number.

The **IF** function returns 2000 if that number is smaller than 20 and 1900 if it isn't.

The number returned by the **IF** function is added to the "YY" number extracted by the **LEFT** function (the second one), and the result is the year number indicated by the "YY" part of the Julian date in cell A2.

The text "1/1/" is joined with the calculated year number into a single string that represents the date of the first day in that year.

The **MOD** function divides the Julian date stored in cell A2 by 1000, and returns the remainder.

Thus, it returns the "JJJ" part of the Julian date, which is the serial number of the day within the year.

Finally, 1 is subtracted from that number (representing a number of days), and the result is added to the date calculated above (the first day of the year represented by "YY").

The result is the calendar date corresponding with the Julian date stored in cell A2.

Time

Entering Times Quickly (1)

➤ **Problem:**

Entering times quickly, without having to use a colon to separate hours and minutes.

➤ **Solution:**

Use the **TIMEVALUE, IF, LEFT,** and **RIGHT** functions as shown in the following formula:

=TIMEVALUE(IF(A2<1000, LEFT(A2,1),LEFT(A2,2))&":"&RIGHT(A2,2))

Enter the above formula in column B and format the cells as "hh:mm".

The formula will convert each numerical value in column A to a properly formatted time value.

	A	B	C	D
1	**Entry**	**Time**		
2	1254	12:54		
3	924	09:24		
4	2005	20:05		
5	1089	11:29		
6				
7	**Formula Syntax in cell B2:**			
8	=TIMEVALUE(IF(A2<1000, LEFT(A2,1),LEFT(A2,2))&":"&RIGHT(A2,2))			
9				

Explanation:

The **IF** function determines whether or not the numerical value in cell A2 is smaller than 1000.

If it is (the hour part of the entry consists of 1 digit), it returns the result of the first **LEFT** function, which extracts the leftmost character of the number in cell A2 (the digit representing the hour). Otherwise, it returns the result if the second **LEFT** function, which extracts the two leftmost characters of the number (the two digits representing the hour).

The hour part of the number in cell A2, returned by the **IF** function, is then joined with the ":" symbol and with the minute part of the number, which is extracted by the **RIGHT** function (extracts the two rightmost characters of the number in cell A2).

Thus, a string representing the time indicated in cell A2 is returned.

Finally, the **TIMEVALUE** function converts that string to a time value.

Entering Times Quickly (2)

➢ **Problem:**

Columns A & B contain pairs of numbers representing minutes and seconds.

Similarly, columns E & F contain pairs of numbers representing hours and minutes.

Some of the minute values in column A and hour values in column E represent time periods greater than 24 hours.

If we were to use simple **TIME** formulas to join each pair of values from columns A:B and E:F into single time values, they would return false results for all values exceeding 24 hours.

Thus, we are unable to simply use the following formulas to achieve our goal of a properly formatted time value:

=TIME(,A2,B2)

=TIME(E2,F2,)

➢ **Solution:**

To join minutes and seconds, use the **TIME** and **INT** functions as shown in the following formula:

=TIME(,A2,B2)+INT(A2/1440)

Enter the above formula in column C and format as "[mm]:ss".

To join hours and minutes, use the **TIME** and **INT** functions as shown in the following formula:

=TIME(E2,F2,) + INT(E2/24)

Enter the above formula in column G and format as "[hh]:mm".

The above formulas will allow the user to enter times quickly, without having to use a colon to separate hours and minutes or minutes and seconds.

	A	B	C	D	E	F	G
1	**Minutes**	**Seconds**	**Result**		**Hours**	**Minutes**	**Result**
2	30	45	30:45		10	50	10:50
3	2	36	02:36		12	75	13:15
4	100	20	100:20		30	20	30:20
5	1000	25.2	1000:25		48	12	48:12
6	1440	12.55	1440:12		1	500	09:20
7	2500	700	2511:40		5	30	05:30
8							
9	**Formula Syntax in cell C2:**						
10	=TIME(,A2,B2)+INT(A2/1440)						
11							
12	**Formula Syntax in cell G2:**						
13	=TIME(E2,F2,) + INT(E2/24)						
14							

Explanation:

Formula for Joining Hours and Minutes (cell G2):

The **TIME** function returns a time value composed of the number of hours in cell E2 and the number of minutes in cell F2.

If the number of hours in cell E2 represents a time period of more than a day (it is greater than 24), the **TIME** function will divide it by 24 and use the remainder as the number of hours.

Thus, in order to create a time value that properly represents an hour value greater than 24, we would have to calculate the number of full days included in it and add it to the time calculated by the **TIME** function.

To calculate the number of full days represented by the hour value in cell E2, it is divided by 24 and the **INT** function rounds the result down to the nearest integer.

The time returned by the **TIME** function is added to the number of full days calculated by the **INT** function.

The result is a time value (hh:mm) that represents the number of hours and minutes listed in cells E2 & F2.

Using the same method, the formula entered in cell C2 calculates the time value (mm:ss) that represents the number of minutes and seconds listed in cells A2 & B2.

Both formulas allow the user to enter times quickly, without having to use a colon to separate hours and minutes or minutes and seconds.

Adding Time Values

➤ **Problem:**

When using a standard **SUM** formula to add the time values in column B (=SUM(B2:B5)), a false result of 4:23 is returned, rather than the actual sum of 28:23.

➤ **Solution:**

Excel's default time format does not allow a time value to exceed 24 hours. This is the cause of the above error.

To properly display a sum exceeding 24 hours, change the format of the cell from "h:mm" to "[hh]:mm".

	A	B	C	D
1		**Times to Sum**		
2		02:32	02:32	
3		10:14	10:14	
4		06:52	06:52	
5		08:45	08:45	
6	**SUM formulas**	04:23	28:23	
7	**Formulas Syntax in Row 6**	=SUM(B2:B5)	=SUM(C2:C5)	
8	**Cells Formatting in Row 6**	h:mm	[hh]:mm	
9				

Adding Text Values Representing Time

➤ **Problem:**

The times listed in column A are formatted as text.

When trying to add them using a simple **SUM** formula (=SUM(A2:A5)), a false result of 0 is returned.

How can we add text values correctly?

> **Solution:**

Use the **SUM** and **TIMEVALUE** functions as shown in the following *Array formula*:

{=SUM(TIMEVALUE(A2:A5))}

☞ To apply *Array formula*:

Select the cell, press **<F2>** and simultaneously press **<Ctrl+Shift+Enter>**.

	A	B	C
1	**Times**	**Result**	
2	00:12	16:08	
3	05:31		
4	08:23		
5	02:02		
6			
7	**Array Formula Syntax in cell B2:**		
8	{=SUM(TIMEVALUE(A2:A5))}		
9			

Explanation:

The **TIMEVALUE** function converts each string in cells A2:A5 to a time value and returns the results in an Array.

The **SUM** function adds all the time values in that Array.

Thus, it returns the sum of the text values from column A that represent times.

Adding Time Values from Separate Hours and Minutes Columns

> **Problem:**

Columns A & B contain numbers representing hours and minutes respectively.

We want to add the numbers from both columns to calculate a single cumulative time value.

➢ **Solution:**

Use the **SUM** and **TIME** functions as shown in the following *Array formula*:

{=SUM(TIME(A2:A4,B2:B4,0))}

☞ To apply *Array formula*:

Select the cell, press **<F2>** and simultaneously press **<Ctrl+Shift+Enter>**.

	A	B	C	D
1	**Hours**	**Minutes**	**Result**	
2	5	20	15:20	
3	6	50		
4	3	10		
5				
6	**Array Formula Syntax in cell C2:**			
7	{=SUM(TIME(A2:A4,B2:B4,0))}			
8				

Explanation:

The **TIME** function creates a time value from each corresponding pair of hour and minute values from columns A (cells A2:A4) and B (cells B2:B4). All the time values created are returned in an Array and the **SUM** function adds them together.

The result is a cumulative time value of the hour and minute values listed in columns A & B.

Adding a Number to a Formatted Time Value

➢ **Problem:**

Creating a formula that will return a time value which is the sum of the time in cell A2 and the number of hours in cell B2.

> **Solution:**

When adding a time value and a number representing hours, we must first divide the number by 24, as shown in the following formula:

=A2+B2/24

Ensure that the result cell is formatted [hh]:mm to correctly display a time.

	A	B	C	D
1	Time	Hours to Add	Result	
2	10:30	4.5	15:00	
3	17:00	5.2	22:12	
4	14:12	0.6	14:48	
5				
6	Formula Syntax in cell C2:			
7	=A2+B2/24			
8				
9	Cells Formatting in column C			
10	[hh]:mm			
11				

Calculating Absolute Difference between Two Time Values

> **Problem:**

Columns A & B contain pairs of time values from the same day.

We want to create a formula that always subtracts the earlier time from the later one, regardless of which column each is in.

> **Solution 1:**

Use the **IF** function as shown in the following formula:

=IF(B2>=A2,B2-A2,A2-B2)

> **Solution 2:**

Use the **ABS** function as shown in the following formula:

=ABS(B2-A2)

❖ **Note:** Apply hh:mm format to cells containing the formulas.

	A	B	C	D
1	**Time1**	**Time2**	**IF Formula**	**ABS Formula**
2	18:30	09:00	9:30	9:30
3	08:00	16:00	8:00	8:00
4				
5				
6	**IF Formula Syntax in cell C2:**			
7	=IF(B2>=A2,B2-A2,A2-B2)			
8				
9	**ABS Formula Syntax in cell D2:**			
10	=ABS(B2-A2)			
11				
12	**Formulas Cells Format**			
13	hh:mm			
14				

Explanation:

☞ **IF Formula:**

The **IF** function determines whether the time value in cell B2 is later than (or equal to) that in cell A2.

If it is, the **IF** function subtracts the time in cell A2 (the earlier time) from that in cell B2 and returns the result.

Otherwise, it subtracts the time value in cell B2 (the earlier time) from that in cell A2 and returns the result.

Thus, the formula always subtracts the earlier time from the later one, regardless of which column each is in.

☞ **ABS Formula:**

The time value in cell A2 is subtracted from the corresponding time value in cell B2.

The **ABS** function returns the absolute value of the result.

Thus, it returns the absolute difference between the time values in cells A2 and B2.

That difference is equivalent to the difference between the later time and the earlier time.

Subtracting Times

➢ **Problem:**

Finding the interval between each pair of start and end times in columns A & B. An error occurs when the end time is "earlier" than the start time, resulting in a negative result.

➢ **Solution:**

Use the **IF** function as shown in the following formula to determine which of the two values is the "earliest", and then subtract accordingly:

=B2-A2+IF(A2>B2,1)

	A	B	C
1	**Start Time**	**End Time**	**Result**
2	10:00	17:00	7:00
3	17:00	2:00	9:00
4	12:00	15:00	3:00
5			
6	**Formula Syntax in cell C2:**		
7	=B2-A2+IF(A2>B2,1)		
8			

Explanation:

The **IF** function determines whether or not the End Time in cell B2 is earlier than the corresponding Start Time.

If it is, the **IF** function returns 1. Otherwise, 0 is returned.

The Start Time in cell A2 is subtracted from the corresponding End Time in cell B2, and the number returned by the **IF** function (1/0) is added to the result.

Thus, if the End Time is earlier than the Start Time, 1 (representing a full day) will be added to the negative difference, converting it to a positive difference.

Hence, the formula calculates the interval between the dates in cells A2 & B2, without resulting in an error caused by a negative result.

Converting a Decimal Value to a Time Value

> ➢ **Problem:**

Converting the decimal values in column A to correctly formatted time values.

> ➢ **Solution:**

Divide each number by 24 as follows:

=A2/24

Format your result cells as custom "[hh]:mm".

	A	B
1	**Decimal Values**	**Times**
2	20.4	20:24
3	2.3333	02:20
4	5.6666	05:40
5	10.75	10:45
6	12.1	12:06
7		
8	**Formula Syntax in cell B2:**	
9	=A2/24	
10		
11	**Format in cell B2:**	
12	[hh]:mm	
13		

Explanation:

Time values are stored in Excel as fractions of 24 (01:00 is stored as 1/24).

Therefore, in order to convert the decimal value stored in cell A2 to a time value ("hh:mm"), we must divide it by 24 and format the result as time ("[hh]:mm").

Converting Text Representing Minutes and Seconds into Numerical Values

> ➤ **Problem:**

Column A contains text strings representing time values in the "Xm Ys" format.

X represents the number of minutes and Y represents the number of seconds.

We want to calculate the total number of seconds represented by each string in column A.

> ➤ **Solution:**

Use the **LEFT**, **FIND**, **LEN**, and **MID** functions as shown in the following formula:

=(LEFT(A2,FIND("m",A2)-1)*60)+LEFT(MID(A2,FIND(" ",A2)+1,99),LEN(MID(A2,FIND(" ",A2)+1,99))-1)

	A	B	C
1	**Times**	**Result**	
2	2m 12.23s	132.23	
3	34m 2s	2,042.00	
4	12m 10.8s	730.80	
5	25m 30.12s	1,530.12	
6	53m 4.2s	3,184.20	
7	5m 4s	304.00	
8			
9	**Formula Syntax in cell B2:**		
10	=(LEFT(A2,FIND("m",A2)-1)*60)+LEFT(MID(A2,FIND(" ",A2)+1,99),LEN(MID(A2,FIND(" ",A2)+1,99))-1)		
11			

Explanation:

The first **LEFT** function extracts the leftmost characters in cell A2 up to the character "m" (based on the position calculated by the **FIND** function).

Those characters are then multiplied by 60, which returns the total number of seconds indicated by the "minutes" ("X") part of the string.

The second **LEFT** function, using the **MID**, **FIND**, and **LEN** functions, extracts all the characters in cell A2 from the character to the right of the space up to the character that is second last, i.e. the "seconds" ("Y") part of the string.

The two results are then added to give the total number of seconds.

Converting Times to Decimal Values

➤ **Problem:**

Converting the time values ("hh:mm") in column A to their decimal equivalents.

➤ **Solution:**

Use the **HOUR** and **MINUTE** functions as shown in the following formula:

=HOUR(A2)+(MINUTE(A2)/60)

	A	B	C
1	**Time**	**Decimal Value**	
2	12:23	12.38	
3	08:00	8.00	
4	16:30	16.50	
5	22:45	22.75	
6			
7	**Formula Syntax in cell B2:**		
8	=HOUR(A2)+(MINUTE(A2)/60)		
9			

Explanation:

The **HOUR** function returns the number of hours in the time value stored in cell A2.

Similarly, the **MINUTE** function returns the number of minutes in that time value.

That number is then divided by 60 to convert it to its decimal equivalent, and the result is added to the number of hours (returned by the **HOUR** function).

Thus, the formula converts the time value in cell A2 to its decimal equivalent.

Calculating Military Time Intervals

➢ **Problem:**

Finding the interval between pairs of times when they are formatted in military style ("hhmm").

➢ **Solution 1:**

Use the **TEXT** function as shown in the following formula:

=(TEXT(B2,"00\:00")-TEXT(A2,"00\:00"))*24

➢ **Solution 2:**

Use the **DOLLARDE** function as shown in the following formula:

=DOLLARDE(B2/100,60)-DOLLARDE(A2/100,60)

	A	B	C	D
1	Time In	Time Out	TEXT Formula	DOLLARDE Formula
2	0800	1730	9.50	9.50
3	1400	1000	-4.00	-4.00
4	0200	0645	4.75	4.75
5				
6	TEXT Formula Syntax in cell C2:			
7	=(TEXT(B2,"00\:00")-TEXT(A2,"00\:00"))*24			
8				
9	DOLLARDE Formula Syntax in cell D2:			
10	=DOLLARDE(B2/100,60)-DOLLARDE(A2/100,60)			
11				

Explanation:

☞ **TEXT Formula:**

The first **TEXT** function formats the military time in cell B2 as "00\:00" (a text value representing time).

The second **TEXT** function formats the military time in cell A2 in the same manner. The second result is subtracted from the first, resulting in a time value that represents the difference between the two military times.

That difference is multiplied by 24 to convert it to its decimal equivalent.

☞ **DOLLARDE Formula:**

The military time in cell B2 is divided by 100.

The first **DOLLARDE** function converts the result, which is a fraction of 60, to its decimal equivalent.

Thus, it returns a decimal number that is equivalent to the military time in cell B2.

Similarly, the second **DOLLARDE** function calculates the decimal equivalent of the military time in cell A2.

The second number is subtracted from the first, resulting in the interval between the military times in cells A2 & B2.

 Analysis ToolPak Add-In:

The **DOLLARDE** function is included in the Analysis ToolPak Add-In. To install the Analysis ToolPak Add-in: Select *Tools → Add-Ins → Analysis ToolPak*, Click OK.

Converting Time Values from One Time Zone to Another

➢ **Problem:**

Listed in cells B1:E2 are several destinations and their hourly time difference with New York.

We want to convert the time value in cell B3 (New York local time) to the equivalent local time in each destination city.

➢ **Solution:**

With destinations in cells C1:E1 and time differences in cells C2:E2, enter the following formula in cell C3, and copy across to cell E3:

=$B$3+(C2/24)*-1

	A	B	C	D	E
1		NY	LA	London	Tokyo
2	**Hour Difference**		3	-5	-14
3	**Local Time**	9:00 AM	6:00 AM	2:00 PM	11:00 PM
4					
5	**Formula Syntax in cell C3:**				
6	=$B$3+(C2/24)*-1				
7					

Explanation:

The hour difference in cell C2 is divided by 24 to convert it to a time value.

The result is then multiplied by -1 to calculate the time that needs to be added to the local time.

Finally, that time is added to (or subtracted from) the local time shown in cell B3.

Creating a World Time Converter

➢ **Problem:**

Finding the equivalent time for the city in cell C5 (Jerusalem) as that shown in cell D2 for the city in cell C2 (New York).

➢ **Solution:**

1. Create a list of cities (column A) and their matching hourly difference (column B) from GMT (Greenwich Mean Time).

2. Use the **VLOOKUP** function as shown in the following formula in cell D5:

=(D2*24-VLOOKUP(C2,A2:B8,2,FALSE)+VLOOKUP(C5,A2:B8,2,FALSE))/24

	A	B	C	D	E
1	**City**	**Hours from GMT**	**City**	**Time to Convert**	
2	Amsterdam	1	New York	11:15 AM	
3	Beijing	7			
4	Melbourne	9	**Desired City**	**Time on Desired City**	
5	New York	-5	Jerusalem	6:15 PM	
6	San Francisco	-8			
7	London	0			
8	Jerusalem	2			
9					
10	**Formula Syntax in cell D5:**				
11	=(D2*24-VLOOKUP(C2,A2:B8,2,FALSE)+VLOOKUP(C5,A2:B8,2,FALSE))/24				
12					

Explanation:

The first **VLOOKUP** function in the above formula looks in the first column of range A2:B8 for the city entered in cell C2 (Jerusalem) and returns the corresponding value from the second column.

Thus, it returns Jerusalem's hourly difference with GMT.

Similarly, the second **VLOOKUP** function returns New York's hourly difference with GMT.

The time value in cell D2 (the time to convert) is multiplied by 24 to convert it to its decimal equivalent.

Jerusalem's hourly difference from GMT (returned by the first **VLOOKUP** function) is then subtracted from the result of that calculation, and New York's hourly difference (returned by the second **VLOOKUP** function) is added.

The result is the decimal equivalent of the time in New York.

In order to convert that decimal number to a time value, it is divided by 24.

Thus, the formula returns the equivalent time for the city in cell C5 (Jerusalem) as that shown in cell D2 for the city in cell C2 (New York).

Rounding Times Down to the Nearest 30 Seconds

➤ **Problem:**

Rounding the times ("hh:mm:ss") in column A down to the nearest 30 seconds.

➤ **Solution 1:**

Use the **ROUNDDOWN** function as shown in the following formula:

=ROUNDDOWN(A2*24*120,0)/(120*24)

➤ **Solution 2:**

Use the **FLOOR** function as shown in the following formula:

=FLOOR(A2,1/(24*120))

	A	B	C
1	Times	ROUNDOWN Formula	FLOOR Formula
2	13:19:45	13:19:30	13:19:30
3	20:30:12	20:30:00	20:30:00
4	05:55:58	05:55:30	05:55:30
5			
6	ROUNDOWN Formula Syntax in cell B2:		
7	=ROUNDDOWN(A2*24*120,0)/(120*24)		
8			
9	FLOOR Formula Syntax in cell C2:		
10	=FLOOR(A2,1/(24*120))		
11			

Explanation:

☞ **ROUNDDOWN Formula:**

The time value entered in cell A2 is multiplied by 24 to convert it to its decimal equivalent, and by 120 to calculate the number of 30 second time periods within that time value (there are 120 periods of 30 seconds in an hour).

The **ROUNDDOWN** function rounds the result down to the nearest integer (0 decimal places).

Finally, the decimal number returned by the **ROUNDDOWN** function is divided by 120*24 in order to convert it back to a time value.

Thus, the formula rounds the time in cell A2 down to the nearest 30 seconds.

☞ **FLOOR Formula:**

The **FLOOR** function rounds the number representing the time value in cell A2 down to the nearest multiple of 1/(24*120). That multiple represents a time value of 30 seconds.

Thus, it rounds the time in cell A2 down to the nearest 30 seconds.

Rounding Times Down to a Specified Time Increment

➢ **Problem:**

Rounding the times in column A down to the nearest 15 minute increment.

➢ **Solution:**

Use the **TIME, FLOOR, HOUR**, and **MINUTE** functions as shown in the following formula:

=TIME(HOUR(A2),FLOOR(MINUTE(A2),15),0)

	A	B	C
1	**Time to Round**	**Result**	
2	18:17	18:15	
3	19:40	19:30	
4	08:55	08:45	
5	10:04	10:00	
6			
7	**Formula Syntax in cell B2:**		
8	=TIME(HOUR(A2),FLOOR(MINUTE(A2),15),0)		
9			

Explanation:

The **HOUR** function returns the hour number of the time value stored in cell A2.

Similarly, the **MINUTE** function returns minute number of that time value.

The **FLOOR** function rounds down that number of minutes to the nearest multiple of 15.

Finally, the **TIME** function returns a time value composed of the hour number returned by the **HOUR** function and the minute number calculated by the **FLOOR** function.

Thus, the formula rounds down the time value stored in cell A2 to the nearest 15 minute increment.

Rounding Hours Up

➤ **Problem:**

Listed in columns B & C are the times that each employee in column A signed in and out of work today.

We want to calculate the number of hours each employee worked, rounded up to the nearest hour.

➤ **Solution:**

Use the **CEILING** functions as shown in the following formula:

=CEILING((C2-B2)*24,1)

	A	B	C	D
1	**Name**	**Time In**	**Time Out**	**# Hours (Rounded Up)**
2	Bill	09:32	12:38	4
3	Joe	05:43	14:32	9
4	Roy	10:17	15:43	6
5				
6	**Formula Syntax in cell D2:**			
7	=CEILING((C2-B2)*24,1)			
8				

Explanation:

The Time Out in cell C2 is subtracted from the corresponding Time in cell B2.

The result is a time value representing the difference between the two times.

That time value is multiplied by 24 to convert it to its decimal equivalent, and the **CEILING** function rounds the result up to the nearest multiple of 1 (the nearest integer, representing the nearest hour).

Thus, it returns the number of hours worked by the employee specified in cell A2, rounded up to the nearest hour.

Rounding Time Intervals to the Nearest Specified Time Increment

➢ **Problem:**

Columns A & B contain times signed in and out of work.

We want to subtract each Time In from its corresponding Time Out, and round the result to the nearest 30 minutes.

➢ **Solution:**

Use the **ROUND** function as shown in the following formula:

=ROUND((B2-A2)/"0:30:00",0)*"0:30:00"

	A	B	C
1	**Time In**	**Time Out**	**Result**
2	10:08	18:27	8:30
3	08:36	17:42	9:00
4	13:52	19:12	5:30
5			
6	**Formula Syntax in cell C2:**		
7	=ROUND((B2-A2)/"0:30:00",0)*"0:30:00"		
8			

Explanation:

The Time Out in cell B2 is subtracted from the corresponding Time In in cell A2.

The result is a time value representing the difference between the two times.

That time value is divided by a time value of 30 minutes ("0:30:00") in order to calculate the number of 30 minute periods within that time.

The **ROUND** function rounds that number to the nearest integer (0 decimal places).

Finally, the number returned by the **ROUND** function is multiplied by a time value of 30 minutes ("0:30:00"), returning a time value that represents the interval between the Time In in cell A2 and the Time Out in cell B2, rounded to the nearest 30 minutes.

Calculating a Building's Occupancy Rate at Specified Times

➤ **Problem:**

Columns B & C show the times that each of a building's tenants left and returned on a particular day.

We want to calculate the building's occupancy rate at each of the times listed in column E.

➢ **Solution:**

Use the **COUNTIF** and **COUNT** functions as shown in the following formula:

=(COUNTIF($C$2:$C$6,">="&E2)-COUNTIF($B$2:$B$6,">"&E2))/
COUNT($A$2:$A$6)

	A	B	C	D	E	F
1	Tenant ID	Time In	Time Out		Base Time	Occupancy Rate
2	1	8:00	12:00		10:00	40%
3	2	9:00	17:30		17:00	60%
4	3	18:00	20:00		19:00	40%
5	4	13:00	23:00		22:00	20%
6	5	11:00	18:30			
7						
8	**Formula Syntax in cell F2:**					
9	=(COUNTIF($C$2:$C$6,">="&E2)-COUNTIF($B$2:$B$6,">"&E2))/COUNT($A$2:$A$6)					
10						

Explanation:

The first **COUNTIF** function returns the number of Time Out values in column C (cells C2:C6) that are later than or equal to the Base Time in cell E2.

Similarly, the second **COUNTIF** function returns the number of Time In values in column B (cells B2:B6) that are later than the Base Time.

The number returned by the second **COUNTIF** function is then subtracted from the number returned by the first **COUNTIF** function.

The result represents the number of tenants who were in the building at the time specified in cell E2.

Finally, that number is divided by the total number of tenants in the building, as calculated by the **COUNT** function (returns the number of values in cells A2:A6).

The result is the building's occupancy rate at the time listed in cell E2.

Date & Time

Creating Date and Time Stamp

➢ **Problem:**

Creating a timestamp for each of the values in List1 (column A).

We want the timestamp to display the date and time that each value was entered or when it was most recently modified.

➢ **Solution:**

1. Go to *Tools → Options → Calculation Tab →* Check the *Iteration* checkbox.

2. Use the **IF** and **NOW** functions as shown in the following formula:
   =IF(A2="","",IF(B2="",NOW(),B2))

3. Apply "mm/dd/yyyy hh:mm" format to column B.

	A	B
1	**List1**	**Timestamp**
2	5	05/31/2005 13:55
3	2	05/31/2005 13:55
4	10	05/31/2005 13:55
5	8	05/31/2005 13:55
6		
7	**Formula Syntax in cell B2:**	
8	=IF(A2="","",IF(B2="",NOW(),B2))	
9		

Explanation:

The first **IF** function determines whether or not cell A2 is blank. If it is, the **IF** function returns a blank cell. Otherwise, it returns the result of the second **IF** function.

The second **IF** function determines whether or not the current cell (cell B2) is blank. If it is, the **IF** function returns the current date and time (returned by the **NOW** function). Otherwise, it returns the value that is currently stored in the cell.

Thus, as long as cell A2 does not contain any data, cell B2 will remain empty.

Once data is entered in cell A2, the **IF** formula in cell B2 will return the current date and time into that cell and that value will remain until the data in cell A2 is cleared.

When the data in cell A2 is cleared in order to modify it, the date and time returned into cell B2 will be cleared as well. The updated date and time will appear as soon as new data is entered into cell A2.

Convert Date and Time from GMT (Greenwich Mean Time) to CST (Central Standard Time)

➢ **Problem:**

Converting the dates and times in column A from GMT (Greenwich Mean Time) to CST (Central Standard Time).

CST is 6 hours earlier than GMT.

➢ **Solution:**

Use the **TIME** function as shown in the following formula:

=A2-TIME(6,0,0)

	A	B	C
1	**Date & Time (GMT)**	**Date & Time (CST)**	
2	05/16/2005 13:00	05/16/2005 07:00	
3	02/02/2005 03:00	02/01/2005 21:00	
4	10/10/2005 22:00	10/10/2005 16:00	
5			
6	**Formula Syntax in cell B2:**		
7	=A2-TIME(6,0,0)		
8			

Explanation:

The **TIME** function returns a time value of 6:00.

That time, representing the hourly difference between GMT and CST (6 hours), is then subtracted from the date and time value stored in cell A2.

The result is the CST equivalent of the GMT date and time shown in cell A2.

Combining Data from Separate Columns into a Single Date and Time Value

➤ **Problem:**

Columns A:F contain values representing month, day, year, hours, minutes and seconds.

We want to combine the numbers from each row into a single date and time value.

➤ **Solution:**

Use the **DATE** and **TIME** functions as shown in the following formula:

=DATE(C2,A2,B2)+TIME(D2,E2,F2)

Format the results (column G) as "mm/dd/yy hh:mm:ss".

	A	B	C	D	E	F	G
1	Month	Day	Year	Hours	Minutes	Seconds	Result
2	3	15	2005	11	33	45	03/15/05 11:33:45
3	8	4	2004	20	7	21	08/04/04 20:07:21
4	12	20	2003	5	20	4	12/20/03 05:20:04
5							
6	Formula Syntax in cell G1:						
7	=DATE(C2,A2,B2)+TIME(D2,E2,F2)						
8							

Explanation:

The **DATE** function returns a date composed of the year number in cell C2, the month number in cell A2, and the day number in cell B2.

The **TIME** function returns a time composed of the hour number in cell D2, the minute number in cell E2, and the second number in cell F2.

The resulting date and time are added and formatted as "mm/dd/yy hh:mm:ss".

Converting Text, Which Represents Date and Time, Into Proper Date and Time Values

➤ **Problem:**

Column A contains strings which represent dates and times that have been formatted as "mmm d yyyy h:mm:ss PM/AM".

We want to extract the date and time from each string, place them in separate cells, and convert them into properly formatted date and time values.

➤ **Solution:**

❖ To extract dates, use the **MID**, **LEFT**, **FIND**, and **SUBSTITUTE** functions as shown in the following formula:

=(--(MID(A2,5,2)&" "&LEFT(A2,3)&" "&MID(A2,FIND(" ",SUBSTITUTE(
A2," ","",1))+2,4)))

Enter the above formula in column B and format as "mm/dd/yyyy".

❖ To extract times, use the **MID**, **FIND**, and **SUBSTITUTE** functions as shown in the following formula:

=(--(MID(A2,FIND(" ",SUBSTITUTE(A2," ","",1))+7,255)))

Enter the above formula in column C and format as "h:mm PM/AM".

	A	B	C	D	E
1	**Strings**	**Date**	**Time**		
2	Mar 4 2005 11:00:00 AM	03/04/2005	11:00 AM		
3	Aug 11 2004 6:55:00 PM	08/11/2004	6:55 PM		
4	Dec 25 2002 11:32:00 PM	12/25/2002	11:32 PM		
5					
6	**Date Formula Syntax in cell B2:**				
7	=(--(MID(A2,5,2)&" "&LEFT(A2,3)&" "&MID(A2,FIND(" ",SUBSTITUTE(A2," ","",1))+2,4)))				
8					
9	**Time Formula Syntax in cell C2:**				
10	=(--(MID(A2,FIND(" ",SUBSTITUTE(A2," ","",1))+7,255)))				
11					

Explanation:

☞ **Formula Extracting Dates:**

The first **MID** function extracts two characters from the string in A2, starting at the 5th character.

Thus, it returns the day number of the date.

The **LEFT** function extracts the three leftmost characters of the string in cell A2.

Thus, it returns the three letters representing the name of the month.

The following expression, using the **FIND** and **SUBSTITUTE** functions, calculates the position (character number) of the second space in the string (the space before the year number):

FIND(" ",SUBSTITUTE(A2," ","",1))+2

The second **MID** function extracts 4 characters from the string in A2, starting at the position calculated by the above expression.

Thus, it extracts the year number of the date.

The day number (returned by the first MID function), the month name (returned by the **LEFT** function) and the year number (returned by the second MID function) are joined into a single string with spaces between them. That string represents the date in cell A2.

The "--" sign converts that string to a proper date value, and thus returns the date in cell A2.

☞ **Formula Extracting Times:**

The **SUBSTITUTE** function returns the string in cell A2 after having its first space removed (replaced by nothing).

The **FIND** function returns the relative position (character number) of the first space in the string returned by the **SUBSTITUTE** function.

That position is equal to the position of the character in cell A2 that is to the left of the second space in the string.

Adding 7 to that position returns the position of the first character in the time part of the string.

The **MID** function extracts as many as 255 characters from cell A2, starting at that calculated position.

Hence, it returns a string representing the time in cell A2.

The "--" sign converts that string to a proper time value, and thus returns the time in cell A2.

Calculating the Number of Weekday Hours between Two Dates

➤ **Problem:**

Calculating the number of hours between Date1 (A2) and Date2 (B2), excluding weekends.

➤ **Solution:**

Use the **NETWORKDAYS** and **MOD** functions as shown in the following formula:

=NETWORKDAYS(A2,B2)-1-MOD(A2,1)+MOD(B2,1)

	A	B	C
1	**Date1**	**Date2**	**Result**
2	04/04/2005 10:30	04/14/2005 19:12	200:42
3			
4	**Formula Syntax in cell C2:**		
5	=NETWORKDAYS(A2,B2)-1-MOD(A2,1)+MOD(B2,1)		
6			

Explanation:

The **NETWORKDAYS** function returns the number of weekdays between the date stored in cell A2 and the one in cell B2.

1 is subtracted from that number to exclude the date in cell B2 from the number of weekdays.

The first **MOD** function divides the value in cell A2 by 1 and returns the remainder, which represents the time part of the date and time value in cell A2. That time is then subtracted from the total time represented by the calculated number of weekdays.

Similarly, the time part of the date and time value in cell B2 (returned by the second **MOD** function) is added to the above total.

The result is a time value, formatted as "[hh]:mm", that represents the weekday hours between the two date and time values in cell A2 & B2.

Analysis ToolPak Add-In:

The **NETWORKDAYS** function is included in the Analysis ToolPak Add-In. To install the Analysis ToolPak Add-in: Select *Tools → Add-Ins → Analysis ToolPak*, Click OK.

Separating Dates and Times

> **Problem**:

The values in column A are combined dates and times.

We want to create two new columns of data: one containing the date and the other containing the time.

> **Solution**:

❖ To extract dates, use the **INT** function as shown in the following formula:

=INT(A2)

Enter the above formula in column B and format as "mm/dd/yyyy".

❖ To extract times, use the **MOD** function as shown in the following formula:

=MOD(A2,1)

Enter the above formula in column C and format as "h:mm".

	A	B	C
1	**Dates & Times**	**Dates**	**Times**
2	05/22/2005 16:12	05/22/2005	16:12
3	06/14/2004 11:37	06/14/2004	11:37
4	03/03/2003 22:43	03/03/2003	22:43
5	10/10/2002 03:25	10/10/2002	3:25
6			
7	**Formula Syntax in cell B2:**		
8	=INT(A2)		
9			
10	**Formula Syntax in cell C2:**		
11	=MOD(A2,1)		
12			

Explanation:

Date and time values are stored in Excel as numbers, where the integer part represents the date, and the fraction part represents the time.

☞ **Formula Extracting Dates (Column B)**

The **INT** function rounds the number representing the date and time value in cell A2 down to the nearest integer.

Thus, it returns the date stored in cell A2.

☞ **Formula Extracting Times (Column C)**

The **MOD** function divides the number representing the date and time value in cell A2 by 1, and returns the remainder (the fraction part of the number).

Thus, it returns the time stored in cell A2.

Creating a Date and Time Matrix

➤ **Problem:**

Listed in column A are the dates and times of doctor's appointments. Column B contains the corresponding patient's name for each appointment.

We want to use this data to create a matrix in cells D1:G10, where each column is a date and each row is a time.

➤ **Solution:**

Use the **INDEX**, **MATCH**, and **TEXT** functions as shown in the following *Array formula*:

{=INDEX($B$2:$B$18,MATCH(TEXT(E$1,"mmddyyyy")&TEXT($D2,"hh:mm"),TEXT($A$2:$A$18,"mmddyyyy")&TEXT($A$2:$A$18,"hh:mm"),0))}

Enter the above formula in cell E2, copy it down the column and across to column G.

☞ To apply *Array formula*:

Select the cell, press **<F2>** and simultaneously press **<Ctrl+Shift+Enter>**.

	A	B	C	D	E	F	G
1	Date & Time	Patient Name		Time/Date	06/01/2005	06/02/2005	06/03/2005
2	06/01/2005 10:00	a		10:00	a	g	#N/A
3	06/01/2005 11:00	b		11:00	b	#N/A	l
4	06/01/2005 13:00	c		12:00	#N/A	h	#N/A
5	06/01/2005 14:00	d		13:00	c	i	m
6	06/01/2005 15:00	e		14:00	d	#N/A	n
7	06/01/2005 17:00	f		15:00	e	j	o
8	06/02/2005 10:00	g		16:00	#N/A	#N/A	p
9	06/02/2005 12:00	h		17:00	f	#N/A	#N/A
10	06/02/2005 13:00	i		18:00	#N/A	k	q
11	06/02/2005 15:00	j					
12	06/02/2005 18:00	k					
13	06/03/2005 11:00	l					
14	06/03/2005 13:00	m					
15	06/03/2005 14:00	n					
16	06/03/2005 15:00	o					
17	06/03/2005 16:00	p					
18	06/03/2005 18:00	q					
19							
20	Array Formula Syntax in cell E2:						
21	{=INDEX($B$2:$B$18,MATCH(TEXT(E$1,"mmddyyyy")&TEXT($D2,"hh:mm"),TEXT($A$2:$A$18,"mmddyyyy")&TEXT($A$2:$A$18,"hh:mm"),0))}						
22							

Explanation:

The first **TEXT** function formats the date in E1 as "mmddyyyy" and converts it to text.

The second **TEXT** function formats the time in D2 as "hh:mm" and converts it to text.

Those two text values are joined into a single string, representing the date and time in E2 and D2.

Similarly, the following expression returns an Array consisting of the string representing each date and time value in column A (A2:A18)

TEXT($A$2:$A$18,"mmddyyyy")&TEXT($A$2:$A$18,"hh:mm").

The format of each string in the Array is identical to the format of the string created above.

The **MATCH** function returns the position of the string created above (representing the date in E2 and the time in D2) within the Array.

If the string does not appear in the Array, it returns the #N/A error.

The **INDEX** function returns the value from B2:B18 (patient name) that is stored in the position calculated by the **MATCH** function.

Thus, it returns the name of the patient whose appointment is on the date stored in E1 and the time specified in D2.

If there is no appointment listed in columns A & B for the date and time in E1 and D2, the formula returns the #N/A error.

To complete the matrix and return the patient name for each date & time combination, copy the formula to range E2:G10 (the references of the cells containing the date and time criteria will update accordingly).

Wages, Shifts & Time Worked

Creating a Timesheet

> ➢ **Problem:**

Creating a timesheet which calculates the number of hours worked each day and a sum of the total hours worked.

> ➢ **Solution:**

Create 3 columns containing the following data:

Date (column A), Time In (column B), Time Out (column C).

In the 4th column (Number of Hours), enter the following formula:

=(C2-B2+(C2<B2))*24

To sum the total number of hours worked, use the **SUM** function as shown in the following formula:

=SUM(D2:D7)

	A	B	C	D
1	**Date**	**Time In**	**Time Out**	**Number of Hours**
2	04/11/2005	9:00	17:00	8.00
3	04/12/2005	10:30	19:00	8.50
4	04/13/2005	8:30	17:30	9.00
5	04/14/2005	11:00	16:00	5.00
6	04/15/2005	12:00	0:30	12.50
7	04/16/2005	9:30	16:45	7.25
8				
9		**Total Hours**		**50.25**
10				
11	**Formula Syntax in cell D2:**			
12	=(C2-B2+(C2<B2))*24			
13				
14	**Formula Syntax in cell D9:**			
15	=SUM(D2:D7)			
16				

Explanation:

☞ **Number of Hours Formula (cell D2):**

The Time In in cell B2 is subtracted from the corresponding Time Out in cell C2, returning a time value that represents the time worked for the date in cell A2.

If that Time Out is earlier than its corresponding Time In, a negative time value is returned.

The following expression returns "1" (TRUE) if the Time Out in cell C2 is earlier than its corresponding Time In (cell B2) and "0" (FALSE) if it isn't:

C2<B2

The number returned by the above expression (1/0) is then added to the time value calculated above.

Thus, if the Time Out is earlier than the Time In, 1 (representing a full day) will be added to the negative time value returned above, and a positive time value will be returned.

Finally, the time value calculated above (time worked) is multiplied by 24 to convert it to its decimal equivalent.

Thus, the number of hours worked for the date in cell A2 will be returned.

☞ **Total Hours Formula (cell D9):**

The **SUM** function adds all the values in the range cells D2:D9, which consists of the number of hours worked for each date in column A.

Finding the First Login and Last Logout Times of Employees

➤ **Problem:**

Range cells A2:C10 contains the IDs and login and logout times of various employees.

Each person can log in and out several times a day.

We want to find the first time each employee logged in and the last time they logged out.

➤ Solution:

❖ To find the first login time for each unique ID in A13:A16, use the **MAX** function as shown in the following *Array formula*:

{=1/MAX((A13=$A$2:$A$10)*($B$2:$B$10<>0)*(1/$B$2:$B$10))}

❖ To find the last logout time for each unique ID in D13:D16, use the **MAX** function as shown in the following *Array formula*:

{=MAX(($A$2:$A$10=D13)*($D$2:$D$10))}

☞ To apply *Array formula*:

Select the cell, press <**F2**> and simultaneously press <**Ctrl+Shift+Enter**>.

	A	B	C	D	E
1	Employee ID	Login Time		Logout Time	
2	1	02:40		03:10	
3	2	00:15		03:20	
4	1	06:20		09:30	
5	3	09:14		11:05	
6	4	11:00		19:30	
7	2	04:05		06:55	
8	3	12:08		17:17	
9	1	10:00		16:20	
10	2	08:12		12:33	
11					
12	Employee ID	First Login Time		Employee ID	Last Logout Time
13	1	02:40		1	16:20
14	2	00:15		2	12:33
15	3	09:14		3	17:17
16	4	11:00		4	19:30
17					
18	Array Formula Syntax in cell B13:				
19	{=1/MAX((A13=$A$2:$A$10)*($B$2:$B$10<>0)*(1/$B$2:$B$10))}				
20					
21	Array Formula Syntax in cell E13:				
22	{=MAX(($A$2:$A$10=D13)*($D$2:$D$10))}				
23					

Explanation:

☞ **First Login Time Formula (cell B13):**

The following expression returns an Array consisting of "1" (TRUE) for each ID in column A (A2:A10) that matches the ID entered in cell A13, and "0" (FALSE) for every ID that doesn't:

A13=$A$2:$A$10

The following expression divides 1 by the number representing each Login Time in column B (B2:B10) and returns the results in a single Array:

1/$B$2:$B$10

The corresponding values in the above Arrays are multiplied and an Array containing the results is returned.

The **MAX** function returns the maximum value in that Array.

That value is the quotient of 1 divided by the number representing the first Login Time of the ID in cell A13.

Finally, 1 is divided by the number returned by the **MAX** function, returning the first Login Time of the ID entered in cell A13.

☞ **Last Logout Time Formula (cell E13):**

The following expression returns an Array consisting of "1" (TRUE) for each ID in column A (A2:A10) that matches the ID entered in cell D13, and "0" (FALSE) for every ID that doesn't:

$A$2:$A$10=D13

Each value (1/0) in that Array, representing an ID in column A, is multiplied by the number representing the corresponding Logout Time in column D, and the products are returned in a single Array.

Thus, that Array includes the Logout time for every ID in column A that matches the ID entered in cell D13, and "0" for every ID that doesn't.

The **MAX** function returns the maximum value in that Array.

Thus, it returns the last Logout Time of the ID entered in cell D13.

Calculating Total Time Worked on a Specific Day

> ➤ **Problem:**

Columns A & B contain the dates and times that a person signed in and out of work.

We want to create a new column containing the date and the calculated time that was worked on that day.

> ➤ **Solution:**

Use the **TEXT** and **TRUNC** functions as shown in the following formula

=TEXT(TRUNC(A2)+(B2-A2),"mm""/""dd""/""yy"" - ""hh"" Hrs ""mm"" Mins """)

The above formula performs the desired time calculation and uses the **TRUNC** function to return the relevant date.

	A	B	C	D
1	**Time In**	**Time Out**	**Date/ Hours worked**	
2	04/04/05 10:00	04/04/05 18:00	04/04/05 - 08 Hrs 00 Mins	
3	03/04/05 11:07	03/04/05 12:16	03/04/05 - 01 Hrs 09 Mins	
4	08/04/05 17:22	08/04/05 17:54	08/04/05 - 00 Hrs 32 Mins	
5				
6	**Formula Syntax in cell C2:**			
7	=TEXT(TRUNC(A2)+(B2-A2),"mm""/""dd""/""yy"" - ""hh"" Hrs ""mm"" Mins """)			
8				

Explanation:

The **TRUNC** function truncates the number representing the date and time in cell A2 (Time In) to an integer.

Thus, it returns the date stored in cell A2.

The date and time value in cell A2 (Time In) is subtracted from the corresponding date and time in cell B2 (Time Out), the difference represents the time worked.

The date returned by the **TRUNC** function and the time calculated above are joined into a single date and time value.

The **TEXT** function formats that date and time value as "mm""/""dd""/""yy"" - ""hh"" Hrs ""mm"" Mins """ and converts it to text.

Thus, it returns a string indicating the date and the time worked with respect to the Time In and Time Out values in cells A2 & B2.

Calculating Hours Worked

➢ **Problem:**

Columns A:C contain ID's, dates and times. Each row indicates the time a particular person signed in or out of work.

We want to determine which of the entries in column C are times signed in and which are times signed out, and then we want to calculate the number of hours worked by each person.

➢ **Solution:**

To determine whether a time represents signing in or out, enter the **CHOOSE**, **MAX**, and **ROW** functions as shown in the following *Array formula* in column D:

{=CHOOSE(MAX((A2=$A$2:$A$9)*(ROW()<>ROW($A$2:$A$9))*((B2&C2)<($B$2:$B$9&$C$2:$C$9)))+1,"Time Out","Time In")}

Thus, "Time In" or "Time Out" will be displayed next to each time shown in column C.

Then, to calculate the number of hours worked by each person, use the **SUM** and **IF** functions as shown in the following *Array formula* in column E:

{=SUM(IF(D2="Time Out",(A2=$A$2:$A$9)*($D$2:$D$9="Time In")*(C2-$C$2:$C$9),0))}

Thus, the number of worked hours will be displayed next to the "Time Out" indicator matching each ID.

☞ To apply *Array formula*:

Select the cell, press <**F2**> and simultaneously press <**Ctrl+Shift+Enter**>.

	A	B	C	D	E
1	ID	Date	Time	Time In/Time Out	Worked Hours
2	1	04/11/2005	10:30	Time In	00:00
3	3	04/15/2005	09:35	Time In	00:00
4	2	04/15/2005	18:15	Time Out	06:30
5	3	04/15/2005	16:00	Time Out	06:25
6	4	04/20/2005	08:45	Time In	00:00
7	2	04/15/2005	11:45	Time In	00:00
8	1	04/11/2005	17:30	Time Out	07:00
9	4	04/20/2005	18:00	Time Out	09:15
10					
11	Time In/Out Array Formula in cell D2:				
12	{=CHOOSE(MAX((A2=$A$2:$A$9)*(ROW()<>ROW($A$2:$A$9))*((B2&C2)<($B$2:$B$9&$C$2:$C$9)))+1,"Time Out","Time In")}				
13					
14	Worked Hours Array Formula in cell E2:				
15	{=SUM(IF(D2="Time Out",(A2=$A$2:$A$9)*($D$2:$D$9="Time In")*(C2-$C$2:$C$9),0))}				
16					

Explanation:

☞ **Formula in Column D:**

The following expression returns an Array consisting of "1" for every row in the range that meets the following three conditions, and "0" for every row that doesn't:

(A2=$A$2:$A$9)*(ROW()<>ROW($A$2:$A$9))*((B2&C2)<($B$2:$B$9&$C$2:$C$9))

1. Column A contains the same ID as in cell A2.

2. The date and time in columns B & C are later than those in cells B2 & C2.

3. The number of the row is different to that of the current row (2).

The **MAX** function returns the maximum number in that Array (1/0).

If "0" is returned, it indicates that there isn't another row in the range that contains an earlier time for the ID in cell A2.

Thus, the time listed in the current row (2) is the Time In for the ID in cell A2.

If "1" is returned, it indicates that, in a different row, there is an earlier time for the ID in cell A2.

Thus, the time listed in the current row (2) is the Time Out for the ID in cell A2.

The **CHOOSE** function returns the Nth string out of the two entered in the formula ("Time Out","Time In"), where N is the number returned by the **MAX** function plus1.

Thus, the formula determines whether the time in cell C2 represents signing in or out, and returns a string indicating the result.

☞ **Formula in Column E:**

The **IF** function determines whether or not the string in cell D2 is "Time Out". If it isn't, it returns 0 (representing a 00:00 time value). If it is, it returns the result of the following expression:

(A2=$A$2:$A$9)*($D$2:$D$9="Time In")*(C2-$C$2:$C$9)

The above expression calculates the difference between the time value in cell C2 (Time Out) and the time value in column C that meets the following two conditions:

1. Its corresponding string in column D is "Time In".

2. Its corresponding ID in column A is the same as that in cell A2.

Thus, it calculates the difference between the Time Out in cell C2 and its matching Time In in column C. That difference represents the time worked by the ID shown in cell A2.

The **IF** function returns the result of the above expression, which is an Array consisting of the time worked, calculated for the time value in column C meeting the above conditions, and a "0" for every other time value in column C.

The **SUM** function adds all the values in the Array returned by the **IF** function, and thus returns the calculated time worked.

Hence, the formula returns a 0:00 time value next to "Time In" indicators in column D, and the time worked for each "Time Out" indicator.

Calculating the Number of Hours Worked Based on a System of Letter Codes

➤ **Problem:**

Column B contains a list of letters which are codes for the hours worked on each of the days listed in column A.

"N" indicates a 9 hour day, "H" indicates a 4 hour day and "V" indicates no hours were worked that day.

We want to calculate the total number of hours worked during the week.

➤ **Solution:**

Use the **COUNTIF** function as shown in the following Formula:

=COUNTIF(B2:B8,"N")*9+COUNTIF(B2:B8,"H")*4

	A	B	C	D
1	**Day**	**Hours Symbol**	**Result**	
2	Monday	N	26	
3	Tuesday	N		
4	Wednesday	H		
5	Thursday	V		
6	Friday	H		
7	Saterday	V		
8	Sunday	V		
9				
10	**Formula Syntax in cell C2:**			
11	=COUNTIF(B2:B8,"N")*9+COUNTIF(B2:B8,"H")*4			
12				

Explanation:

The first **COUNTIF** function counts the number of values in column B that are equal to "N". The result is then multiplied by 9.

The second **COUNTIF** function counts the number of values in column B that are equal to "H". The result is then multiplied by 4.

Finally, the results of those calculations are added together, creating the total number of worked hours.

Calculating Total Pay, Based on Hours Worked Per Day and Hourly Rates

➤ **Problem:**

Listed in columns A & B are the times an employee signed in and out of work each day.

Column C contains the rate per hour for that particular day.

We want to calculate the employee's total pay.

➤ **Solution 1:**

To calculate the number of hours worked per day, enter the following formula in column D:

=B2-A2+(A2>B2)

Then calculate the pay per day by entering the following formula in column E:

=C2*D2*24

Finally, use the **SUM** function as shown in the following formula to sum the results from column E:

=SUM(E2:E7)

	A	B	C	D	E
1	Time In	Time Out	Rate	Worked Hours	Result
2	8:00 AM	3:45 PM	$6.00	7:45	$46.50
3	6:00 PM	9:00 AM	$10.00	15:00	$150.00
4	12:30 PM	10:00 PM	$10.00	9:30	$95.00
5	9:30 AM	6:00 PM	$10.00	8:30	$85.00
6	2:00 PM	8:00 PM	$6.00	6:00	$36.00
7	8:00 AM	12:30 PM	$12.00	4:30	$54.00
8					
9	**Total Pay**			**Formula Syntax in cell A10:**	
10	$466.50			=SUM(E2:E7)	
11					
12	**Formula Syntax in Column D:**			**Formula Syntax in Column E:**	
13	=B2-A2+(A2>B2)			=C2*D2*24	
14					

> **Solution 2:**

Use the **SUM** function as shown in the following *Array formula*:

{=SUM((B2:B7-A2:A7+(A2:A7>B2:B7))*24*C2:C7)}

☞ To apply *Array formula*:

Select the cell, press **\<F2\>** and simultaneously press **\<Ctrl+Shift+Enter\>**.

	A	B	C	D	E
1	Time In	Time Out	Rate		Total Pay
2	8:00 AM	3:45 PM	$6.00		$466.50
3	6:00 PM	9:00 AM	$10.00		
4	12:30 PM	10:00 PM	$10.00		
5	9:30 AM	6:00 PM	$10.00		
6	2:00 PM	8:00 PM	$6.00		
7	8:00 AM	12:30 PM	$12.00		
8					
9	**Array Formula Syntax in cell E2:**				
10	{=SUM((B2:B7-A2:A7+(A2:A7>B2:B7))*24*C2:C7)}				
11					

Explanation to Solution 1:

☞ **Worked Hours Formula (Column D):**

The Time In in cell A2 is subtracted from the corresponding Time Out in cell B2, returning a time value that represents the time worked for that day.

If that Time Out is earlier than its corresponding Time In, a negative time value is returned.

The following expression returns "1" (TRUE) if the Time Out in cell B2 is earlier than its corresponding Time In (A2) and "0" (FALSE) if it isn't.

A2>B2

The number returned by the above expression is then added to the time value calculated above.

Thus, if the Time Out is earlier than the Time In, 1 (representing a full day) will be added to the negative time value returned above (the difference), and a positive time value (time worked) will be returned.

☞ **Pay per Day Formula (Column E):**

The time worked, stored in cell D2, is multiplied by 24 to convert it to its decimal equivalent.

Then, it is multiplied by the hourly rate in cell C2 to calculate the pay for that day of work.

☞ **Total Pay Formula (cell A10):**

The **SUM** function adds the values in the range E2:E7, which consists of the pay for each day of work.

Thus, it returns the total pay.

Explanation to Solution 2:

The following expression returns an Array consisting of the difference between each Time Out in column B (cells B2:B7) and the corresponding Time In from column A:

B2:B7-A2:A7

Thus, an Array of time values is returned, representing the time worked on each day.

If a particular Time Out is earlier than its corresponding Time In, a negative time worked will be calculated.

The following expression returns an Array consisting of "1" (TRUE) for each Time Out in column B that is earlier than its corresponding Time In column A and "0" (FALSE) for each Time Out that isn't:

A2:A7>B2:B7

The corresponding values in the two above Arrays are added together, and a single Array containing the results is returned.

Thus, 1 (representing a full day) will be added to any negative time values in the first Array, converting them to positive values.

Each result in the Array, representing the time worked for a particular day, is then multiplied by 24 to convert it to its decimal equivalent, and also by the corresponding rate from column C (cells C2:C7).

Thus, an Array is returned consisting of the pay for each day.

The **SUM** function adds the values in that Array and returns the total pay.

Calculating Daily Pay, Incorporating Variable Hourly Rates

> ➤ **Problem:**

Columns B & C contain the times signed in and out of work for each date in column A.

Column D contains the following formula, which calculates the number of worked hours per day:

=(C2-B2)*24

Range A11:B12 contains 2 types of hourly rates - one for weekdays and one for weekends.

In addition, for both of those types there is an overtime rate (cells C11:C12), which is paid for every hour over 8 daily hours.

We want to calculate the daily pay for each of the dates listed in column A.

➢ **Solution:**

Use the **WEEKDAY**, **MAX**, and **MIN** functions as shown in the following formula:

=IF(WEEKDAY(A2,2)<=5,MAX(D2-8,0)*$C$11+MIN(D2,8)*$B$11,MAX(D2-8,0)*$C$12+MIN(D2,8)*$B$12)

	A	B	C	D	E
1	Date	Start Time	End Time	Hours	Result
2	05/23/2005	10:30	20:00	9.5	$98.00
3	05/24/2005	09:00	16:00	7	$70.00
4	05/25/2005	12:00	21:20	9.333333333	$96.00
5	05/26/2005	10:45	18:10	7.416666667	$74.17
6	05/27/2005	09:00	14:30	5.5	$55.00
7	05/28/2005	15:00	17:30	2.5	$37.50
8	05/29/2005	10:20	13:45	3.416666667	$51.25
9					
10		Rate	Overtime Rate		
11	Weekday	$10.00	$12.00		
12	Weekend	$15.00	$20.00		
13					
14	Formula Syntax in cell D2:				
15	=(C2-B2)*24				
16					
17	Formula Syntax in cell E2:				
18	=IF(WEEKDAY(A2,2)<=5,MAX(D2-8,0)*$C$11+MIN(D2,8)*$B$11,MAX(D2-8,0)*$C$12+MIN(D2,8)*$B$12)				
19					

Explanation:

The following expression calculates the pay for the worked hours in cell D2, based on the weekday rate:

MAX(D2-8,0)*$C$11+MIN(D2,8)*$B$11

8 is subtracted from the number of worked hours in cell D2, in order to calculate the number of overtime hours.

If the number of worked hours is smaller than 8 (no overtime), a negative number is returned.

The **MAX** function returns the maximum of the calculated number of overtime hours and 0.

The number returned by the **MAX** function is then multiplied by the weekday overtime rate in cell C11, in order to calculate the pay for overtime hours.

The **MIN** function returns the minimum of the number of worked hours in cell D2 and 8.

Thus, it returns the number of normal (non-overtime) worked hours.

That number is then multiplied by the weekday normal rate to calculate the pay for normal hours.

Finally, the overtime pay calculated above and the normal pay is added together, returning the total pay for the hours worked in cell D2.

Similarly, the following expression calculates the pay for the worked hours in cell D2, based on the weekend rate:

MAX(D2-8,0)*$C$12+MIN(D2,8)*$B$12

The **WEEKDAY** function returns a number between 1 & 7, representing the day of the week that corresponds with the date in cell A2 (1 representing Monday).

If the number returned by the **WEEKDAY** function is smaller than 5 (Friday) or equal, the **IF** function returns the result of the first expression (weekday pay). Otherwise, it returns the result of the second expression (weekend pay).

Thus, the daily pay is returned for the date in cell A2.

Determining Whether a Person Worked a Full or Partial Shift

➤ **Problem:**

Columns A & B contain times signed in and out of work.

A full shift includes at least 8 hours; any period less than 8 hours is considered a partial shift.

We want to determine the type of shift corresponding with each pair of time values.

➤ **Solution:**

Use the **IF** and **TIME** functions as shown in the following formula:

=IF(IF(B2<A2,B2+1-A2,B2-A2)>TIME(8,0,0),"Full Shift","Partial Shift")

	A	B	C	D	E
1	**Time In**	**Time Out**	**Result**		
2	08:00	16:20	Full Shift		
3	20:00	02:10	Partial Shift		
4	10:00	13:30	Partial Shift		
5	22:00	07:00	Full Shift		
6					
7	**Formula Syntax in cell C2:**				
8	=IF(IF(B2<A2,B2+1-A2,B2-A2)>TIME(8,0,0),"Full Shift","Partial Shift")				
9					

Explanation:

The second **IF** function determines whether or not the Time Out in cell B2 is earlier than its corresponding Time In in cell A2.

If it is, the **IF** function calculates the difference between cells B2 and A2 (the time worked) and adds 1 (representing a full day) to convert it from negative to positive.

Otherwise, it simply calculates the difference between cells B2 and A2.

Thus, it returns a time value representing the time worked.

The **TIME** function returns a time value representing 8 hours (8:00).

The first **IF** function determines whether the time worked (returned by the second **IF** function) is greater than 8 hours (returned by the **TIME** function). If it is, the string "Full Shift" is returned. Otherwise, "Partial Shift" is returned.

Thus, the formula determines the type of shift that corresponds with the pair of time values in cells A2 & B2, and returns a string indicating the result.

Determining Whether a Worked Shift Was Morning, Afternoon or Night

➤ **Problem:**

We want to use the sign-in times from column A to determine whether a person was starting a morning, an afternoon, or a night shift.

For times before 12:00, the formula should return "Morning Shift".

For times between 12:00 and 16:00 the formula should return "Afternoon Shift".

For times after 16:00, the formula should return "Night Shift".

➤ **Solution:**

Use the **IF** and **TIME** functions as shown in the following formula:

=IF(A2<TIME(12,0,0),"Morning Shift",IF(A2<TIME(16,0,0),"Afternoon Shift","Night Shift"))

	A	B	C	D	E	F	G
1	**Times In**	**Result**					
2	09:00	Morning Shift					
3	14:00	Afternoon Shift					
4	18:00	Night Shift					
5	10:00	Morning Shift					
6	16:40	Night Shift					
7	12:00	Afternoon Shift					
8							
9	**Formula Syntax in cell B2:**						
10	=IF(A2<TIME(12,0,0),"Morning Shift",IF(A2<TIME(16,0,0),"Afternoon Shift","Night Shift"))						
11							

Explanation:

The first **TIME** function returns the time value "12:00".

The first **IF** function determines whether or not the Time In in cell A2 is earlier than 12:00.

If it is, the **IF** function returns the string "Morning Shift". Otherwise, it returns the result of the second **IF** function.

The second **IF** function determines whether or not the Time In shown in cell A2 is earlier than 16:00 (returned by the second **TIME** function).

If it is, the **IF** function returns the string "Afternoon Shift". Otherwise, it returns "Night Shift".

Counting the Number of Shifts in a Specified Week that an Employee Worked Overtime

➤ **Problem:**

Each row in columns A & B represents a shift worked during the first week of the year.

Column A identifies an employee, and column B lists the number of hours that employee worked on that shift.

Each employee may work any number of shifts per week, and they may be of variable length.

Columns C & D contain similar information for the second week of the year, and so on.

For any given employee and week number (cells A12:B14), we want to be able to calculate the number of overtime shifts (i.e. over 8 hours) that were worked.

➤ **Solution:**

Use the **SUMPRODUCT** and **OFFSET** functions as shown in the following formula:

=SUMPRODUCT((OFFSET($A$3:$A$9,0,2*(B12-1))=A12)*(OFFSET($B$3:$B$9,0,2*(B12-1))>8))

	A	B	C	D	E	F	G	H
1	**Week1**		**Week2**		**Week3**		**Week4**	
2	Employee	# Hours	Employee	# Hours	Employee	# Hours	Employee	# Hours
3	A	9	A	9	B	10	A	9
4	B	7	C	8	B	9	A	7
5	C	6	B	6	C	8	B	6
6	A	5	B	9	C	11	B	5
7	B	8	B	10	A	8	A	10
8	C	9	A	7	A	9	C	8
9	A	10	A	9	B	7	A	9
10								
11	Employee	# Week	Result					
12	A	1	2					
13	C	3	1					
14	B	2	2					
15								
16	Formula Syntax in cell C12:							
17	=SUMPRODUCT((OFFSET($A$3:$A$9,0,2*(B12-1))=A12)*(OFFSET($B$3:$B$9,0,2*(B12-1))>8))							
18								

Explanation:

The first **OFFSET** function offsets column A (cells A3:A9) by as many columns to the right as calculated by the following expression:

$2*(B12-1)$

The result of that expression represents the number of columns between columns A and the ID column for the week specified in cell B12.

Thus, the **OFFSET** function returns the reference of the ID column for the week specified in cell B12.

Every value (ID) in that column is compared with the ID entered in cell A12. That comparison yields an Array consisting of "1" (TRUE) for each value that matches that ID and "0" (FALSE) for each value that doesn't.

Similarly, the second **OFFSET** function returns the reference of the Hours column for the week specified in cell B12.

Every value (# Hours) in that column is compared with 8. That comparison yields an additional Array consisting of "1" for each value that is greater than 8 and "0" for each value that isn't.

The **SUMPRODUCT** function adds the products of the corresponding values (1/0) in the two Arrays created above.

The result represents the number of overtime shifts (i.e. over 8 hours) that the employee shown in cell A12 worked in the week specified in cell B12.

Calculating the Number of Hours per Month, Allowing for Daylight-Saving Shifts

➢ **Problem:**

Calculating the number of hours that constitute each month (serial number) listed in column A.

One hour should be subtructed to April due to the shift to daylight saving time.

Similarly, one hour should be added from October's total due to the shift back to standard time.

➢ **Solution:**

Use the **DAY**, **EOMONTH**, and **DATE** functions as shown in the following formula:

=DAY(EOMONTH(DATE(2005,A2,1),0))*24-(A2=4)+(A2=10)

	A	B	C	D
1	**Month**	**# Hours**		
2	1	744		
3	2	672		
4	3	744		
5	4	719		
6	5	744		
7	6	720		
8	7	744		
9	8	744		
10	9	720		
11	10	745		
12	11	720		
13	12	744		
14				
15	**Formula Syntax in cell B2:**			
16	=DAY(EOMONTH(DATE(2005,A2,1),0))*24-(A2=4)+(A2=10)			
17				

Explanation:

The **DATE** function returns the date of the first day of the month specified in cell A2, for the year 2005.

The **EOMONTH** function calculates the date 0 months after the date returned by the **DATE** function, and returns the last day of the month per that date. Thus, it returns the date of the last day of the month specified in cell A2.

The **DAY** function returns the day part of that date, thus representing the number of days in the month entered in cell A2.

That number of days is then multiplied by 24 to calculate the total number of hours constituting the month in cell A2.

The following expression returns "1" (TRUE) if the month number in cell A2 equals 4 (April) and "0" (FALSE) if it doesn't:

A2=4

Similarly, the following expression returns "1" (TRUE) if the month number in cell A2 equals 10 (October) and "0" (FALSE) if it isn't:

A2=10

The result of the first expression (returning "1" for April), is subtracted from the total number of hours calculated above, and the result of the second expression (returning "1" for October) is added.

Thus, if the month in cell A2 is April (4), one hour is subtracted from the total due to the shift to daylight saving time.

If the month is October (10) one hour is added due to the shift back to standard time.

Thus, the formula calculates the number of hours in the month in cell A2, allowing for daylight-saving shifts.

 Analysis ToolPak Add-In:

The **EOMONTH** function is included in the Analysis ToolPak Add-In. To install the Analysis ToolPak Add-in: Select *Tools → Add-Ins → Analysis ToolPak*, Click OK.

Counting Vacation or Sick Days within a Specified Time Period

➤ **Problem:**

Listed in column A are dates when an employee was absent.

Column B contains a letter, indicating the type of each absence (V for vacation, S for sick).

We want to count the number of vacation days that occurred during the last 90 days.

➤ **Solution:**

Use the **SUM** and **TODAY** functions in the *Array formula*:

{=SUM(((TODAY()-A2:A8)<=90)*(B2:B8=C2))}

☞ To apply *Array formula*:

Select the cell, press <**F2**> and simultaneously press <**Ctrl+Shift+Enter**>.

	A	B	C
1	**Absence Date**	**Absence Type**	**Counted Absence Type**
2	03/12/2004	V	V
3	01/05/2005	S	
4	01/13/2005	V	**Result**
5	05/08/2005	S	3
6	05/09/2005	V	
7	05/10/2005	V	**Today's Date**
8	05/11/2005	V	07/13/2005
9			
10	**Array Formula Syntax in cell C5:**		
11	{=SUM(((TODAY()-A2:A8)<=90)*(B2:B8=C2))}		
12			

Explanation:

The **TODAY** function returns today's date.

The following expression returns an Array consisting of the difference between today's date and each date in column A (cells A2:A8):

TODAY()-A2:A8

Each value in that Array, representing the number of days between today's date and a particular date in column A, is compared with 90.

That comparison yields an Array consisting of "1" (TRUE) for every number in the Array that is smaller than or equal to 90, and "0" (FALSE) for every number that isn't.

The following expression returns an additional Array consisting of "1" (TRUE) for every value in column B (cells B2:B8) that matches the absence type specified in cell C2 ("V") and "0" (FALSE) for every value that doesn't:

B2:B8=C2

The corresponding values (1/0) in the two Arrays created above are multiplied and a single Array, consisting of the results, is returned.

The **SUM** function adds the values in that Array.

The result represents the number of vacation days in column B (absence type ="V") that occurred during the last 90 days.

Calculating Hourly Productivity

➢ **Problem:**

Column B contains time values representing the hours worked by each salesperson in column A.

Column C shows the number of items each salesperson sold during that time.

We want to calculate the hourly productivity (Items Sold/Hours Worked) for each salesperson.

➢ **Solution:**

As time values in Excel are stored as fractions of 24 (an entire day), we must first multiply the times in column B by 24 in order to convert them to decimal values.

Hence, we calculate productivity as shown in the following formula:

=C2/(B2*24)

	A	B	C	D
1	Salesperson ID	Hours Worked	Items Sold	Result (Items per Hour)
2	1	05:45	7	1.22
3	2	07:30	10	1.33
4	3	03:20	5	1.50
5				
6	Formula Syntax in cell D2:			
7	=C2/(B2*24)			
8				

Chapter 4

Lookup

About This Chapter

This chapter provides information on the issues and problems involved with the use of Lookup formulas, and includes the following sections:

☞ **Retrieving Data Using Text References, page 160:** The formulas in this section retrieve data using row & column references, defined names, sheet names, and dates as references. You will learn how to retrieve data from a specific cell in multiple sheets and from another Excel workbook by using text references.

☞ **Retrieving Data Using One Criterion, page 170:** This section contains more than 20 examples of retrieving data using one criterion and includes: retrieving by position or by maximum/minimum value in a list, retrieving from a dynamic list, retrieving every nth value, and more.

☞ **Retrieving Data Using Two Criteria, page 196:** This section contains formulas that retrieve items using two criteria. For example, retrieving sale price using item name and color.

☞ **Retrieving an Entire Row of Data, page 201:** The formulas in this section retrieve the data from all cells in a row.

☞ **Retrieving Data from Two Different Lists, page 204:** This section contains a formula that uses criteria to retrieve data from two different lists.

☞ **Complex Retrieval Problems, page 206:** This section deals with formulas that use column or row headers to retrieve data. There is also a formula that retrieves values from a grid.

Retrieving Data Using Text References

Retrieving Values Using References Based on Row and Column Numbers

➤ **Problem:**

Columns C & D contain pairs of row and column numbers representing some of the cells in Data Range (A2:B5).

We want to create a cell reference from each pair of numbers in columns C & D and then retrieve the value stored in that cell.

➤ **Solution:**

Use the **INDIRECT** and **ADDRESS** functions as shown in the following formula:

=INDIRECT(ADDRESS(C2,D2))

	A	B	C	D	E	F
1	Data Range		Row	Column	Result	
2	50	ab	3	1	10/05/2005	
3	10/05/2005	20	2	2	ab	
4	cdg	45	4	1	cdg	
5	5:56 PM	12	5	2	12	
6						
7	Formula Syntax in cell E2:					
8	=INDIRECT(ADDRESS(C2,D2))					
9						

Explanation:

The **ADDRESS** function returns a text value representing a cell reference based on the row and column numbers in cells C2 & D2.

The **INDIRECT** function returns the data stored in the reference indicated by that text value.

Retrieving Each Second Number from Two Lists

> ## Problem:

Columns A & B contain two lists of numbers.

We want to create a formula that first retrieves a value from List1, then one from List2, and so on down the columns.

> ## Solution:

Use the **INDIRECT, IF, MOD,** and **ROW** functions as shown in the following formula:

=INDIRECT(IF(MOD(ROW(),2)=0,"A"&ROW(),"B"&ROW()))

	A	B	C	D	E	F
1	**List1**	**List2**	**Result**			
2	1	2	1			
3	4	3	3			
4	5	6	5			
5	8	7	7			
6	9	10	9			
7						
8	**Formula Syntax in cell C2:C6:**					
9	=INDIRECT(IF(MOD(ROW(),2)=0,"A"&ROW(),"B"&ROW()))					
10						

Explanation:

The **ROW()** function returns the row number of the current cell. The **MOD** function then divides that number by 2 and returns the remainder.

If the row number is even (remainder=0), the **IF** function returns a string composed of the letter "A" and the current row number.

Otherwise, it returns a string composed of the letter "B" and the current row number.

Finally, the **INDIRECT** function returns the reference indicated by the result of the **IF** function.

Retrieving Values Using Range Names as References (1)

➤ **Problem:**

Column A contains two range Names that have been defined for two cells in Sheet1 of Book1.xls.

We want to create a formula to retrieve the values stored in each of these range Names.

➤ **Solution:**

Use the **INDIRECT** function as shown in the following formula:

=INDIRECT("[Book1.xls]Sheet1'!"&A2&"")

❖ **Note:** Book1.xls must be open.

	A	B	C
1	**Range Name**	**Value Retrieved**	
2	DeadLine	05/05/2005	
3	Rate	$10.00	
4			
5	**Formula Syntax in cell B2:**		
6	=INDIRECT("[Book1.xls]Sheet1'!"&A2&"")		
7			

Explanation:

The Workbook name, Sheet name, and Range name (entered in cell A2) are joined into a single text value.

The **INDIRECT** function returns the reference indicated by that text value.

Retrieving Values Using Range Names as References (2)

➤ **Problem:**

First3 and Last3 are the defined Names for ranges A2:A4 and A5:A7 respectively.

We want to create a formula that will look up each of the values listed in column B for one of the defined Names listed in column C.

➤ **Solution:**

Use the **VLOOKUP** and **INDIRECT** functions as shown in the following formula:

=VLOOKUP(B2,INDIRECT(C2),1,FALSE)

	A	B	C	D	E
1	List1	Value to Look	Range to Look	Result	
2	5	2	First3	2	
3	2	4	Last3	#N/A	
4	4	8	Last3	8	
5	7	7	First3	#N/A	
6	6				
7	8				
8					
9	Formula Syntax in cell D2:				
10	=VLOOKUP(B2,INDIRECT(C2),1,FALSE)				
11					

Explanation:

The **INDIRECT** function returns the range reference indicated by the text value in cell C2 (Named Range).

The **VLOOKUP** function then looks in the first column of that range for the value stored in cell B2 and returns it if a match is found.

Retrieving Values from Different Sheets Using the Sheet Name as a Reference

➤ **Problem:**

Listed in columns A & B are first and last names.

Each of those names has a matching worksheet, named in the following format: "FirstName LastName".

We want to create a formula to retrieve the cell A1 from the sheet that matches each name.

➤ **Solution:**

Use the **INDIRECT** function as shown in the following formula:

=INDIRECT("'"&A2&" "&B2&"'!A1")

	A	B	C
1	**First Name**	**Last Name**	**Result**
2	Jerry	Seinfeld	Seinfeld
3	John	Lennon	Beatles
4	Michael	Jordan	Chicago Bulls
5			
6	**Formula Syntax in cell C2:**		
7	=INDIRECT("'"&A2&" "&B2&"'!A1")		
8			

Explanation:

The first name (cell A2), last name (cell B2), and cell reference (cell A1) are combined into a single string, which represents a sheet name and cell reference to retrieve.

The **INDIRECT** function then returns the reference indicated by that text value.

Retrieving Values from another Sheet Using Date as Sheet Name Reference

➢ **Problem:**

The dates entered in column A ("mmm-yy") refer to sheets with corresponding names (mmyy).

We want to create a formula to retrieve value in cell A1 from a sheet referred to by each of the dates in column A.

➢ **Solution:**

Use the **INDIRECT** and **TEXT** functions as shown in the following formula:

=INDIRECT(TEXT(A2,"mmyy")&"'!A1")

	A	B	C	D
1	**Date**	**Result**		
2	Jan-05	100		
3	Feb-05	50		
4	Mar-05	2		
5				
6	**Formula Syntax in cell B2:**			
7	=INDIRECT(TEXT(A2,"mmyy")&"!A1")			
8				

Explanation:

The **TEXT** function formats the date in cell A2 to as "mmyy" and converts it to a text value. That text is combined with the text "A1" to represent the worksheet and cell reference to retrieve.

The **INDIRECT** function returns the reference indicated by that string.

Retrieving a Specific Cell from Multiple Sheets

➤ **Problem:**

We want to copy the contents of cell A1 from Sheets1-5 into row 2 of the current sheet.

That is, cell C2 of the current sheet is to contain the value stored in cell A1 of Sheet1, cell D2 is to contain the value from Sheet2, and so on.

➤ **Solution:**

Use the **INDIRECT** and **COLUMN** functions as shown in the following formula:

=INDIRECT("Sheet" & COLUMN()-COLUMN($C$2)+1 & "'!$A$1")

	A	B	C	D	E	F	G
1	Sheet1		Cell A1 in Sheet1 to Sheet5				
2	10		10	5	12	4	9
3							
4	Sheet2						
5	5						
6							
7	Sheet3						
8	12						
9							
10	Sheet4						
11	4						
12							
13	Sheet5						
14	9						
15							
16	Formula Syntax in C2:G2						
17	=INDIRECT("Sheet" & COLUMN()-COLUMN($C$2)+1 & "'!$A$1")						
18							

Explanation:

The **COLUMN** functions return the column number of the current cell (**COLUMN**()) and of cell C2 (COLUMN ($C$2)).

Those column numbers are then used to calculate a sheet number.

The text value "Sheet" is combined with the calculated sheet number and the desired cell reference ("$A$1") to create a single string.

The **INDIRECT** function returns the reference indicated by that string.

Retrieving Values from another Excel Workbook Using Text References

> ## Problem:

Listed in column A are the path, file name, sheet name, and cell reference for a range containing pairs of numbers and letters.

We want to lookup each of the numbers in column C in the range specified in column A and retrieve the matching letters.

> ## Solution:

To retrieve the values listed in column C in the range specified in column A, use the **VLOOKUP** and **INDIRECT** function as shown in the following formula:

=VLOOKUP(C2,INDIRECT("'"&$A$2&"\["&$A$5&".xls]"&$A$8&"'!"&$A$11),2,FALSE)

❖ **Note:** Book5.xls must be open.

	A	B	C	D	E	F
1	**Path**		**Number to Lookup**	**Result**		
2	C:\ExcelFiles		2	AAA		
3			4	CCC		
4	**File Name**		3	300		
5	Book5					
6			**$A$1:$B$4 in Sheet1 of Book5:**			
7	**Sheet Name**		1	100		
8	Sheet1		2	AAA		
9			3	300		
10	**Cell Reference**		4	CCC		
11	$A$1:$B$4					
12						
13	**Formula Syntax in Column D**					
14	=VLOOKUP(C2,INDIRECT("'"&$A$2&"\["&$A$5&".xls]"&$A$8&"'!"&$A$11),2,FALSE)					
15						
16	**INDIRECT Workbook Reference Syntax**					
17	'Drive:\Folder\[WorkbookName.xls]SheetName'!Range					

Explanation:

Use the **INDIRECT** function to create a reference from the data in column A.

To refer to a range in a different workbook, use the following syntax in the **INDIRECT** formula:

'Drive:\Folder\[WorkbookName.xls]SheetName'!Range

Note that the full path (Drive:\Folder\[WorkbookName.xls]SheetName) is enclosed in single quotes and followed by the "!" sign, separating it from the range.

The workbook name must be enclosed in brackets ("[]") and include the ".xls" ending.

All of these elements are required in order for **INDIRECT** to return the proper information when referring to a different workbook.

(Drive and folder may be omitted if they are the same as those of the file currently in use).

The following **INDIRECT** formula refers to the range specified in column A:

=INDIRECT("'"&$A$2&"\["&$A$5&".xls]"&$A$8&"'!"&$A$11)

The data in cells A2, A5, A8 & A11 is joined into a single string, which represents a range reference in a different workbook.

The **INDIRECT** function returns the reference indicated by that string.

The **VLOOKUP** function looks for the value stored in cell C2 in the first column (column A) of the range reference returned by the **INDIRECT** function, and retrieves the corresponding value from the second column (column B).

Retrieving the Price for a Specified Item and a Specified Brand

➤ **Problem:**

Retrieving the matching price of the item shown in cell A2, for the specific brand entered in cell B2.

Following are the prices for each possible combination:

Item,Brand,Price

Jeans, Diesel, $85

Jeans, Levis, $80

Jeans, Lee, $70

T-Shirt, Sacks, $7

T-Shirt, Gap, $5

T-Shirt, Old Navy, $3

➢ **Solution:**

Use the **IF** and **LOOKUP** functions as shown in the following formula:

=IF(A2="Jeans",LOOKUP(B2,{"Diesel","Lee","Levis";85,70,80}),IF(A2="T-Shirt",LOOKUP(B2,{"Gap","Old Navy","Sacks"},{5,3,7})))

	A	B	C	D	E	F
1	**Item**	**Brand**	**Price**			
2	T-Shirt	Old Navy	$3.00			
3						
4	**Formula Syntax in cell C2:**					
5	=IF(A2="Jeans",LOOKUP(B2,{"Diesel","Lee","Levis";85,70,80}),IF (A2="T-Shirt",LOOKUP(B2,{"Gap","Old Navy","Sacks"},{5,3,7})))					
6						

Explanation:

Each **LOOKUP** function (one for each item type) searches in its respective Array for the brand entered in cell B2 and returns the matching price.

Depending on the item type stored in cell A2, the **IF** functions determine which of the two **LOOKUP** functions is used.

Retrieving Data Using One Criterion

Retrieving from List by Position

> ➤ **Problem:**

Sorting List1 (column A) according to position numbers as shown in column B.

> ➤ **Solution:**

Use the **INDEX** function as shown in the following formula:

=INDEX($A$2:$A$6,B2)

	A	B	C
1	**List1**	**Position**	**Result**
2	Mike	5	Rachel
3	Ron	4	Mischelle
4	David	3	David
5	Mischelle	2	Ron
6	Rachel	1	Mike
7			
8	**Formula Syntax in cell C2:**		
9	=INDEX($A$2:$A$6,B2)		
10			

Explanation:

The **INDEX** function returns the value from List1 at the position specified in cell B2.

Ranking Salespeople According to Sales Figure

> ➤ **Problem:**

Range A1:B6 contains salespeople's names and their total number of sales.

We want to rank the top 3 salespeople according to their sales performance.

➤ **Solution:**

Use the **INDEX**, **MATCH**, and **LARGE** functions as shown in the following formula:

=INDEX($A$2:$A$6,MATCH(LARGE($B$2:$B$6,A9),$B$2:$B$6,0))

	A	B	C	D
1	**Name**	**Total**		
2	Mike	500		
3	Donna	1000		
4	David	700		
5	Mischelle	300		
6	John	1200		
7				
8	**Rank**	**Result**		
9	1	John		
10	2	Donna		
11	3	David		
12				
13	**Formula Syntax in cell B9:**			
14	=INDEX($A$2:$A$6,MATCH(LARGE($B$2:$B$6,A9), $B$2:$B$6,0))			
15				

Explanation:

The **LARGE** function returns the kth highest sales figure in cells B2:B6, where kth is the rank specified in cell A9.

The **MATCH** function returns the position (row number) of that sales figure within column B.

Finally, the **INDEX** function returns the name stored in the corresponding position in column A.

Retrieving the Player Who Scored the Highest Number of Points

➢ **Problem:**

Column B contains the number of points scored by each player listed in column A.

We want to retrieve the name of the player who scored the highest number of points.

➢ **Solution:**

Use the **INDEX**, **MATCH**, and **MAX** functions in the following formula:

=INDEX(A2:A9,MATCH(MAX(B2:B9),B2:B9,0))

	A	B	C	D
1	**Player**	**Score**		**Top Score By**
2	Michael	18		Adam
3	David	12		
4	Anthony	7		
5	Dan	5		
6	Ron	20		
7	Jim	15		
8	Adam	22		
9	Kevin	2		
10				
11	**Formula Syntax in cell D2:**			
12	=INDEX(A2:A9,MATCH(MAX(B2:B9),B2:B9,0))			
13				

Explanation:

The **MAX** function returns the maximum value in column B (cells B2:B9).

The **MATCH** function returns the position of that value within cells B2:B9.

Finally, the **INDEX** function returns the value stored in the corresponding position in column A (cells A2:A9).

Thus, it returns the name of the player who scored the highest number of points.

Retrieving File Name by Matching a Given Page Number in a Book

➢ **Problem:**

The typed manuscript of a book was divided into five files.

Columns B & C contain the numbers of the first and last page included in each of the files.

We want to retrieve the file name corresponding to each page number listed in column E.

➢ **Solution:**

Use the **INDEX** and **MATCH** functions as shown in the following formula:

=INDEX($A$2:$A$6,MATCH(E2,$B$2:$B$6))

	A	B	C	D	E	F
1	**File Name**	**Start Page**	**End Page**		**Page #**	**Result**
2	File 1	1	35		93	File 3
3	File 2	36	85		22	File 1
4	File 3	86	120		195	File 5
5	File 4	121	178		161	File 4
6	File 5	179	230			
7						
8	**Formulas Syntax in cell F2:**					
9	=INDEX($A$2:$A$6,MATCH(E2,$B$2:$B$6))					
10						

Explanation:

The **MATCH** function returns the position (row number within column B) of the start page that is closest to (and smaller than) the page number in cell E2.

The **INDEX** function returns the file name that is stored in the corresponding position in column A.

Retrieving Grade Value for Corresponding Mark

➢ **Problem:**

Column B contains the mark matching each of the grades shown in column A.

We want to grade each mark in column D by finding the mark closest to it in column B, and then retrieving the corresponding grade from column A.

➢ **Solution:**

Use the **INDEX**, **MIN**, **IF**, **ABS**, and **ROW** functions as shown in the following *Array formula*:

{=INDEX($A$2:$A$6,MIN(IF(ABS($B$2:$B$6-D2)=MIN(ABS($B$2:$B$6-D2)),ROW($B$2:$B$6)-ROW($B$2)+1)),1)}

☞ To apply *Array formula:*

Select the cell, press **<F2>** and simultaneously press **<Ctrl+Shift+Enter>**.

	A	B	C	D	E
1	Grade	Mark		Mark to Grade	Grade
2	A	100		95	A
3	B	90		88	B
4	C	80		72	D
5	D	70		55	F
6	F	60			
7					
8	**Array Formula Syntax in cell E2:**				
9	{=INDEX($A$2:$A$6,MIN(IF(ABS($B$2:$B$6-D2)=MIN(ABS($B$2:$B$6-D2)),ROW($B$2:$B$6)-ROW($B$2)+1)),1)}				
10					

Explanation:

The **ABS** function returns an Array containing the absolute differences between each mark in column B and the mark to grade in cell D2.

The second **MIN** function returns the smallest number in that Array.

Thus, it calculates the minimal absolute difference between any mark in column B and the mark to grade in cell D2.

The **IF** determines whether or not the difference between each mark in column B and the mark entered in cell D2 equals that minimal difference, and returns an Array of the row numbers (calculated by the **ROW** function) of all the marks that satisfy that condition.

The **MIN** function then returns the smallest number in that Array, which is the row number of the mark in column B that is closest to the one entered in cell D2.

Finally, the **INDEX** function retrieves the grade from column A that is stored in the position indicated by that row number.

Thus returning the grade that corresponds to the mark that is closest to the one entered in cell D2.

Retrieving the Most Frequent Occurrence for Each Category

➤ **Problem:**

Each number in column B is designated to one of the categories A, B, or C. In different instances, the same number can be ascribed to any of the three categories.

Column A shows the category for each of the numbers in column B.

We want to find the number that occurs most frequently for each category.

> ➤ **Solution:**

Use the **MODE** and **IF** functions as shown in the following *Array formula*:

{=MODE(IF($A$2:$A$12=D2,$B$2:$B$12))}

☞ To apply *Array formula:*

Select the cell, press <**F2**> and simultaneously press <**Ctrl+Shift+Enter**>.

	A	B	C	D	E
1	Category	Number		Category	Result
2	A	1		B	5
3	B	2		C	3
4	C	3		A	1
5	C	1			
6	B	5			
7	A	2			
8	C	3			
9	B	5			
10	A	1			
11	C	4			
12	A	3			
13					
14	**Array Formula Syntax in cell E2:**				
15	{=MODE(IF($A$2:$A$12=D2,$B$2:$B$12))}				
16					

Explanation:

The **IF** function returns an Array containing all the numbers in column B having a corresponding value in column A that matches the criteria stored in cell D2.

The **MODE** function returns the value within that Array that occurs most frequently.

Retrieving the Last Value and the Last Character in a Row

➢ **Problem:**

Range B2:F7 contains characters and numbers, each in an individual cell. Some of the cells in the range may be empty.

We want to retrieve both the last value (of any type) and the last character that appears in each row of the range.

➢ **Solution:**

❖ To find the last character for each row, use the **HLOOKUP** and **REPT** functions as shown in the following formula in column H:

=HLOOKUP(REPT("z",10),B2:F2,1)

❖ To find the last value (of any type) in each row, use the **INDEX**, **MAX**, **IF**, and **COLUMN** functions as shown in the following *Array formula* in column I:

{=INDEX(B2:F2,1,MAX(IF(B2:F2<>"",COLUMN(B2:F2)))-COLUMN(B2)+1)}

☞ To apply *Array formula:*

Select the cell, press **<F2>** and simultaneously press **<Ctrl+Shift+Enter>**.

	A	B	C	D	E	F	G	H	I
1								**Last Character**	**Last Value**
2		a	b					b	b
3		n	3					n	3
4		3	n	7	p			p	p
5		1	2	y	o	z		z	z
6		4	10	t	0			t	0
7		x				y		y	y
8									
9	**Last Character Formula Syntax in cell H2:**								
10	=HLOOKUP(REPT("z",10),B2:F2,1)								
11									
12	**Last Value Formula Syntax in cell I2:**								
13	{=INDEX(B2:F2,1,MAX(IF(B2:F2<>"",COLUMN(B2:F2)))-COLUMN(B2)+1)}								
14									

Explanation:

☞ **Last Character Formula:**

The **REPT** function returns a string in which the letter "z" is repeated 10 times ("zzzzzzzzzz").

The **HLOOKUP** function then looks for that string in row 2 (cells B2:F2), and returns the character closest to it within the row (i.e. the last character in the row).

☞ **Last Value Formula:**

The **IF** function returns an Array consisting of the column numbers (calculated by the **COLUMN** functions) of all the non-blank cells in row 2 (cells B2:F2).

The **MAX** function returns the largest number in that Array (i.e. the column number of the last non-blank cell in the row).

The **INDEX** function retrieves the value from row 2 that is stored in the position indicated by that column number.

Retrieving the Last Value in a Dynamic List

➤ **Problem:**

Column A contains a list of numbers that is being continually added to at its base.

We want to create a formula that will retrieve the last value in the column and automatically update when a new number is added.

➤ **Solution:**

Use the **OFFSET** and **COUNTA** functions as shown in the following formula:

=OFFSET(A1,COUNTA($A:$A)-1,0)

❖ **Note:**

The formula will only work correctly when there are no empty cells within the list.

	A	B	C	D	E
1	10	**Result**			
2	A	8			
3	20				
4	C	**Formula Syntax in cell B2:**			
5	2	=OFFSET(A1,COUNTA($A:$A)-1,0)			
6	8				
7					

Explanation:

The **COUNTA** function returns the number of values (non-blank cells) in column A.

The **OFFSET** function offsets the reference "A1" as many rows as the number calculated by the **COUNTA** function, minus 1.

Thus, the reference of the last non-blank cell in the column is returned.

Retrieving the Value of the First Non-Blank Cell in a List

➤ **Problem:**

Retrieving the value of the first non-blank cell in Range1 (cells A2:A7).

➤ **Solution:**

Use the **INDEX** and **MATCH** functions as shown in the following *Array formula*:

{=INDEX(A2:A7,MATCH(TRUE,A2:A7<>"",0))}

☞ To apply *Array formula:*

Select the cell, press <**F2**> and simultaneously press <**Ctrl+Shift+Enter**>.

	A	B	C	D
1	**Range1**			
2				
3				
4	X			
5				
6	Y			
7	Z			
8				
9	Result	X		
10				
11	**Array Formula Syntax in cell B9:**			
12	{=INDEX(A2:A7,MATCH(TRUE,A2:A7<>"",0))}			
13				

Explanation:

The **MATCH** function returns the position (row number) of the first cell in Range1 for which "TRUE" is the result of the following expression:

A2:A7<>""

(i.e. the position of the first non-blank cell).

The **INDEX** function then returns the value from Range1 stored in that position.

Retrieving the Most Recent Payment Made by Client

➢ **Problem:**

Columns A & B list all the pay dates of various clients.

We want to retrieve the date of the most recent payment made by each of the clients listed in column D.

➢ **Solution:**

Use the **MAX** and **IF** functions as shown in the following *Array formula*:

{=MAX(IF($A$2:$A$8=D2,$B$2:$B$8))}

☞ To apply *Array formula:*

Select the cell, press **<F2>** and simultaneously press **<Ctrl+Shift+Enter>**.

	A	B	C	D	E
1	**Client**	**PayDates**		**Client**	**Result**
2	A	02/10/2004		B	04/20/2005
3	B	04/16/2005		A	05/18/2004
4	A	10/16/2003		C	08/11/2002
5	C	08/11/2002			
6	A	05/18/2004			
7	B	04/20/2005			
8	C	07/11/2002			
9					
10	**Array Formula Syntax in cell E2:**				
11	{=MAX(IF($A$2:$A$8=D2,$B$2:$B$8))}				
12					

Explanation:

The **IF** function returns an Array containing the pay dates (column B) corresponding to all the values in column A that match the client criteria (cell D2).

The **MAX** function returns the maximum date within that Array.

Retrieving the Closest Larger / Closest Smaller Values from a List when there is No Exact Match

➤ **Problem:**

Listed in cells B2:B5 are values to look up in column A.

We want to create formulas to look up each value and, in the case of there being no exact match, return the closest larger and the closest smaller number that is in the list.

➢ **Solution:**

❖ To find the closest larger number or an exact match in column A, use the **SMALL** and **COUNTIF** functions as shown in the following formula:

=SMALL($A$2:$A$7,COUNTIF($A$2:$A$7,"<"&B2)+1)

❖ To find the closest smaller number or an exact match in column A, use the **LARGE** and **COUNTIF** functions as shown in the following formula:

=LARGE($A$2:$A$7,COUNTIF($A$2:$A$7,">"&B2)+1)

	A	B	C	D
	List1	Value to look	Closest Larger Value	Closest Smaller Value
2	2	3	4	2
3	5	5	5	5
4	4	7	10	6
5	10	9	10	6
6	1			
7	6			
8				
9	Formula for Closest Larger Value in cell C2:			
10	=SMALL($A$2:$A$7,COUNTIF($A$2:$A$7,"<"&B2)+1)			
11				
12	Formula for Closest Smaller Value in cell D2:			
13	=LARGE($A$2:$A$7,COUNTIF($A$2:$A$7,">"&B2)+1)			
14				

Explanation:

☞ **Formula for Closest Larger Value:**

The **COUNTIF** function returns the number of values in column A that are smaller than the lookup value in cell B2.

The **SMALL** function returns the kth smallest number in column A, where kth is the number calculated by the **COUNTIF** function, plus 1.

☞ **Formula for Closest Smaller Value:**

The **COUNTIF** function returns the number of values in column A that are larger than the lookup value in cell B2.

The **LARGE** function returns the kth largest number in column A, where kth is the number calculated by the **COUNTIF** function, plus 1.

Retrieving the First Value in a List that is Greater / Smaller than a Specified Number

➢ **Problem:**

We want to use each of the numbers in column C as criteria when searching through List1 (column A). For each search, we want to retrieve the first number from the list that is greater than the current criteria, and also the first number that is smaller.

➢ **Solution:**

Use the **INDEX** and **MATCH** functions as shown in the following *Array formulas*:

First greater value -
{=INDEX($A$2:$A$7,MATCH(TRUE,$A$2:$A$7>C2,0))}

First smaller value -
{=INDEX($A$2:$A$7,MATCH(FALSE,$A$2:$A$7>C2,0))}

☞ To apply *Array formula*:

Select the cell, press **<F2>** and simultaneously press **<Ctrl+Shift+Enter>**.

	A	B	C	D	E
1	**List1**		**Criteria**	**First Greater Value**	**First Smaller Value**
2	8		10	20	8
3	5		4	8	#N/A
4	20		7	8	5
5	15		25	#N/A	8
6	6				
7	12				
8					
9	**Array Formula Syntax in cell D2:**				
10	{=INDEX($A$2:$A$7,MATCH(TRUE,$A$2:$A$7>C2,0))}				
11					
12	**Array Formula Syntax in cell E2:**				
13	{=INDEX($A$2:$A$7,MATCH(FALSE,$A$2:$A$7>C2,0))}				
14					

Explanation:

☞ **Formula for First Greater Value:**

The **MATCH** function returns the position (row number) of the first cell in column A for which "TRUE" is the result of the following expression:

$A$2:$A$7>C2

(i.e. the first cell containing a value larger than the criteria in cell C2).

The **INDEX** function then returns the value from column A stored in that position.

☞ **Formula for First Smaller Value:**

The **MATCH** function returns the position (row number) of the first cell in column A for which "FALSE" is the result of the following expression:

$A$2:$A$7>C2

(i.e. the first cell containing a value smaller than the criteria in cell C2).

The **INDEX** function then returns the value from column A stored in that position.

Finding the Maximal / Minimal String, Based on Alphabetic Order

➤ **Problem:**

Finding the maximal and minimal name (text) within List1 (column A), based on alphabetic order of the first character of each name (text).

➤ **Solution:**

❖ To retrieve the maximal name within column A, use the **INDEX**, **MATCH**, **MAX**, and **COUNTIF** functions as shown in the following *Array formula*:

{=INDEX(A2:A8,MATCH(MAX(COUNTIF(A2:A8,"<"&A2:A8)),COUNTIF(A2:A8,"<"&A2:A8),0))}

❖ To retrieve the minimal name within column A, use the **INDEX**, **MATCH**, **MIN**, and **COUNTIF** functions as shown in the following *Array formula*:

{=INDEX(A2:A8,MATCH(MIN(COUNTIF(A2:A8,"<"&A2:A8)),COUNT IF(A2:A8,"<"&A2:A8),0))}

☞ To apply *Array formula*:

Select the cell, press <**F2**> and simultaneously press <**Ctrl+Shift+Enter**>.

	A	B	C	D	E
1	List1		Max	Min	
2	Emily		Sean	Adam	
3	Sean				
4	Kevin				
5	Joan				
6	Adam				
7	Kate				
8	Ben				
9					
10	Array Formula Syntax in cell C2:				
11	{=INDEX(A2:A8,MATCH(MAX(COUNTIF(A2:A8,"<"&A2 :A8)),COUNTIF(A2:A8,"<"&A2:A8),0))}				
12					
13	Array Formula Syntax in cell D2:				
14	{=INDEX(A2:A8,MATCH(MIN(COUNTIF(A2:A8,"<"&A2: A8)),COUNTIF(A2:A8,"<"&A2:A8),0))}				
15					

Explanation:

The **COUNTIF** function returns an Array containing the number of names in column A that are smaller (based on alphabetic order) than each name listed in the column.

The **MAX/MIN** function returns the largest/ smallest number in that array, representing the largest/ smallest name.

The **MATCH** function then returns the position (row number) of that number within the Array returned by the **COUNTIF** function.

Finally, the **INDEX** function returns the name from column A that is stored in the row number returned by the **MATCH** function.

Retrieve Value Using Case-Sensitive Lookups

➢ **Problem:**

Listed in the range A2:B7 are characters and their corresponding ASCII codes.

Note that upper and lower case forms of the same letter are assigned different codes.

We want to be able to find the code from cells B2:B7 that provides a case-sensitive match for each character in cells A11:A13.

➢ **Solution:**

Use the **INDEX**, **MATCH**, and **EXACT** functions as shown in the following *Array formula*:

{=INDEX($B$2:$B$7,MATCH(TRUE,EXACT(A11,$A$2:$A$7),0))}

☞ To apply *Array formula*:

Select the cell, press **<F2>** and simultaneously press **<Ctrl+Shift+Enter>**.

	A	B	C	D	E
1	CHAR Formula	ASCII Code			
2	A	65			
3	a	97			
4	B	66			
5	b	98			
6	C	67			
7	c	99			
8					
9					
10	Character	Array Formula			
11	A	65			
12	b	98			
13	C	67			
14					
15	Array Formula Syntax in cell B11:				
16	{=INDEX($B$2:$B$7,MATCH(TRUE,EXACT(A11,$A$2:$A$7),0))}				
17					
18	Formula Syntax in cell A2:				
19	=CHAR(B2)				

Explanation:

The **EXACT** function checks whether the character in cell A11 is an exact (case sensitive) match of any of the characters in cells A2:A7.

It then returns an Array of TRUE/FALSE results, one for each character in cells A2:A7.

The **MATCH** function returns the position of the first "TRUE" within that Array. (i.e. the position of the first character in cells A2:A7 that is an exact match of the one in cell A11).

Finally, the **INDEX** function returns the code from column B that is stored in the corresponding position.

Retrieving the Minimal / Maximal Values from a Filtered List

➤ **Problem:**

An auto filter is set for List1 (column A) and List2 (column B).

When setting the filter of List1 to "2", the number "5" is the minimal value displayed in List2.

However, when using the **MIN** function, a minimal value of "2" is returned, which is not among the filtered data.

We want to create a formula to find the true minimal value within the filtered data, one that updates with every change of filter.

➤ **Solution:**

❖ To retrieve the minimal value use the **SUBTOTAL** function as shown in the following formula:
=SUBTOTAL(5,B13:B21)

❖ To retrieve the maximal value use the **SUBTOTAL** function as shown in the following formula:
=SUBTOTAL(4,B13:B21)

	A	B	C	D	E	F	G
1	**Full Range**			**Result**	**Formula Syntax in column D:**		
2				12	Minimal value	=SUBTOTAL(5,B13:B21)	
3	**List1**	**List2**		15	Maxmimal value	=SUBTOTAL(4,B13:B21)	
4	1	12					
5	1	15					
6	2	10					
7	2	5					
8	3	2					
9	3	8					
10							
11	**Filtered Range**						
12							
13	**List1**	**List2**					
14	1	12					
15	1	15					

Explanation:

The **SUBTOTAL** function returns a subtotal for a list or database.

To add a subtotal to a filtered list and ignore any hidden values, use the numbers 1-11 as the first argument of the function (new from Excel version 2003).

To include hidden numbers in your subtotal, use the numbers 101-111 as the first argument.

The screenshot (Excel 2003 version) provides an explanation of the various argument numbers that are available to be used in the **SUBTOTAL** function.

Function_num (includes hidden values)	Function_num (ignores hidden values)	Function
1	101	AVERAGE
2	102	COUNT
3	103	COUNTA
4	104	MAX
5	105	MIN
6	106	PRODUCT
7	107	STDEV
8	108	STDEVP
9	109	SUM
10	110	VAR
11	111	VARP

Retrieving Smallest Nth Value Match within a List

➤ **Problem:**

Columns A & B contain matching pairs of numbers and letters.

Each number in column A may appear multiple times, on each occasion with a different corresponding letter.

We want to search the data and retrieve the letter corresponding to the nth match of specified numbers from column A. Column C specifies the number to search for, and column D specifies the particular match required.

➤ **Solution:**

Use the **INDEX**, **SMALL**, **IF**, and **ROW** functions as shown in the following *Array formula*:

{=INDEX($B$2:$B$12,SMALL(IF($A$2:$A$12=C2,ROW($B$2:$B$12)-ROW($B$2)+1),D2))}

☞ To apply *Array formula:*

Select the cell, press <**F2**> and simultaneously press <**Ctrl+Shift+Enter**>.

	A	B	C	D	E	F
1	**Number**	**Letter**	**Number to Look For**	**Match to Retrieve**	**Result**	
2	1	A	2	2	F	
3	2	B	1	3	H	
4	1	C	3	1	D	
5	3	D	3	2	J	
6	5	E				
7	2	F				
8	4	G				
9	1	H				
10	5	I				
11	3	J				
12	2	K				
13						
14	**Array Formula Syntax in cell E2:**					
15	{=INDEX($B$2:$B$12,SMALL(IF($A$2:$A$12=C2,ROW($B$2:$B$12)-ROW($B$2)+1),D2))}					
16						

Explanation:

The **IF** function returns an Array containing the positions (returned by ROW function) of all the values in column A that are equal to the number in cell C2.

The **SMALL** function returns the kth smallest number within that array, where kth is the match number to retrieve (cell D2).

Finally, the **INDEX** function returns the value from column B that is stored in the row number returned by the **SMALL** function.

Finding Every Third Number and Returning the Largest of Them

> **Problem:**

We want to scan List1 (Column A) for every third number and then determine which of them is the largest.

➤ **Solution:**

Use the **MAX**, **IF**, **MOD**, and **ROW** functions as shown in the following *Array formula*:

{=MAX(IF(MOD(ROW($A$2:$A$10)-ROW($A$2)+1,3)=0,$A$2:$A$10))}

☞ To apply *Array formula*:

Select the cell, press **<F2>** and simultaneously press **<Ctrl+Shift+Enter>**.

	A	B	C	D
1	List1	Result		
2	5	4		
3	1			
4	2			
5	7			
6	8			
7	4			
8	10			
9	12			
10	3			
11				
12	**Array Formula Syntax in B2:**			
13	{=MAX(IF(MOD(ROW($A$2:$A$10)-ROW($A$2)+1,3)=0,$A$2:$A$10))}			
14				

Explanation:

The **ROW** functions are used to calculate the serial numbers matching each value in List1, based on the row number of each value.

The **MOD** function divides each of those serial numbers by 3, and returns the remainder.

The **IF** function returns an Array containing all the values in column A which calculated serial numbers are divisible by 3 (i.e. an Array containing every third value from List1).

The **MAX** function returns the largest value in that Array.

Retrieving the Nth Value in a Row / Column

➢ **Problem:**

For each value of n from column C, we want to retrieve the nth value in row 1 (B1:I1), as well as the nth value in column A (A4:A11).

➢ **Solution:**

❖ To retrieve the nth value in the column, use the **OFFSET** function as shown in the following formula in column D:

=OFFSET($B$1,0,C4-1)

❖ To retrieve the nth value in the row, use the **OFFSET** function as shown in the following formula in column E:

=OFFSET($A$4,C4-1,0)

	A	B	C	D	E	F	G	H	I
1	Row	5	7	8	9	10	12	2	3
2									
3	Column		n	n^{th} Value in Row	n^{th} Value in Column				
4	6		1	5	6				
5	4		3	8	7				
6	7		5	10	1				
7	11		8	3	5				
8	1								
9	15								
10	8								
11	5								
12									
13	Formula Syntax in cell D4:								
14	=OFFSET($B$1,0,C4-1)								
15									
16	Formula Syntax in cell E4:								
17	=OFFSET($A$4,C4-1,0)								
18									

Explanation:

The **OFFSET** function returns a reference that is offset from the given reference ($B$1/$A$4) by as many columns/rows as the number in cell C4, minus 1.

Retrieving Every Nth Value in a Range

> ➤ **Problem:**

Creating a new list (List2), which consists of every 3rd value from List1.

> ➤ **Solution:**

Use the **INDEX** and **ROW** functions as shown in the following formula:

=INDEX($A$2:$A$13,(ROW()-2)*3+3)

	A	B	C	D
1	List1	List2		
2	A	C		
3	B	F		
4	C	I		
5	D	L		
6	E			
7	F			
8	G			
9	H			
10	I			
11	J			
12	K			
13	L			
14				
15	**Formula Syntax in cell B2:**			
16	=INDEX($A$2:$A$13,(ROW()-2)*3+3)			
17				

Explanation:

The **ROW()** function returns the row number of the current cell.

That number is then used to calculate the next position (row number) that is a multiple of 3.

The **INDEX** function returns the value in List1 that is stored in that position.

Retrieve the Distance between Any Two Cities from Distance Table

➢ **Problem:**

Range A1:G7 contains a table of the respective distances (miles) between 6 cities.

We want to use that table to retrieve the distance between each origin and destination pair shown in cells A10:B13.

➢ **Solution:**

Use the **INDEX** and **MATCH** functions as shown in the following formula:

=INDEX($A$1:$G$7,MATCH(A10,$A$1:$A$7,0),MATCH(B10,$A$1:$G$1,0))

	A	B	C	D	E	F	G
1		Chicago	New York	Los Angeles	Miami	Atlanta	Seattle
2	Chicago		1275	3250	2220	1150	3330
3	New York	1275		4505	2060	1390	4600
4	Los Angeles	3250	4505		4405	3515	1835
5	Miami	2220	2060	4405		1070	5415
6	Atlanta	1150	1390	3515	1070		4485
7	Seattle	3330	4600	1835	5415	4485	
8							
9	Origin	Destination	Result				
10	New York	Seattle	4600				
11	Miami	Chicago	2220				
12	Atlanta	Los Angeles	3515				
13	Chicago	Atlanta	1150				
14							
15	Formula Syntax in cell C10:						
16	=INDEX($A$1:$G$7,MATCH(A10,$A$1:$A$7,0),MATCH(B10,$A$1:$G$1,0))						
17							

Explanation:

The first **MATCH** function (used as the row_num argument of the **INDEX** function) returns the position (row number) of the origin (cells A1:A7) entered in cell A10. The second **MATCH** function (used as the column_num argument of the **INDEX** function) returns the position (column number) of the destination (cells A1:G1) entered in cell B10.

To discuss the formula presented, visit: www.exceltip.com/fx-194

The **INDEX** function retrieves the value from cells A1:G7 that is stored at the intersection of the row and column numbers calculated by the **MATCH** functions.

Retrieving Matching Values from Not Adjacent List

➤ **Problem:**

Columns A & B contain numbers and matching letters.

However, rather than being adjacent, each letter in column B is shifted down one row with respect to its matching number in column A.

We want to retrieve the matching letter for each number.

➤ **Solution:**

Use the **INDEX** and **MATCH** functions as shown in the following formula:

=INDEX($B$2:$B$7,MATCH(C2,$A$2:$A$7,0)+1)

	A	B	C	D
1	**Numbers**	**Letters**	**Value to Look For**	**Result**
2	1		1	A
3	2	A	3	C
4	3	B	5	E
5	4	C		
6	5	D		
7		E		
8				
9	**Formula Syntax in cell D2:**			
10	=INDEX($B$2:$B$7,MATCH(C2,$A$2:$A$7,0)+1)			
11				

Explanation:

The **MATCH** function returns the position (row number) in column A of the lookup value (cell C2).

The **INDEX** function returns the letter in column B that is stored one row down from that position.

Retrieving Data Using Two Criteria

Retrieving an Item from a List that Meets Multiple Criteria (1)

➤ **Problem:**

Range1 (A3:C7) contains file names with their matching types and sizes.

Range2 (A12:B16) contains a similar list of file names but with matching types only.

We want to find the appropriate file sizes from Range1 by matching each pair of file names and types from both ranges.

➤ **Solution:**

Use the **INDEX** and **MATCH** functions as shown in the following *Array formula*:

{=INDEX($C$3:$C$7,MATCH(A12&B12,$A$3:$A$7&$B$3:$B$7,0))}

☞ To apply *Array formula*:

Select the cell, press **<F2>** and simultaneously press **<Ctrl+Shift+Enter>**.

	A	B	C	D	E
1	Range1				
2	**File Name**	**File Type**	**Size (KB)**		
3	file1	xls	500		
4	file2	doc	80		
5	file3	ppt	800		
6	file4	xls	400		
7	file1	ppt	1200		
8					
9					
10	Range2				
11	**File Name**	**File Type**	**Size (KB) from Range1**		
12	file1	xls	500		
13	file2	doc	80		
14	file3	ppt	800		
15	file4	xls	400		
16	file1	ppt	1200		
17					
18	**Formula Syntax in cell C12:**				
19	{=INDEX($C$3:$C$7,MATCH(A12&B12,$A$3:$A$7&$B$3:$B$7,0))}				
20					

Explanation:

The **MATCH** function looks in Range1 ($A$3:$A$7&$B$3:$B$7) for each pair of file names and types from Range2 (A12&B12).

On finding a match, it returns the position (row number) of that value within Range1.

The **INDEX** function then returns the value found in the corresponding position in column C of Range1 ($C$3:$C$7).

Retrieving an Item from a List that Meets Multiple Criteria (2)

> ➤ **Problem:**

Range A2:C7 contains a list of items and their corresponding colors and prices.

We want to find the name of the first Blue item that costs less than $200.

> ➤ **Solution:**

Use the **INDEX** and **MATCH** functions as shown in the following *Array formula*:

{=INDEX(A2:A7,MATCH(1,(B2:B7=D2)*(C2:C7<D3)))}

> ☞ To apply *Array formula*:
>
> Select the cell, press **<F2>** and simultaneously press **<Ctrl+Shift+Enter>**.

	A	B	C	D	E
1	Item	Color	Price	Criteria	Result
2	Shoes	Red	$140	Blue	Shoes
3	Jacket	Brown	$300	$200	
4	Shoes	Blue	$199		
5	T-Shirt	Green	$10		
6	Jeans	Blue	$150		
7	Shoes	Black	$99		
8					
9	**Array Formula Syntax in cell E2:**				
10	{=INDEX(A2:A7,MATCH(1,(B2:B7=D2)*(C2:C7<D3)))}				
11					

Explanation:

The **MATCH** function returns the position (row number) of the first pair of Color & Price values that meet the criteria in cells D2 & D3 (Blue, costs less than $200).

The **INDEX** function then returns the Item in column A from the corresponding position.

Retrieving Sale Price Based on Item and Color Criteria

> ➤ **Problem:**

Cells A1:C5 contain color and price data for a range of items.

We want to find the matching price for each pair of item and color values entered in cells A9:B11.

> ➤ **Solution:**

Use the **INDEX** and **MATCH** functions as shown in the following *Array formula*:

{=INDEX($C$2:$C$5,MATCH(1,($A$2:$A$5=A9)*($B$2:$B$5=B9),0))}

> ☞ To apply *Array formula*:

Select the cell, press **<F2>** and simultaneously press **<Ctrl+Shift+Enter>**.

	A	B	C	D
1	**Item**	**Color**	**Price**	
2	Jeans	Blue	$50	
3	Sneakers	Red	$70	
4	T-Shirt	Green	$10	
5	Skirt	Orange	$30	
6				
7				
8	**Item**	**Color**	**Price**	
9	Sneakers	Red	$70	
10	Jeans	Blue	$50	
11	T-Shirt	Yellow	#N/A	
12				
13	**Array Formula in cell C9:**			
14	{=INDEX($C$2:$C$5,MATCH(1,($A$2:$A$5=A9) *($B$2:$B$5=B9),0))}			
15				

Explanation:

The **MATCH** function returns the position (row number) of the first pair of Item & Color values that meet the criteria in cells A9 & B9 (Sneakers, Red).

The **INDEX** function then returns the Price found in the corresponding position in column C.

Retrieving a Price from a List that Matches both Category and Item Criteria

> ➤ **Problem:**

Columns A:C contain the prices of various items in different categories.

We want to retrieve the price matching each category/item pair shown in columns E & F.

> ➤ **Solution:**

Use the **INDEX** and **MATCH** functions as shown in the following *Array formula*:

{=INDEX($C$2:$C$6,MATCH(E2&F2,$A$2:$A$6&$B$2:$B$6,0))}

☞ To apply *Array formula*:

Select the cell, press <**F2**> and simultaneously press <**Ctrl+Shift+Enter**>.

	A	B	C	D	E	F	G
1	Category	Item	Price		Category to Look For	Item to Look For	Result
2	A	1	$50.00		A	2	$30.00
3	A	2	$30.00		B	3	$20.00
4	B	1	$40.00		C	3	$10.00
5	B	3	$20.00				
6	C	3	$10.00				
7							
8	Array Formula Syntax in cell G2:						
9	{=INDEX($C$2:$C$6,MATCH(E2&F2,$A$2:$A$6&$B$2:$B$6,0))}						
10							

Explanation:

The **MATCH** function returns the position (row number) of the first pair of Category & Item values in columns A & B that meet the criteria in cells E2 & F2.

The **INDEX** function returns the value (Price) found in the corresponding position in column C.

Retrieving an Entire Row of Data

Retrieving the Entire Row of a Matched Value

➤ **Problem:**

The range A1:E6 contains ID, name, gender, and age data for a group of people.

We want to lookup the data range for each ID listed in column G and retrieve all data from the matching row.

➤ **Solution 1:**

Use the **VLOOKUP** function as shown in the following *Array formula*:

{=VLOOKUP(G2,$A$2:$E$6,{2,3,4,5},FALSE)}

Select range H2:K2 and enter the above *Array formula*.

Then, copy/paste the formula from cells H2:K2 to H3:K4.

☞ To apply *Array formula*:

Select the cell, press <**F2**> and simultaneously press <**Ctrl+Shift+Enter**>.

➤ **Solution 2:**

Use the **INDEX** and **MATCH** functions as shown in the following formula in cell H7:

=INDEX(B$2:B$6,MATCH($G2,$A$2:$A$6,0),1)

Copy the formula and paste it to all cells in the range H7:K9.

	A	B	C	D	E	F	G	H	I	J	K
1	ID	First Name	Last Name	Gender	Age		ID to Look	VLOOKUP Formula			
2	1	John	Doe	Male	22		2	Kate	Adams	Female	19
3	2	Kate	Adams	Female	19		4	Michael	Walsh	Male	35
4	3	Kim	Wood	Female	43		3	Kim	Wood	Female	43
5	4	Michael	Walsh	Male	35						
6	5	Dave	Martin	Male	72			INDEX Formula			
7								Kate	Adams	Female	19
8								Michael	Walsh	Male	35
9	ARRAY VLOOKUP Formula Syntax in cell H2:							Kim	Wood	Female	43
10	{=VLOOKUP(G2,$A$2:$E$6,{2,3,4,5},FALSE)}										
11											
12	INDEX Formula Syntax in cell H7:										
13	=INDEX(B$2:B$6,MATCH($G2,$A$2:$A$6,0),1)										
14											

Explanation to Solution 1:

The **VLOOKUP** function searches the first column of range A2:E6 for the ID entered in G2 and returns the corresponding values from the next four columns, as follows:

The value in column B (first name) is returned into cell H2.

The value in column C (last name) is returned into cell I2.

The value in column D (gender) is returned into cell J2.

The value in column E (age) is returned into cell K2.

Explanation to Solution 2:

The **MATCH** function returns the position (row number) within column A of the ID entered in cell G2.

The **INDEX** function returns the value found in the corresponding position in column B (i.e. the First Name matching the ID in cell G2).

On copying the formula to the next cell in the row (from cell H7 to cell I7)), the **INDEX** function will update accordingly and return a value from the next column in the range (i.e. the Last Name from column C).

Returning the Entire Contents of the Row Containing the Highest Math Grade

➢ **Problem:**

Each row of columns B:E contains data on a student's ID, year, subject, and grade.

We want to find the highest math mark in the data range and retrieve all the information from that particular row.

➢ **Solution:**

Use the **INDEX**, **MATCH**, and **MAX** functions as shown in the following *Array formula*:

{=INDEX(B2:B6,MATCH(MAX(($E$2:$E$6)*($D$2:$D$6="Math")),$E$2:$E$6,0))}

Copy the formula from cell B8 to cells C8:E8.

☞ To apply *Array formula*:

Select the cell, press <F2> and simultaneously press <Ctrl+Shift+Enter>.

	A	B	C	D	E	F	G
1		ID	Year	Subject	Grade		
2		1	12	Math	85		
3		2	11	Science	95		
4		3	12	Math	92		
5		4	12	Math	70		
6		5	10	Science	62		
7							
8	**Highest score**	3	12	Math	92		
9							
10	**Array Formula Syntax in cell B8:**						
11	{=INDEX(B2:B6,MATCH(MAX(($E$2:$E$6)*($D$2:$D$6="Math")),$E$2:$E$6,0))}						
12							

Explanation:

The **MAX** function returns the highest Grade for those IDs that have "Math" values in column D.

The **MATCH** function returns the position (row number) of that grade within column E.

Finally, the **INDEX** function returns the value stored in the same position in column B (Student ID).

The column from which the **INDEX** function returns a value will change to match the column containing the formula. Thus, on copying the formula to cell C8, the **INDEX** function will retrieve the corresponding year from column C, and so on.

Retrieving Data from Two Different Lists

Retrieving a Price Value by Looking at Two Difference Data Tables

➤ **Problem:**

Listed in range1 (A4:B6) and range2 (D4:E6) are clothing items and their prices.

Cell B9 contains the name of an item from one of the ranges.

We would like to perform a lookup on both ranges, find the relevant item, and return the matching price.

➤ **Solution:**

Use the **ISNA** and **VLOOKUP** functions as shown in the following formula:

=IF(ISNA(VLOOKUP(B9,A4:B6,2,FALSE)),VLOOKUP(B9,D4:E6,2,FALSE), VLOOKUP(B9,A4:B6,2,FALSE))

	A	B	C	D	E	F	G
1	**Range1**			**Range2**			
2							
3	**Item**	**Price**		**Item**	**Price**		
4	Shoes	$80		Jeans	$70		
5	Skirt	$30		T-Shirt	$10		
6	Socks	$5		Sneakers	$100		
7							
8	**Item to look**	Jeans					
9	**Price**	$70					
10							
11	**Formula Syntax in cell B9:**						
12	=IF(ISNA(VLOOKUP(B9,A4:B6,2,FALSE)),VLOOKUP(B9,D4:E6,2,FALSE),VLOOKUP(B9,A4:B6,2,FALSE))						
13							

Explanation:

The first **VLOOKUP** function looks up the first column of range1 (A4:B6) for the item entered in cell B9, and returns its matching price.

Similarly, the second **VLOOKUP** function looks up range2 (D4:E6) for the same item.

If the lookup value is not found in the lookup range, the function returns the #N/A error.

The **ISNA** function determines whether or not the value calculated by the first **VLOOKUP** function is the #N/A error, and returns TRUE/FALSE accordingly.

If the result of the ISNA function is TRUE (i.e. the item was not found in range1), the **IF** function returns the result of the second **VLOOKUP** function. Otherwise (i.e. the item was found in range1), the result of the first **VLOOKUP** function is returned.

Complex Retrieval Problems

Retrieving the Column Header of the Next Non-Blank Cell in a Row

➤ **Problem:**

Row 2 lists amounts payable over a twelve month period.

A blank cell in the row indicates that no payment is due that month.

We want to create a new row that, for each month, will display the name of the month in which the next payment is due.

➤ **Solution:**

Use the **INDEX, MATCH, MIN, IF,** and **COLUMN** functions as shown in the following *Array formula*:

{=INDEX(C1:M1,MATCH(MIN(IF(C2:M2<>" ",COLUMN(C2:M2))),COLUMN(C2:M2)))}

Enter the formula in cell B3 and copy/paste it across the row from cell B3 up to cell M3.

☞ To apply *Array formula:*

Select the cell, press <**F2**> and simultaneously press <**Ctrl+Shift+Enter**>.

	A	B	C	D	E	F	G	H	I	J	K	L	M
1		Jan	Feb	Mar	Apr	May	Jun	Jul	Aug	Sep	Oct	Nov	Dec
2	Payment	$200		$500				$300			$800		$200
3	Next Payment	Mar	Mar	Jul	Jul	Jul	Jul	Oct	Oct	Oct	Dec	Dec	#N/A
4													
5	Array Formula Syntax in cell B3:												
6	{=INDEX(C1:M1,MATCH(MIN(IF(C2:M2<>"",COLUMN(C2:M2))),COLUMN(C2:M2)))}												
7													

Explanation:

The **IF** function returns an Array containing the column numbers (calculated by the **COLUMN** function) of all the non-blank cells in cells C2:M2.

To discuss the formula presented, visit: www.exceltip.com/fx-206

The **MIN** function returns the smallest value in that Array.

The **MATCH** function returns the position of that number within the Array of column numbers, which is the position of the first non-blank cell within cells C2:M2.

The **INDEX** function returns the value that is stored in the corresponding position in cells C1:M1 (i.e. the header of the next non-blank cell).

Finding the First Value in a Row and Retrieving the Header for That Column

➤ **Problem:**

Columns B:G contain the monthly payments for the first half of the year that were made for each investment in column A.

The payments for each investment may start or end on any of the months.

We want to retrieve the month on which payments for each investment started.

➤ **Solution:**

Use the **INDEX**, **MIN**, **IF**, and **COLUMN** functions as shown in the following *Array formula*:

{=INDEX($B$1:$G$1,MIN(IF(B2:G2<>"",COLUMN($B$1:$G$1)-COLUMN(B1)+1)))}

☞ To apply *Array formula*:

Select the cell, press <**F2**> and simultaneously press <**Ctrl+Shift+Enter**>.

	A	B	C	D	E	F	G	H
1		Jan	Feb	Mar	Apr	May	Jun	Result
2	Investment 1		200	200	200	200	200	Feb
3	Investment 2	100	100	100	100			Jan
4	Investment 3						400	Jun
5	Investment 4			300	300	300	300	Mar
6	Investment 5				500	500	500	Apr
7								
8	**Array Formula Syntax in cell H2:**							
9	{=INDEX($B$1:$G$1,MIN(IF(B2:G2<>"",COLUMN($B$1:$G$1)-COLUMN(B1)+1)))}							
10								

Explanation:

The **IF** function returns an Array containing the positions (column numbers, calculated by the **COLUMN** functions) of all the non-blank cells in cells B2:G2

The **MIN** function returns the smallest value in that Array, which is the position of the first non-blank cell in row 2.

The **INDEX** function returns the value stored in the corresponding position in row 1 (i.e. the column header of the first non-blank cell in row 2).

Retrieving the Column Header that Corresponds with a Matched Value

➢ **Problem:**

Looking up the range A2:C5 for each of the values listed in column E, and retrieving the corresponding column header for each match.

➢ **Solution:**

Use the **INDEX**, **SUMPRODUCT**, **MAX**, and **COLUMN** functions as shown in the following formula:

=INDEX($A$1:$C$1,
SUMPRODUCT(MAX(($A$2:$C$5=E2)*(COLUMN($A$2:$C$5))))-
COLUMN($A$1)+1)

	A	B	C	D	E	F
1	**Numbers**	**Lettters**	**Signs**		**Value to Look For**	**Result**
2	5	Z	*		2	Numbers
3	2	G	$		*	Signs
4	3	D	!		D	Lettters
5	10	E	#		#	Signs
6						
7	**Formula Syntax in cell F2:**					
8	=INDEX($A$1:$C$1, SUMPRODUCT(MAX(($A$2:$C$5=E2)*(COLUMN($A$2:$C$5))))-COLUMN($A$1)+1)					
9						

Explanation:

The following expression returns an Array containing the column number of each value in cells A2:C5 that matches the look up value (cell E2), and a "0" (FALSE) for each value that does not.

($A$2:$C$5=E2)*(COLUMN($A$2:$C$5))

The **MAX** function returns the largest number in that Array (the column number).

The **SUMPRODUCT** function returns that column number after having the column number of the first cell in the range (calculated by the second **COLUMN** function) subtracted from it and adding 1.

Thus, the position of that column within range A2:C5 is returned.

Finally, the **INDEX** function retrieves the value in row 1 that is stored in the corresponding position (i.e. the column header of the matched value).

Retrieving the Column Header of the Largest Value in a Row

➤ **Problem:**

Range A1:E5 contains four players' scores in four games.

Each column from B to E contains the scores of one player for each of the four games listed in column A. The column header corresponds to the name of that particular player.

We want to add a new column (F) that contains the name of the winner of each game.

➤ **Solution:**

Use the **INDEX**, **MATCH**, and **MAX** functions as shown in the following formula:

=INDEX($B$1:$E$1,1,MATCH(MAX(B2:E2),B2:E2,0))

	A	B	C	D	E	F
1		Anthony	John	Kate	Lily	Winner
2	Game1	20	18	15	13	Anthony
3	Game2	14	19	18	20	Lily
4	Game3	10	15	12	8	John
5	Game4	15	17	19	16	Kate
6						
7	Formula Syntax in Column F					
8	=INDEX($B$1:$E$1,1,MATCH(MAX(B2:E2),B2:E2,0))					
9						

Explanation:

The **MAX** function returns the highest value from cells B2:E2.

The **MATCH** function returns the position (column number) of that value within cells B2:E2.

The **INDEX** function returns the value stored in the corresponding position in row 1 (i.e. the header of the highest score in Game1).

Thus, the name of the winner is returned in cell F2.

Retrieving a Value from a Reference Grid, Using Indexes Listed in another Range

➢ **Problem:**

The numbers in Data Range (A1:E6) are arrayed in a reference grid of 4 columns and 5 rows.

Each row in Index Range (A9:B12) contains a pair of values referring to the row and column of a number in Data Range.

We want to find the number in Data Range referred to by each pair of indexes in Index Range.

➢ **Solution 1:**

Use the **OFFSET** and **MATCH** functions as shown in the following formula:

=OFFSET($A$1,MATCH(B9,$A$1:$A$6,0)-1,MATCH(A9,$A$1:$E$1,0)-1)

➢ **Solution 2:**

Use the **INDEX** and **MATCH** functions as shown in the following *Array formula*:

{=INDEX($A$1:$E$6,MATCH(B9,$A$1:$A$6),MATCH(A9,$A$1:$E$1))}

☞ To apply *Array formula:*

Select the cell, press **<F2>** and simultaneously press **<Ctrl+Shift+Enter>**.

	A	B	C	D	E
1	A	B	C	D	
2	1	9	1	28	76
3	2	18	7	56	58
4	3	6	4	10	43
5	4	30	70	2	12
6	5	25	66	34	0
7					
8	**Column**	**Row**	**OFFSET Function**	**INDEX function**	
9	A	4	30	30	
10	C	3	10	10	
11	D	5	0	0	
12					
13	**Formula Syntax in cell C9:**				
14	=OFFSET($A$1,MATCH(B9,$A$1:$A$6,0)-1,MATCH(A9,$A$1:$E$1,0)-1)				
15					
16	**Formula Syntax in cell D9:**				
17	{=INDEX($A$1:$E$6,MATCH(B9,$A$1:$A$6),MATCH(A9,$A$1:$E$1))}				
18					

Explanation to Solution1:

The first **MATCH** function returns the position (row number) within column A (the index column) of the index value entered in cell B9.

The second **MATCH** function returns the position (column number) within row 1 (the index row) of the index value entered in cell A9.

The **OFFSET** function offsets the reference "A1" by as many rows as the number calculated by the first **MATCH** function, minus 1, and as many columns as the number calculated by the second **MATCH** function, minus 1.

Thus, the reference of the cell referred to by the pair of indexes is returned.

Explanation to Solution 2:

The first **MATCH** function returns the position (row number) within column A (the grid's index column) of the row index value entered in cell B9.

The second **MATCH** function returns the position (column number) within row 1 (the grid's index row) of the column index value entered in cell A9.

The **INDEX** function retrieves the value from cells A1:E6 that is stored at the intersection of the row and column calculated by the **MATCH** functions.

Chapter 5

Logical & Errors

About This Chapter

This chapter deals with formulas that use Logical functions and also those that are used for the handling of Errors. It includes the following sections:

☞ **Reducing Complexity of IF Functions, Page 216:** This section contains three examples of how to reduce the number of IF functions used when creating logical formulas.

☞ **Using OR, AND Functions, Page 221:** This section contains formulas that use the OR & AND logical functions to meet multiple criteria.

☞ **Handling Errors, Page 224:** This section provides solutions for avoiding errors such as #VALUE! and #DIV/0! when using formulas.

☞ **Handling Errors with the VLOOKUP Function, Page 234**: This section demonstrates techniques on preventing errors when using the VLOOKUP function.

Reducing Complexity of IF Functions

Simplifying Formulas by Reducing the Complexity of IF Functions (1)

> **Problem:**

The range A2:C8 contains rows of numbers. For each row, we want an indication of how many of the following conditions are met:

1. Num1 (column A) = 2

2. Num2 (column B) = 4

3. Num3 (column C) = 6

The following formula based on nested **IF** functions, is very complex:

=IF(A2=2,IF(B2=4,IF(C2=6,"All Conditions","Two Conditions"),IF(C2=6,"Two Conditions","One Condition")),

IF(B2=4,IF(C2=6, "Two Conditions","One Condition"),IF(C2=6,"One Condition","None of the Conditions")))

Is there a simpler way to achieve the same results?

> **Solution:**

Use the **CHOOSE** function as shown in the following formula:

=CHOOSE((A2=2)+(B2=4)+(C2=6)+1,"None of the Conditions","One Condition","Two Conditions","All Conditions")

	A	B	C	D	E	F	G
1	Num1	Num2	Num3	CHOOSE Formula	IF Formula		
2	5	4	6	Two Conditions	Two Conditions		
3	2		6	Two Conditions	Two Conditions		
4	1	0	6	One Condition	One Condition		
5	2	4	8	Two Conditions	Two Conditions		
6	2	7	3	One Condition	One Condition		
7	2	4	6	All Conditions	All Conditions		
8	0	4	9	One Condition	One Condition		
9							
10	CHOOSE Formula Syntax in cell D2:						
11	=CHOOSE((A2=2)+(B2=4)+(C2=6)+1,"None of the Conditions","One Condition","Two Conditions","All Conditions")						
12							
13	IF Formula Syntax in cell E2:						
14	=IF(A2=2,IF(B2=4,IF(C2=6,"All Conditions","Two Conditions"),IF(C2=6,"Two Conditions","One Condition")),IF(B2=4,IF(C2=6,"Two Conditions","One Condition"),IF(C2=6,"One Condition","None of the Conditions")))						
15							

Explanation:

The **CHOOSE** function returns the nth item in a list of values.

The first argument of the function is N, while the rest of the arguments are a list of values comprising the results to be returned.

N, in this case, is the result of the following calculation:

Each of the following three expressions returns "1" (TRUE) if the value stored in the specified cell equals the indicated number, and "0" (FALSE) if it doesn't:

A2=2

B2=4

C2=6

The results of the three expressions are added together (creating a count of the met conditions) and 1 is added to the total.

Depending on the value of N (1 to 4), the **CHOOSE** function returns the nth member of the list of strings making up the return arguments.

Thus, in this case, the **CHOOSE** function returns an appropriate string indicating how many conditions have been met by each row.

Simplifying Formulas by Reducing the Complexity of IF Functions (2)

> **Problem:**

The range A2:A4 lists the three primary colors.

To find which of the various colors in column B are primary colors, we could use the following IF formula:

=IF(OR(B2=A2,B2=A3,B2=A4),"Primary Color","Not a Primary Color").

However, such a formula would become increasingly complex as the number of values in column A increases.

> **Solution:**

Use the **IF** and **OR** functions as shown in the following *Array formula*:

{=IF(OR(B2=$A$2:$A$4),"Primary Color","Not a Primary Color")}

☞ To apply *Array formula*:

Select the cell, press **<F2>** and simultaneously press **<Ctrl+Shift+Enter>**.

	A	B	C	D
1	**Primary Colors**	**Colors**	**Is a Primary Color?**	
2	Red	Green	Not a Primary Color	
3	Blue	Black	Not a Primary Color	
4	Yellow	Blue	Primary Color	
5		Orange	Not a Primary Color	
6		Red	Primary Color	
7				
8	**Array Formula Syntax in cell C2:**			
9	{=IF(OR(B2=$A$2:$A$4),"Primary Color","Not a Primary Color")}			
10				

Explanation:

The following expression returns an Array consisting of TRUE for every value in cells A2:A4 that equals the value stored in cell B2 and FALSE for every other value:

B2=$A$2:$A$4

The **OR** function returns TRUE if any of the results in that Array are TRUE. Otherwise, it returns FALSE.

Thus, it returns TRUE if the color in cell B2 appears in the Primary Colors list (cells A2:A4) and FALSE if it doesn't.

If TRUE is returned, the **IF** function returns the string "Primary Color". Otherwise, it returns "Not a Primary Color".

Hence, the *Array formula* allows us to compare one value with a range of other values, without having to specify each individual comparison, as was the case in the original formula.

Create Conditional Formula

➢ **Problem:**

We want to create a conditional formula that will return TRUE if there is at least one number in List1 greater than the value in cell D1. Otherwise the formula will return FALSE.

➢ **Solution 1:**

Use the following formula:

=($A$2>D1)+($A$3>D1)+($A$4>D1)>0

➢ **Solution 2:**

Use the **OR** function as shown in the following *Array formula*:
{=OR($A$2:$A$4>D1)}

☞ To apply *Array formula:*

Select the cell, press <**F2**> and simultaneously press <**Ctrl+Shift+Enter**>.

	A	B	C	D	E
1	List1		Number to Compare:	20	
2	8				
3	2		Formula	FALSE	
4	3		Formula Syntax in cell D3:	=($A$2>D1)+($A$3>D1)+($A$4>D1)>0	
5					
6			Array Formula	FALSE	
7			Array Formula Syntax in cell D6:	{=OR($A$2:$A$4>D1)}	
8					

Explanation to Solution 1:

Each of the following three expressions returns "1" (TRUE) if the value stored in the specified cell is greater than the value in cell D1, and "0" (FALSE) if it isn't:

$A$2>D1

$A$3>D1

$A$4>D1

If the sum of all three expressions is greater than 0, TRUE is returned. Otherwise, FALSE is returned.

Thus, TRUE will be returned if there is at least one number in List1 greater than the number in cell D1.

Explanation to Solution 2:

The following expression returns an Array consisting of TRUE for every value in cells A2:A4 that is greater than the value stored in cell D1 and FALSE for every value that isn't:

$A$2:$A$4>D1

The **OR** function returns TRUE if any of the results in that Array are TRUE. Otherwise, it returns FALSE.

Thus, TRUE will be returned if there is at least one number in List1 greater than the number in cell D1.

Using OR, AND Functions

Nesting OR & AND Functions to Meet Multiple Criteria (1)

➢ **Problem:**

We want to create a formula that returns "1" if Num1=10 and either Num2=5 or Num3=2.

Otherwise, the formula is to return "0".

➢ **Solution:**

Use the **IF**, **AND**, and **OR** functions as shown in the following formula:

=IF(AND(A2=10,OR(B2=5,C2=2)),1,0)

	A	B	C	D
1	**Num1**	**Num2**	**Num3**	
2	10	5	2	
3				
4	**Result**	1		
5				
6	**Formula Syntax in cell B4:**			
7	=IF(AND(A2=10,OR(B2=5,C2=2)),1,0)			
8				

Explanation:

The **OR** function returns TRUE if either cell B2 equals 5 or cell C2 equals 2. Otherwise, it returns FALSE.

The **AND** function returns TRUE if both cell A2 equals 10 and the result of the **OR** function is TRUE.

If TRUE is returned by the **AND** function, the **IF** function returns "1". Otherwise, it returns "0".

Nesting OR & AND Functions to Meet Multiple Criteria (2)

➤ **Problem:**

We want to check whether or not each value in List1 (column A) meets both of the following criteria:

1. The number must be even.

2. The number must be smaller than 3 or larger than 8.

➤ **Solution:**

Use the **AND**, **MOD**, and **OR** functions as shown in the following formula:

=AND(MOD(A2,2)=0,OR(A2<3,A2>8))

	A	B	C
1	**List1**	**Result**	
2	2	TRUE	
3	5	FALSE	
4	4	FALSE	
5	10	TRUE	
6			
7	**Formula Syntax in cell B2:**		
8	=AND(MOD(A2,2)=0,OR(A2<3,A2>8))		
9			

Explanation:

The **MOD** function divides the number in cell A2 by 2 and returns the remainder. Even numbers will have a remainder of 0.

The **OR** function returns TRUE if the number in cell A2 is either smaller than 3 or greater than 8.

The **AND** function returns TRUE only if the **MOD** function equals 0 and the **OR** function is TRUE. Otherwise, FALSE is returned.

Checking for the Presence of Specified Values within a Range.

> ## Problem:

Creating a formula that will return TRUE if each number in column E appears at least once in the range A2:C6.

If any of the specified numbers are missing, the formula will return FALSE.

> ## Solution:

Use **AND** and **COUNTIF** functions in the following *Array formula*:

{=AND(COUNTIF(A2:C6,E2:E10))}

☞ To apply *Array formula*:

Select the cell, press **<F2>** and simultaneously press **<Ctrl+Shift+Enter>**.

	A	B	C	D	E
1					**Numbers to Check**
2	9	1	3		1
3	2	6	8		2
4	5	4	7		3
5	10	15	12		4
6	33	2	9		5
7					6
8	**Result**	TRUE			7
9					8
10	**Array Formula Syntax in cell B8:**				9
11	{=AND(COUNTIF(A2:C6,E2:E10))}				
12					

Explanation:

The **COUNTIF** function returns an Array consisting of the number of times each value in column E (cells E2:E10) appears in the range A2:C6.

A count of 0 represents a number in column E that does not appear in cells A2:C6, and any other count represents a number that does.

The **AND** function returns TRUE if all the numbers (counts) in the Array are not equal to 0 (0 represents a FALSE argument in logical functions). Otherwise (if there is at least one 0 in the Array), it returns FALSE.

Thus, the formula returns TRUE if each of the numbers in column E appears at least once in range A2:C6, and FALSE if any of them are missing.

Handling Errors

Ignoring Blank Cells when Performing Calculations

➤ **Problem:**

Columns A & B contain numbers as well as empty cells.

We want to be able to multiply each number in column A with the matching number in Column B without getting false results or errors.

➤ **Solution:**

Use **IF**, **AND**, and **ISNUMBER** functions in the following formula:

=IF(AND(ISNUMBER(A2), ISNUMBER(B2)),A2*B2,"")

	A	B	C	D	E
1	**List1**	**List2**	**Result**		
2	2	3	6		
3	5				
4		8			
5	11	4	44		
6					
7	**Fomrula Syntax in cell C2:**				
8	=IF(AND(ISNUMBER(A2), ISNUMBER(B2)),A2*B2,"")				
9					

Explanation:

The first **ISNUMBER** function determines whether or not the value stored in cell A2 is a number and returns TRUE/FALSE accordingly.

The second **ISNUMBER** function determines whether or not the value stored in cell B2 is a number and returns TRUE/FALSE accordingly.

The **AND** function returns TRUE only if both **ISNUMBER** functions returned TRUE (both cell A2 and cell B2 contain numbers).

Otherwise, it returns FALSE.

If TRUE is returned by the **AND** function, the **IF** function multiplies cell A2 by cell B2 and returns the result. Otherwise, it returns a blank cell (" ").

Thus, if one or both of the cells in columns A & B are blank, the formula returns a blank cell, rather than an error or 0.

Avoiding the #VALUE! Error when Adding Cells that May Contain Blanks

➢ **Problem:**

The following formula:

=IF(A5>0,B5+C5-A5)

Returns the #VALUE! error because an inadvertent blank space is stored in cell B5.

➢ **Solution:**

Use the **IF** and **SUM** functions as shown in the following formula:

=IF(A5>0,SUM(B5:C5)-A5)

	A	B	C	D
1	**Num 1**	**Num 2**	**Num3**	**Result**
2	5	3	7	5
3	0	6	9	FALSE
4	2		4	2
5	2		4	2
6				
7	**Formula Syntax in cell D2:**			
8	=IF(A2>0,SUM(B2:C2)-A2)			
9				

Explanation:

The **SUM** function adds all the values in range B5:C5, disregarding any cells that contain blanks.

Thus, the blank in cell B5 does not cause any errors.

The **IF** function determines whether or not the value in cell A5 is greater than 0.

If so, the **IF** function returns the result of the **SUM** function after subtracting the value stored in cell A5.

Otherwise, it returns FALSE.

Avoiding #DIV/0! Errors when Dividing by Zero

➢ **Problem:**

The following simple formula, which divides Num1 (column A) by Num2 (column B):

=A2/B2

Returns a #DIV/0! error whenever Num2 is empty or equals zero.

We want to avoid these errors being displayed.

➢ **Solution:**

Use the **IF** function as shown in the following formula:

=IF(B2=0,"",A2/B2)

	A	B	C
1	**Num1**	**Num2**	**Result**
2	5	2	2.5
3	6	0	
4	8	4	2
5			
6		5	0
7	14	2	7
8	6		
9			
10	Formula Syntax in cells C2:C8		
11	=IF(B2=0,"",A2/B2)		
12			

Explanation:

The **IF** function determines whether or not cell B2 equals zero (i.e. the value stored in B2 = 0 or the cell is empty).

If so, the **IF** function returns a blank value (" "). Otherwise, cell A2 is divided by cell B2 and the result returned.

Thus, the display of #DIV0! errors for invalid values is prevented.

Ignoring #DIV/0! Errors when Performing Calculations

> **Problem:**

Column C contains a formula that divides each number in column A by the corresponding number in column B:

=A2/B2

The formula returns the #DIV/0! error for each empty cell in column B.

When using the **AVERAGE** function to calculate an average for column C (=AVERAGE(C2:C7)), the errors present within the range prevent the formula from calculating a correct result, and it returns #DIV/0! as well.

Therefore, we want to create a formula that ignores the cells containing #DIV/0! errors when averaging the results in column C.

➢ **Solution:**

Use **AVERAGE**, **IF**, and **ISERROR** functions in the following *Array formula*:

{=AVERAGE(IF(ISERROR(C2:C7),"",C2:C7))}

☞ To apply *Array formula:*

Select the cell, press **<F2>** and simultaneously press **<Ctrl+Shift+Enter>**.

	A	B	C	D	E
1	**Num1**	**Num2**	**Num1/Num2**		**Result**
2		2	0		2.5
3	6	2	3		
4	1		#DIV/0!		
5	4	2	2		
6	10	2	5		
7	8		#DIV/0!		
8					
9	**Array Formula Syntax in cell E2:**				
10	{=AVERAGE(IF(ISERROR(C2:C7),"",C2:C7))}				
11					

Explanation:

The **ISERROR** function returns an Array containing TRUE for each value in column C (C2:C7) that is an error and FALSE for each value that isn't.

For each TRUE in the **ISERROR** Array, the **IF** function returns a blank (" "). For each FALSE, it returns the corresponding number from column C.

Thus, it returns an Array containing all the valid values in column C and blanks for all the non-valid values.

The **AVERAGE** function returns the average of all the values in that Array, disregarding the blanks.

Hence, it ignores the cells containing #DIV0! errors when averaging the results in column C.

Eliminating Errors Resulting from If Functions with Multiple Conditions

➢ **Problem:**

The following formula returns FALSE, even though both conditions are true (i.e. cell A2=5 and cell B2=8):

=IF(A2=5&B2=8,TRUE,FALSE)

➢ **Solution:**

Use the **IF** and **AND** functions as shown in the following formula:

=IF(AND(A2=5,B2=8),TRUE,FALSE)

	A	B	C	D
1	**Num1**	**Num2**		**Result**
2	5	8		TRUE
3				
4	**Formula Syntax in cell D2:**			
5	=IF(AND(A2=5,B2=8),TRUE,FALSE)			
6				

Explanation:

The "&" symbol cannot be used in Excel to express a combination of conditions.

To express such a combination, use the **AND** function.

The **AND** function returns TRUE only if both cell A2 equals 5 and cell B2 equals 8.

If TRUE is returned, the **IF** function returns the text TRUE, otherwise, it returns the text FALSE.

Avoiding Errors when Using the And Function to Combine Multiple Conditions in Array Formulas

➢ **Problem:**

The following *Array formula* was designed to calculate the average difference between each pair of values in columns A & B (providing both cells are not empty):

{=AVERAGE(IF(AND(ISNUMBER(A1:B5),ISNUMBER(A1:B5)),A1:A5-B1:B5))}

However, an incorrect result of "0" is returned.

➢ **Solution:**

Use the **AVERAGE**, **IF**, and **ISNUMBER** functions as shown in the following *Array formula*:

{=AVERAGE(IF(ISNUMBER(A1:A5)*ISNUMBER(B1:B5),A1:A5-B1:B5))}

☞ To apply *Array formula*:

Select the cell, press **\<F2\>** and simultaneously press **\<Ctrl+Shift+Enter\>**.

	A	B	C	D	E
1	**List1**	**List2**	**Result**	**Difference**	**Formula Syntax in column D**
2	5	3	3	2	=IF(AND(A2>0,B2>0),A2-B2,0)
3	8	4		4	
4	2			0	
5		6		0	
6	10	7		3	
7				9	=SUM(D2:D6)
8					
9	**Array Formula Syntax in cell C2:**				
10	{=AVERAGE(IF(ISNUMBER(A1:A5)*ISNUMBER(B1:B5),A1:A5-B1:B5))}				
11					

Explanation:

In order to express a combination of multiple conditions in an *Array formula*, use the "*" operator rather than the **AND** function.

The two **ISNUMBER** functions in the formula determine whether or not each cell in column A and column B contains a numeric value and return TRUE/FALSE accordingly.

The **IF** function returns an Array containing the difference between each pair of cells in columns A & B, for which TRUE was returned by both **ISNUMBER** functions (i.e. the cells in column A and column B both contain numeric values).

The **AVERAGE** function returns the average of the numbers in that Array.

Thus, the formula returns the average difference between each pair of values in columns A & B (providing both cells are not empty).

Avoiding Errors when Counting Date Values that Meet Specified Criteria

➢ **Problem:**

The range A2:B9 contains a series of dates and the corresponding number of hours worked on each of them.

An empty cell in column B that matches a date in column A indicates that 0 hours were worked on that day.

The range may also include blank rows.

The following formula was created to count the number of days in January for which 0 hours were worked:

=SUMPRODUCT((MONTH(A2:A9)=1)*(ISBLANK(B2:B9)))

However, an incorrect result of 3 was returned.

➢ **Solution:**

Use the **SUMPRODUCT**, **MONTH**, **ISBLANK**, and **ISNUMBER** functions as shown in the following formula:

=SUMPRODUCT((MONTH(A2:A9)=1)*(ISBLANK(B2:B9))*(ISNUMBER(A2:A9)))

	A	B	C	D
1	**Date**	**Hours Worked**	**Result**	
2	1 Jan	8	1	
3				
4	4 Apr	5		
5	3 Mar	4		
6				
7	5 Jan			
8	8 Feb			
9	10 Jan	2		
10				
11	**Formula Syntax in cell C2:**			
12	=SUMPRODUCT((MONTH(A2:A9)=1)*(ISBLANK(B2:B9))* (ISNUMBER(A2:A9)))			
13				

Explanation:

The incorrect result occurs because Excel considers empty date cells to be January 1900 dates.

Thus, each empty cell in column A was included in the count of January dates.

To avoid that error and ignore empty cells, the **ISNUMBER** function was added to the formula.

The **MONTH** function returns the month number of each date in column A.

If that number equals "1" (January), TRUE is returned; all other months return FALSE.

The **ISBLANK** function determines whether or not each value in column B is blank, and returns TRUE/FALSE accordingly.

The **ISNUMBER** function determines whether or not each value in column A is numeric, and returns TRUE/FALSE accordingly.

Finally, the **SUMPRODUCT** function returns the count of all the rows in range A2:B9 for which all three expressions returned TRUE.

Thus, a count is returned of all the days in January for which 0 hours were worked.

Avoiding Errors when Subtracting Times

➢ **Problem:**

In order to calculate the difference between two time values, the earlier time must be subtracted from the later one.

However, when the later time refers to the following day (with respect to the earlier time), an error will result.

We want to create a formula that avoids these errors when calculating the difference between any two time values.

➢ **Solution:**

Use the **MOD** function as shown in the following formula:

=MOD(B2-A2,1)

❖ **Note:**

Apply hh:mm format to all cells containing the formula.

	A	B	C
1	**Time In**	**Time Out**	**Result**
2	10:30	19:00	08:30
3	18:00	01:00	07:00
4	17:00	04:30	11:30
5	23:00	08:15	09:15
6			
7	**Formula Syntax in cell C2:**		
8	=MOD(B2-A2,1)		
9			
10	**Format in cells in column C:**		hh:mm
11			

Explanation:

As time values are stored in Excel as fractions of 24 (1 hour=1/24), the result of B2-A2 is a positive or negative fraction.

The **MOD** function divides that fraction by 1 (representing 24 hours) and returns the remainder.

When dividing a fraction (positive or negative) by 1, the remainder is the absolute value of that fraction.

Thus, the **MOD** function always returns a positive time difference.

Handling Errors with the VLOOKUP Function

Preventing a VLOOKUP Function from Returning an Error when an Exact Match is Not Found

➤ **Problem:**

We want to create a formula to check whether each number in column B appears in List 1 (Column A).

For each successful search, the formula should return that number.

However, if an exact match is not found, the formula should return a text message to that effect, rather than an error.

➤ **Solution:**

Use the **IF**, **ISERROR**, and **VLOOKUP** functions as shown in the following formula:

=IF(ISERROR(VLOOKUP(B2,$A$2:$A$9,1,FALSE)),"Number Not Found",VLOOKUP(B2,$A$2:$A$9,1,FALSE))

	A	B	C	D
1	**List1**	**Numbers to Check**	**Result**	
2	8	2	Number Not Found	
3	5	7	7	
4	3	10	Number Not Found	
5	7	6	6	
6	4			
7	9			
8	6			
9	1			
10				
11	**Formula Syntax in cell C2:**			
12	=IF(ISERROR(VLOOKUP(B2,$A$2:$A$9,1,FALSE)),"Number Not Found",VLOOKUP(B2,$A$2:$A$9,1,FALSE))			
13				

Explanation:

The **VLOOKUP** function looks up column A for the number stored in B2 and returns that value if a match is found. If the value is not found, the function returns the #N/A error.

The **ISERROR** function determines whether or not the result of the **VLOOKUP** function was an error (i.e. whether or not the search was successful), and returns TRUE/FALSE accordingly.

If TRUE, the **IF** function returns the string "Number Not Found".

Otherwise, it returns the result of the **VLOOKUP** function.

Thus, if there is no exact match, the formula returns the text "Number Not Found", rather than an error.

Avoiding the Occurrence of Unexpected VLOOKUP #N/A Errors

➤ **Problem:**

List1 (A2:A4) and List2 (B2:B4) appear to contain the same values.

However, when using a **VLOOKUP** function to find values in List2 that match each value in List1, #N/A errors are returned for each search.

> ## Solutions:

There are several possible solutions:

❖ Use the **TRIM** function to remove any redundant spaces from the values in List1 : =TRIM(A2)

❖ Use the **ROUND** function to round the numbers in List1 to the nearest integer: =ROUND(A3,0)

❖ Use the **VALUE** function to convert text-formatted numbers to actual numbers : =VALUE(A4)

	A	B	C	D	E
1	List1	List2	VLOOKUP Formula can't match values in List2		
2	Excel	500	#N/A		
3	500	700	#N/A		
4	`700	Excel	#N/A		
5					
6					
7	Corrected List1	Formula Syntax in cells A8:A10	VLOOKUP matches values in List2	Formula Syntax in cells C8:C10	
8	Excel	=TRIM(A2)	Excel	=VLOOKUP(A8,$B$2:$B$4,1,FALSE)	
9	500	=ROUND(A3,0)	500	=VLOOKUP(A9,$B$2:$B$4,1,FALSE)	
10	700	=VALUE(A4)	700	=VLOOKUP(A10,$B$2:$B$4,1,FALSE)	
11					

Explanation:

The most likely cause of error is that the values from both lists are not 100% identical.

They may have invisible differences such as different formatting, redundant spaces, etc.

In this case:

☞ The text in cell A2 has a redundant space at the beginning. Therefore it does not match the text in cell B4.

Using the **TRIM** function will remove the space and enable the **VLOOKUP** function to find a match.

☞ Cell A3 apparently contains the number 500. However, the number stored in that cell is actually 500.2. Therefore, it does not match the number in cell B2.

Rounding the value in cell A3 to 0 decimal places (using the **ROUND** function) will enable the **VLOOKUP** function to find a match.

☞ Cell A4 contains the number 700, but it is formatted as text.

Therefore, it is different than the value in cell B3, which is formatted as a number.

Using the **VALUE** function on cell A4 will convert it from text to a number, which will enable the **VLOOKUP** function to find a match.

Using a VLOOKUP Formula to Check If a Value Exists

➢ **Problem:**

Column B contains values to look up in List1 (Column A).

We want to modify the results returned by the **VLOOKUP** function to include the lookup term as well as an indication of whether or not the value was found.

➢ **Solution:**

Use the **IF**, **ISNA**, and **VLOOKUP** functions as shown in the following formula:

=IF(ISNA(VLOOKUP(B2,$A$2:$A$7,1,FALSE)),B2&"Not Found",VLOOKUP(B2,$A$2:$A$7,1,FALSE)&"Found")

	A	B	C
1	**List1**	**Values to look for**	**Result**
2	Blue	Pink	Pink Not Found
3	Red	Blue	Blue Found
4	Green	White	White Not Found
5	Black	Purple	Purple Not Found
6	Yellow	Red	Red Found
7	Orange		
8			
9	**Formula Syntax in cell C2:**		
10	=IF(ISNA(VLOOKUP(B2,$A$2:$A$7,1,FALSE)),B2&" Not Found",VLOOKUP(B2,$A$2:$A$7,1,FALSE)&" Found")		
11			

Explanation:

The **VLOOKUP** function searches List1 for the value stored in cell B2 and returns it if there is a match.

If that color is not found, the **VLOOKUP** function returns the #N/A error.

The **ISNA** function determines whether or not the result of the **VLOOKUP** function is the #N/A error and returns TRUE/FALSE accordingly.

If TRUE, the **IF** function returns a string composed of the look up value (the color) and the text "Not Found".

Otherwise, it returns a string composed of the result of the **VLOOKUP** function (the matched color) and the text "Found".

Thus, in all cases, a string is returned that includes the lookup term as well as an indication of whether or not the value was found.

Checking If Matching Numbers Exist in Different Ranges

➤ **Problem:**

Column A in Range1 contains numbers. Columns A & B in Range2 contain numbers and their matching text.

For each number in Range1, we want to find a match in Range2 and then copy that number's corresponding text to column B for Range1.

➢ **Solution:**

Use the **IF**, **ISNA**, and **VLOOKUP** functions as shown in the following formula:

=IF(ISNA(VLOOKUP(A3,$A$9:$B$14,1,FALSE)),"Not Found",VLOOKUP(A3,$A$9:$B$14,2,FALSE))

	A	B	C	D	E
1	**Range1**				
2	**Number**	**Result**			
3	1	One			
4	9	Not Found			
5	3	Three			
6					
7	**Range2**				
8	**Number**	**Text**			
9	4	Four			
10	5	Five			
11	3	Three			
12	6	Six			
13	1	One			
14					
15	**Formula Syntax in cell B3:**				
16	=IF(ISNA(VLOOKUP(A3,$A$9:$B$14,1,FALSE)),"Not Found",VLOOKUP(A3,$A$9:$B$14,2,FALSE))				
17					

Explanation:

The **VLOOKUP** function searches the first column of Range2 for the number stored in cell A3 (Range1). If successful, the corresponding value from the second column is returned.

If a match is not found, the **VLOOKUP** function returns the #N/A error.

The **ISNA** function determines whether or not the result of the **VLOOKUP** function is the #N/A error, and returns TRUE/FALSE accordingly.

If TRUE is returned, the **IF** function returns the string "Not Found".

Otherwise, it returns the result of the **VLOOKUP** function (i.e. the text matching the look up value).

Chapter 6

Counting

About This Chapter

This chapter provides information on the issues and problems involved with the use of COUNT formulas, and includes the following sections:

The COUNT Functions

Using the COUNT Functions

➢ **Problem:**

How can we count the cells in List1 (column A) according to the following criteria:

1. Cell contains a number.
2. Cell is not empty.
3. Cell is empty.
4. Cell contains a number larger than 5.
5. Cell contains text.
6. Cell contains the string "Excel".
7. Cell contains 3 characters only.

➢ **Solution:**

Use the **COUNT, COUNTA, COUNTBLANK,** and **COUNTIF** functions as shown in the following formulas:

1. =COUNT(A2:A13)
2. =COUNTA(A2:A13)
3. =COUNTBLANK(A2:A13)
4. =COUNTIF(A2:A13,">5")
5. =COUNTIF(A2:A13,"*")
6. =COUNTIF(A2:A13,"*Excel*")
7. =COUNTIF(A2:A13,"???")

To replace the criteria specified in the **COUNTIF** function with a cell reference containing the desired criteria, include the following operators: <, >, and = within quotation marks and use the "&" operator to join (concatenate) them with the cell reference.

The same method can be applied when using the "*" operator (wildcard) to count cells containing a particular substring.

Thus, with the information stored in C11:C14, the above **COUNTIF** functions (4-7) could be modified, as follows:

1. =COUNTIF(A2:A13,">"&C11)

2. =COUNTIF(A2:A13,C12)

3. =COUNTIF(A3:A13,"*"&C13&"*")

4. =COUNTIF(A2:A13,C14)

	A	B	C	D	E
1	**List1**		**Criteria**	**Result**	**Formula Syntax**
2	8		Cell contains a number.	6	=COUNT(A2:A13)
3	Excel Tip		Cell is not empty.	10	=COUNTA(A2:A13)
4	20		Cell is empty.	2	=COUNTBLANK(A2:A13)
5	2		Cell contains a number larger than 5.	4	=COUNTIF(A2:A13,">5")
6			Cell contains text.	4	=COUNTIF(A2:A13,"*")
7	abc		Cell contains the string "Excel".	2	=COUNTIF(A2:A13,"*Excel*")
8	XY		Cell contains 3 characters only.	1	=COUNTIF(A2:A13,"???")
9	6				
10	Microsoft Excel		**Cell References as COUNTIF Criteria**	**Result**	**Formula Syntax**
11	10		5	4	=COUNTIF(A2:A13,">"&C11)
12			*	4	=COUNTIF(A2:A13,C12)
13	1		Excel	2	=COUNTIF(A3:A13,"*"&C13&"*")
14			???	1	=COUNTIF(A2:A13,C14)

Counting Using One Criterion

Counting Unique Numeric Values or Unique Data in a List

> ➤ **Problem:**
>
> Counting the number of unique numeric values or unique data in List1, disregarding blank cells.

> ➤ **Solution1:**
>
> To count the number of unique values use the **SUM**, **IF**, and **FREQUENCY** functions as shown in the following formula:
>
> = SUM(IF(FREQUENCY(A2:A13,A2:A13)>0,1))

> ➤ **Solution 2:**
>
> To count the number of unique data use the **SUMPRODUCT** and **COUNTIF** functions as shown the following formula:
>
> =SUMPRODUCT((A2:A13<>"")/COUNTIF(A2:A13,A2:A13&""))

	A	B	C	D	E	F
1	**List1**					
2	4		**Number of unique values**	6		
3	1					
4	2		**FREQUENCY Syntax Formula in cell D2:**			
5	Excel		=SUM(IF(FREQUENCY(A2:A13,A2:A13)>0,1))			
6	6					
7			**Number of unique data**	7		
8	4					
9	Excel		**SUMPRODUCT Syntax Formula in cell D7:**			
10			=SUMPRODUCT((A2:A13<>"")/COUNTIF(A2:A13,A2:A13&""))			
11	5					
12	3					
13	1					

Explanation:

☞ **Explanation to Solution 1:**

The **FREQUENCY** function returns an Array consisting of the frequency within the list of each numeric value in List1 (cells A2:A13).

For the first occurrence of a specific value, the function returns the number of occurrences of that value. For each occurrence of that same value after the first, the function returns a zero. Thus, each "0" in the **FREQUENCY** Array represents a duplicate of a value that has already been processed.

The **IF** function returns an Array consisting of "1" for each value in the **FREQUENCY** Array that is greater than 0, and "0" for each value that isn't.

The **SUM** function adds all the numbers in the Array returned by the **IF** function.

The result represents the number of unique numeric values in List1.

☞ **Explanation to Solution 2:**

The **COUNTIF** function returns an Array containing the number of times each value (of any type) in List1 (cells A2:A13) appears within a modified version of List1 which has had a blank (" ") added to the end of each value.

The blank is added in order to convert any empty cells in List1 to blanks and, thus, avoid errors in the formula.

The following expression returns an Array consisting of "1" (TRUE) for every non-blank cell in List1 and "0" (FALSE) for every blank one:

A2:A13<>""

Each value in that Array, representing a value in List1, is then divided by the corresponding value (count) from the **COUNTIF** Array, and a new Array, containing the results, is returned.

The **SUM** function adds the numbers in that Array.

The result represents the number of unique values (of any type) in List1.

Counting the Number of Values Below or Above Average

➤ **Problem:**

Counting the number of values in List1 (column A) that are below the range's average, as well as the number of values above average.

➤ **Solution:**

Use the **COUNTIF** and **AVERAGE** functions as shown in the following formulas:

To count values below average:

=COUNTIF(A2:A9,"<"&AVERAGE(A2:A9))

To count values above average:

=COUNTIF(A2:A9,">"&AVERAGE(A2:A9))

	A	B	C
1	**List1**	**Number below Average**	**Number above Average**
2	20	5	3
3	12		
4	3		
5	6		
6	8		
7	5		
8	10		
9	4		
10			
11	**Number below Average Formula Syntax in cell B2:**		
12	=COUNTIF(A2:A9,"<"&AVERAGE(A2:A9))		
13			
14	**Number above Average Formula Syntax in cell C2:**		
15	=COUNTIF(A2:A9,">"&AVERAGE(A2:A9))		
16			

Explanation:

☞ **Formula for Values below Average:**

The **AVERAGE** function returns the average of all the values in List1 (cells A2:A9).

The **COUNTIF** function returns the number of values in List1 that are smaller than the number returned by the **AVERAGE** function.

☞ **Formula for Values above Average:**

The **AVERAGE** function returns the average of all the values in List1 (cells A2:A9).

The **COUNTIF** function returns the number of values in List1 that are greater than the number returned by the **AVERAGE** function.

Counting Values that Appear Only Once in a List

➢ **Problem:**

Counting the number of values in List1 (column A) that appear only once within the list.

➢ **Solution:**

Use the **SUM**, **IF**, and **COUNTIF** functions as shown in the following *Array formula*:

{=SUM(IF(COUNTIF(A2:A7,A2:A7&"")=1,1,0))}

☞ To apply *Array formula:*

Select the cell, press **<F2>** and simultaneously press **<Ctrl+Shift+Enter>**.

	A	B	C	D	E
1	**List1**	**Result**			
2	3	2			
3	1				
4	2				
5	2				
6	1				
7	4				
8					
9	**Array Formula Syntax in cell B2:**				
10	{=SUM(IF(COUNTIF(A2:A7,A2:A7&"")=1,1,0))}				
11					

Explanation:

The **COUNTIF** function returns an Array containing the number of times each value in List1 (cells A2:A7) appears within a modified version of List1 which has had a blank (" ") added to the end of each value.

The blank is added in order to convert any empty cells in List1 to blanks and, thus, avoid errors in the formula.

The **IF** function returns an Array consisting of "1" for each count in the **COUNTIF** Array that equals 1 (representing a value in List1 that appears only once within the list) and "0" for each count that doesn't.

The **SUM** function adds the values in the Array returned by the **IF** function.

The result represents the number of values in List1 that appear only once within the list.

Counting the Number of Times a Specified Substring Appears within a Range of Strings

➤ **Problem:**

Counting the total number of times each of the substrings listed in column B appears within any of the strings in column A.

➢ **Solution:**

Use the **SUMPRODUCT**, **LEN**, and **SUBSTITUTE** functions as shown in the following formula:

=SUMPRODUCT(LEN($A$2:$A$6)- LEN(SUBSTITUTE($A$2:$A$6,B2," ")))/LEN(B2)

	A	B	C
1	**Strings**	**Substrings to Count**	**Result**
2	abc	abc	5
3	abcdeabcd	cd	2
4	dddabc	e	3
5	edd	dd	2
6	eabc		
7			
8	**Formula Syntax in cell C2:**		
9	=SUMPRODUCT(LEN($A$2:$A$6)-LEN(SUBSTITUTE($A$2:$A$6,B2,"")))/LEN(B2)		
10			

Explanation:

The **SUBSTITUTE** function returns an Array consisting of all the strings in column A after they have been modified by having each occurrence of the substring stored in cell B2 replaced by nothing.

The **LEN** function creates an Array containing the lengths of all the strings in the Array returned by the **SUBSTITUTE** function.

That Array is subtracted from another Array which contains the lengths of all the original strings in column A.

Thus, an Array is created that contains the difference in length between each original string in column A and the one returned by the **SUBSTITUTE** function.

Each item in that Array is then divided by the length of the substring in cell B2 (calculated by the **LEN** function).

Finally, the **SUMPRODUCT** function adds the results of that calculation, which returns the total number of times the substring in cell B2 appears within any of the strings in column A.

Counting the Number of Cells Containing Text (1)

> **Problem:**

Counting the number of cells containing text values in the range A1:B5.

> **Solution:**

Use the **SUM, IF,** and **ISTEXT** functions as shown in the following *Array formula*:

{=SUM(IF(ISTEXT(A1:B5),1,0))}

☞ To apply *Array formula:*

Select the cell, press **<F2>** and simultaneously press **<Ctrl+Shift+Enter>**.

	A	B	C	D	E
1	2	abc		**Result**	
2	A	John		5	
3	20	5			
4	5/23/2005	18:28			
5	Excel	*.*			
6					
7					
8	**Array Formula Syntax in cell D2:**				
9	{=SUM(IF(ISTEXT(A1:B5),1,0))}				
10					

Explanation:

The **ISTEXT** function returns an Array consisting of TRUE for every cell in range A1:B5 that contains a text value and FALSE for every cell that doesn't.

The **IF** function returns an Array consisting of "1" for each TRUE value in the **ISTEXT** Array and "0" for every FALSE value in that Array.

The **SUM** function adds all the values in the Array returned by the **IF** function.

Each value in that Array is multiplied by the corresponding value from the Array returned by the expression DynamicRange<>"" and the results are added by the **SUM** function.

Thus resulting in the current number of names that have both first and last names beginning with the same letter.

That number will update upon the removal or addition of names.

Counting the Number of Times a Substring Appears Within a String

➢ **Problem:**

Counting the number of times each of the substrings listed in column B appears within the corresponding string in column A.

➢ **Solution:**

Use the **LEN** and **SUBSTITUTE** functions as shown in the following formula:

=(LEN(A2)-LEN(SUBSTITUTE(A2,B2,""))))/LEN(B2)

	A	B	C	D
1	**String**	**Substring to Count**	**Result**	
2	abcdabcfabc	abc	3	
3	12XY3XZ	XY	1	
4	700A	0	2	
5	wwwwww	ww	2	
6				
7				
8	**Formula Syntax in cell C2:**			
9	=(LEN(A2)-LEN(SUBSTITUTE(A2,B2,""))))/LEN(B2)			
10				

Explanation:

The **SUBSTITUTE** function returns the string in cell A2 after it has been modified by having each occurrence of the substring stored in cell B2 replaced by a blank (" ").

The **LEN** function (the second one in the formula) returns the length of that string.

That length is then subtracted from the length of the original string in cell A2, calculated by the first **LEN** function.

The result is then divided by the length of the substring in cell B2 (calculated by the third **LEN** function).

The result of that calculation represents the number of times the substring in cell B2 appears within the corresponding string in cell A2.

Counting the Number of Strings which Contain Numbers Meeting Criteria

➢ **Problem:**

List1 (column A) contains strings composed of the letter "T" and a number (i.e. T1,T2,,,,T100).

We want to count the number of strings in List1 which contain a number smaller than the one in a specified string of the same format.

➢ **Solution:**

Use the **SUMPRODUCT, SUBSTITUTE**, and **VALUE** functions as shown in the following formula:

=SUMPRODUCT(--(VALUE((SUBSTITUTE($A$2:$A$7,"T",""))))<VALUE (SUBSTITUTE(B2,"T",""))))

	A	B	C	D
1	List1	Criteria	Result	
2	T2	T10	4	
3	T10	T5	2	
4	T5			
5	T16			
6	T4			
7	T8			
8				
9	Formula Syntax in cell C2:			
10	=SUMPRODUCT(-- (VALUE((SUBSTITUTE($A$2:$A$7,"T",""))) <VALUE(SUBSTITUTE(B2,"T",""))))			
11				

Explanation:

The first **SUBSTITUTE** function returns an Array consisting of each string in List1qual (cells A2:A7) which has had the "T" removed (replaced with a blank).

The first **VALUE** function converts each string in that Array to a numeric value.

Thus, it returns an Array consisting of the numbers included within each string in List1.

Similarly, the second **VALUE** and **SUBSTITUTE** functions return the number included within the string stored in cell B2 (criteria).

Each number in the Array created above is compared with the criteria number, creating an Array that consists of TRUE for each number that is smaller than the criteria and FALSE for each number that isn't.

The "--" symbol converts each TRUE/FALSE value in that Array to "1"/"0" accordingly, and the **SUMPRODUCT** function adds all the values in the Array.

The result represents the number of strings in List1 which contain a number smaller than the one within the string stored in cell B2.

Counting Date Values by Specified Date Criteria

➢ **Problem:**

Counting the number of dates in column A that are equal and later than 01/01/2005.

➢ **Solution:**

Use the **COUNTIF** and **DATE** functions as shown in the following formula:

=COUNTIF(A2:A10,">="&DATE(2005,1,1))

	A	B	C	D	E
1	**Dates**		**Result**		
2	01/01/2004		3		
3	02/02/2005				
4	03/03/2004				
5	04/04/2003				
6	05/05/2002				
7	06/06/2006				
8	07/07/2005				
9	08/08/2000				
10	09/09/2001				
11					
12	**Formula Syntax in cell C2:**				
13	=COUNTIF(A2:A10,">="&DATE(2005,1,1))				
14					

Explanation:

The **DATE** function returns the date value that corresponds with the year, month, and day specified in the formula (2005, 1, and 1), i.e. 01/01/2005.

The **COUNTIF** function returns the number of dates in column A (cells A2:A10) that are later than or equal to that date.

Counting the Number of Dates with Matching Month Criteria

➢ **Problem:**

The following formula was written to count the number of dates in column A that matched the month criteria in cell B2.

=COUNTIF(MONTH(A2:A6),B2)

However, on entry, an error occurred and the formula could not be used.

➢ **Solution 1:**

Use the **SUMPRODUCT** and **MONTH** functions as shown in the following formula:

=SUMPRODUCT(--(MONTH(A2:A6)=B2))

> ## Solution 2:

Use the **SUM**, **IF,** and **MONTH** functions as shown in the following *Array formula*:

{=SUM(IF(MONTH(A2:A6)=B2,1))}

☞ To apply *Array formula:*

Select the cell, press <**F2**> and simultaneously press <**Ctrl+Shift+Enter**>.

	A	B	C	D
			SUMPRODUCT	
1	**Dates**	**Month Criteria**	**Formula**	**Array Formula**
2	05/18/2005	5	3	3
3	01/01/2005			
4	05/11/2004			
5	05/10/2005			
6	08/05/2005			
7				
8	**SUMPRODUCT Formula Syntax in cell C2:**			
9	=SUMPRODUCT(--(MONTH(A2:A6)=B2))			
10				
11	**Array Formula Syntax in cell D2:**			
12	{=SUM(IF(MONTH(A2:A6)=B2,1))}			
13				

Explanation:

The reason for the above error is that an array of values (MONTH(A2:A6)) was entered as the first argument of the **COUNTIF** function.

The first argument of the **COUNTIF** function (and **SUMIF** function as well) must be a range reference.

☞ **SUMPRODUCT Formula (cell C2):**

The **MONTH** function returns an Array consisting of the month number (1-12) that corresponds with each date in column A (cells A2:A6).

Each month number in that Array is compared with the month criteria in cell B2, creating an Array that consists of TRUE for every month number that equals the criteria and FALSE for every month number that doesn't.

The "--" sign converts every TRUE/FALSE in that Array to 1/0 accordingly.

The **SUMPRODUCT** function adds all the values in the Array, and, thus, returns the number of dates in column A that match the month criteria in cell B2.

☞ **Array Formula (cell D2):**

The **MONTH** function returns an Array consisting of the month number (1-12) that corresponds with each date in column A (cells A2:A6).

Each month number in that Array is compared with the month criteria in cell B2, creating an Array that consists of TRUE for every month number that equals the criteria and FALSE for every month number that doesn't.

The **IF** function returns an Array that consists of "1" for each TRUE value in the above Array.

Finally, the **SUM** function adds all the values in the Array returned by the **IF** function, and, thus, returns the number of dates in column A that match the month criteria in cell B2.

Counting Time Values in Terms of Hourly Increments

➤ **Problem:**

Counting the number of time values in List1 (column A) that occur between each pair of successive hours listed in column B.

➤ **Solution:**

Use the **COUNTIF** function as shown in the following formula:

=COUNTIF($A$2:$A$7,">"&B2)-COUNTIF($A$2:$A$7,">"&B3)

	A	B	C	D	E	F
1	**List1**	**Hour**	**Result**			
2	11:05	11:00	2			
3	11:50	12:00	1			
4	12:10	13:00	3			
5	13:10	14:00				
6	13:35					
7	13:55					
8						
9						
10	**Formula Syntax in cell C2:**					
11	=COUNTIF($A$2:$A$7,">"&B2)-COUNTIF($A$2:$A$7,">"&B3)					
12						

Explanation:

The first **COUNTIF** function returns the number of time values in List1 (cells A2:A7) that are greater than the time value in cell B2.

The second **COUNTIF** function returns the number of time values in List1 that are greater than the time value in cell B3.

The number (count) returned by the second **COUNTIF** function is then subtracted from the number returned by the first one.

The result of that calculation represents the number of time values in List1 that occur between the pair of hours listed in cells B2:B3.

Counting the Number of Values Meeting Criteria, but Only for Every 3rd Cell in a Range

> **Problem:**

We want to count the number of values in row 1 that are greater than the criteria specified in cell A4, but only for every 3rd cell in the range.

> **Solution:**

Use the **SUMPRODUCT, MOD,** and **COLUMN** functions as shown in the following formula:

=SUMPRODUCT(--(MOD(COLUMN($A$1:$J$1)-
COLUMN($A$1)+1,3)=0)*($A$1:$J$1>$A$4))

	A	B	C	D	E	F	G	H	I	J
1	13	1	8	2	12	5	4	3	9	6
2										
3	Criteria	Result								
4	7	2								
5										
6	Formula Syntax in cell B. ·									
7	=SUMPRODUCT((MOD(COLUMN($A$1:$J$1)-COLUMN($A$1)+1,3)=0)*($A$1:$J$1>$A$4))									
8										

Explanation:

The **COLUMN** functions in the following expression return the column numbers of each value in row 1 (cells A1:J1) and of the first value in the row (cell A1): (MOD(COLUMN($A$1:$J$1)-COLUMN($A$1)+1,3)=0)

Those column numbers are then used to calculate serial numbers matching each value in row 1.

The **MOD** function divides each of those serial numbers by 3 and returns the remainder.

The result of the expression is an Array consisting of "1" (TRUE) for every value in row 1 where the serial number is divisible by 3 (the remainder calculated by the **MOD** function is 0) and "0" (FALSE) for all other values.

The following expression returns an additional Array consisting of "1" (TRUE) for every value in row 1 that is greater than the criteria in cell A4 and "0" (FALSE) for every value that isn't:

$A$1:$J$1>$A$4

The **SUMPRODUCT** function adds the products of the corresponding items in the Arrays returned by the above expressions.

The result represents the number of values in row 1 that are greater than the criteria specified in cell A4 and also members of the set of every 3rd value in the range.

Counting Rows of Even Numbers in Two Parallel Ranges

➢ **Problem:**

Counting the number of times that a row has an even number in both columns A and B.

➢ **Solution:**

Use the **SUMPRODUCT** and **MOD** functions as shown in the following formula:

=SUMPRODUCT((MOD(A2:A7,2)=0)*(MOD(B2:B7,2)=0))

	A	B	C	D	E	F
1	List1	List2		Result		
2	2	6		2		
3	5	10				
4	30	8				
5	40	11				
6	33	20				
7	1	7				
8						
9	Formula Syntax in cell D2:					
10	=SUMPRODUCT((MOD(A2:A7,2)=0)*(MOD(B2:B7,2)=0))					
11						

Explanation:

The first **MOD** function divides each number in column A (cells A2:A7) by 2 and returns an Array consisting of the remainder of each them.

The following expression returns an Array consisting of "1" for each remainder in the **MOD** Array that equals 0 and "0" for each remainder that doesn't: (MOD(A2:A7,2)=0)

Hence, the Array consists of "1" for every even number in column A and "0" for every odd one.

A similar expression is used to evaluate column B.

The **SUMPRODUCT** function adds the products of the corresponding items in the two Arrays created above.

The result represents the number of times that a row has an even number in both columns A and B.

Counting the Number of Values from Multiple Worksheets that Match Criteria

➤ **Problem:**

Counting the total number of values from the range A1:B3 on Sheets 1, 2 & 3 that are greater than the criteria specified in cell A2.

➤ **Solution:**

Use the **SUM, COUNTIF,** and **INDIRECT** functions as shown in the following formula:

=SUM(COUNTIF(INDIRECT("Sheet"&{1,2,3}&"!A1:B3"),">"&A2))

	A	B	C	D	E	F	G	H
1	**Criteria**	**Result**						
2	7	5						
3								
4	**Sheet1**			**Sheet2**			**Sheet3**	
5	10	8		9	0		5	13
6	5	6		3	2		4	7
7	2	1		7	5		3	8
8								
9	**Formula Syntax in cell B2:**							
10	=SUM(COUNTIF(INDIRECT("Sheet"&{1,2,3}&"!A1:B3"),">"&A2))							
11								

Explanation:

The text "Sheet" is joined with each of the numbers 1, 2, & 3, and the text "!A1:B3".

The result is an Array consisting of three strings that represent the reference of range A1:B3 in Sheets 1, 2, & 3.

The **INDIRECT** function returns an Array consisting of the three references indicated by those three strings.

For each range reference returned by the **INDIRECT** function, the **COUNTIF** function returns the number of values in that range that are greater than the criteria specified in cell A2.

Thus, it returns an Array that consists of the number of values meeting criteria in each of the three sheets.

The **SUM** function adds the values in that Array and returns the total number of values from range A1:B3 on Sheets 1, 2, & 3 that are greater than the criteria specified in cell A2.

Counting Using Two Criteria

Counting Rows that Match Specific Criteria for Each Column

➤ **Problem:**

Range A2:C7 contains the ID's, genders and ages of all the people in the room.

Cells F1:F2 contains the criteria according to which we would like to count.

As different counting criteria are required, we would vary the values stored in cells F1:F2.

What single formula will count the number of rows matching the variable criteria stored in cells F1:F2?

➤ **Solution:**

Use the **SUMPRODUCT** function as shown in the following formula:

=SUMPRODUCT((B2:B7=F1)*(C2:C7=F2))

	A	B	C	D	E	F
1	**ID**	**Gender**	**Age**		**Gender**	Female
2	1	Female	25		**Age**	25
3	2	Male	34		**Result**	2
4	3	Female	32			
5	4	Male	21			
6	5	Female	25			
7	6	Female	36			
8						
9	**Formula Syntax in cell F3:**					
10	=SUMPRODUCT((B2:B7=F1)*(C2:C7=F2))					
11						

Explanation:

The following expression returns an Array consisting of "1" (TRUE) for each value in column B (cells B2:B7) that matches the gender criteria in F1 and "0" (FALSE) for each value that doesn't:

B2:B7=F1

Similarly, the following expression returns an Array consisting of "1" (TRUE) for each value in column C (cells C2:C7) that equals the age criteria in cell F2 and "0" (FALSE) for each value that doesn't:

C2:C7=F2

The **SUMPRODUCT** function adds the products of the corresponding items in the two Arrays created above.

The result represents the number of rows in range A2:C7 that match the criteria stored in cells F1 & F2.

Counting the Number of Values between Two Specified Values in a List

➤ **Problem:**

Finding the number of values in List1 (Column A) that are between each two successive values in List2 (Column B).

➢ **Solution:**

To count the numbers in List1 that are, for example, between 1 and 2 (B2:B3), use the **COUNTIF** function as shown in the following formula:

=COUNTIF($A$2:$A$10,">="&B2)-COUNTIF($A$2:$A$10,">"&B3)

	A	B	C	D	E
1	**List1**	**List2**	**Result**		
2	2.4	1	3		
3	3.8	2	2		
4	1.3	3	2		
5	4.3	4	2		
6	3.5	5	0		
7	2.6				
8	1.2				
9	1.9				
10	4.5				
11					
12	**Formula Syntax in cell C2:**				
13	=COUNTIF($A$2:$A$10,">="&B2)-COUNTIF($A$2:$A$10,">"&B3)				
14					

Explanation:

The first **COUNTIF** function returns the number of values in List1 (cells A2:A10) that are greater than or equal to the value stored in cell B2.

The second **COUNTIF** function returns the number of values in List1 that are greater than the value stored in cell B3.

The number returned by the second **COUNTIF** function is then subtracted from the number returned by the first one.

The result of that calculation represents the number of values in List1 that are between the values in cells B2 & B3.

Counting the Number of Values between Upper and Lower Limits

➤ **Problem:**

Finding the number of values in List1 (Column A) that are larger than 20 and smaller than 50.

➤ **Solution 1:**

Use the **COUNTIF** function as shown in the following formula:

=COUNTIF(A2:A7,">20")-COUNTIF(A2:A7,">=50")

➤ **Solution 2:**

Use the **SUMPRODUCT** function as shown in the following formula:

=SUMPRODUCT((A2:A7>20)*(A2:A7<50))

	A	B	C	D
1	List1		COUNTIF Formula	2
2	30		COUNTIF Formula Syntax in cell D1:	
3	10		=COUNTIF(A2:A7,">20")-COUNTIF(A2:A7,">=50")	
4	60			
5	40		SUMPRODUCT Formula	2
6	15		SUMPRODUCT Formula Syntax in cell D5:	
7	55		=SUMPRODUCT((A2:A7>20)*(A2:A7<50))	
8				

Explanation:

☞ **COUNTIF Formula:**

The first **COUNTIF** function returns the number values in List1 (cells A2:A7) that are greater than 20.

The second **COUNTIF** function returns the number of values in List1 that are greater than or equal to 50.

The number returned by the second **COUNTIF** function is then subtracted from the number returned by the first one.

The result of that calculation represents the number of values in List1 that are greater than 20 and smaller than 50.

☞ **SUMPRODUCT Formula:**

The following expression returns an Array consisting of "1" (TRUE) for each value in List1 (cells A2:A7) that is greater than 20 and "0" (FALSE) for each value that isn't:

A2:A7>20

Similarly, the following expression returns an Array consisting of "1" (TRUE) for each value in List1 that is smaller than 50 and "0" (FALSE) for each value that isn't:

A2:A7<50

The **SUMPRODUCT** function adds the products of the corresponding items in the two Arrays created above.

The result represents the number of values in List1 that are greater than 20 and smaller than 50.

Counting the Number of Unique Items Sold by Each Salesperson

➤ **Problem:**

Columns A:B contain a list of items sold and the ID of the salesperson who sold each of them.

We want to count the number of different items sold by each salesperson listed in column D.

➤ **Solution:**

Use the **SUM**, **MMULT**, **IF**, and **TRANSPOSE** functions as shown in the following *Array formula*:

{=SUM(($A$2:$A$13=D2)/(($A$2:$A$13<>D2)+MMULT(--(IF($A$2:$A$13=D2,$B$2:$B$13)=TRANSPOSE($B$2:$B$13)),--($A$2:$A$13=D2)))))}

☞ To apply *Array formula:*

Select the cell, press <F2> and simultaneously press **<Ctrl+Shift+Enter>**.

	A	B	C	D	E
1	**Salesperson ID**	**Item Sold**		**Salesperson ID**	**Result**
2	1	A		1	3
3	1	B		2	2
4	1	A		3	1
5	2	A			
6	3	C			
7	1	B			
8	2	D			
9	1	A			
10	3	C			
11	1	D			
12	2	D			
13	3	C			
14					
15					
16	**Array Formula Syntax in cell E1:**				
17	{=SUM(($A$2:$A$13=D2)/(($A$2:$A$13<>D2)+MMULT(-- (IF($A$2:$A$13=D2,$B$2:$B$13)=TRANSPOSE($B$2:$B$13)),-- ($A$2:$A$13=D2))))}				
18					

Explanation:

The **MMULT** function, using the **IF** and **TRANSPOSE** functions, returns an Array consisting of the number of times each item in column B (cells B2:B13) appears next to the salesperson specified in cell D2.

The following expression returns an Array consisting of "1" (TRUE) for each ID in column A that is different than the one stored in cell D2 and "0" (FALSE) for each ID that isn't:

$A$2:$A$13<>D2

The corresponding values in the two above Arrays are added, and the results are returned in a single Array.

Thus, an Array is created that consists of the total number of times each ID & Item combination appears in columns A & B.

The following expression returns an additional Array consisting of "1" (TRUE) for each ID in column A that is the same as the one stored in cell D2 and "0" (FALSE) for each ID that isn't:

$A$2:$A$13=D2

Each value in that Array is then divided by the corresponding value in the Array calculated above and the **SUM** function adds the results.

Thus, the formula returns the number of unique items sold by the salesperson listed in cell D2.

Counting the Number of Players According to Their Score in a Particular Quarter

➢ **Problem:**

Finding the number of players (column A) who scored over 3 points (column C) in the first quarter (column B).

➢ **Solution:**

Use the **SUMPRODUCT** function as shown in the following formula:

=SUMPRODUCT((B2:B17=F2)*(C2:C17>F3))

	A	B	C	D	E	F
1	Player	Quarter	Score		Result	Criteria
2	1	1	5		2	1
3		2	2			3
4		3	6			
5		4	3			
6	2	1	2			
7		2	1			
8		3	3			
9		4	2			
10	3	1	4			
11		2	5			
12		3	3			
13		4	2			
14	4	1	1			
15		2	4			
16		3	3			
17		4	3			
18						
19	Formula Syntax in cell E2:					
20	=SUMPRODUCT((B2:B17=F2)*(C2:C17>F3))					
21						

Explanation:

The following expression returns an Array consisting of "1" (TRUE) for each quarter number in column B (cells B2:B17) that equals the quarter criteria in cell F2 (1) and "0" (FALSE) for each quarter number that doesn't:

B2:B17=F2

Similarly, the following expression returns an Array consisting of "1" (TRUE) for each score in column C (cells C2:C17) that is higher than the score criteria in F3 (3) and "0" (FALSE) for each score that isn't:

C2:C17>F3

The **SUMPRODUCT** function adds the products of the corresponding items in the two Arrays created above.

The result represents the number of players in column A who scores over 3 points (cell F3) in the first quarter (cell F2).

Counting the Number of Students who Answered "A" to the Second Question

➤ **Problem:**

Listed in columns A:C are students' IDs and their answers to the first two questions of a test.

An empty cell indicates an unanswered question.

We want to count the number of students who answered both questions and answered "A" to the second question.

➤ **Solution:**

Use the **SUMPRODUCT** function as shown in the following formula:

=SUMPRODUCT((B2:B5<>"")*(C2:C5="A"))

	A	B	C	D	E
1	Student ID	Answer1	Answer2		Result
2	1	C	A		2
3	2	D	B		
4	3		A		
5	4	B	A		
6					
7					
8	Formula Syntax in cell E2:				
9	=SUMPRODUCT((B2:B5<>"")*(C2:C5="A"))				
10					

Explanation:

The following expression returns an Array consisting of "1" (TRUE) for each non-blank cell in cells B2:B5 (an answered question) and "0" (FALSE) for each blank cell (an unanswered question):

B2:B5<>""

Similarly, the following expression returns an Array consisting of "1" (TRUE) for each answer in cells C2:C5 that equals "A" and "0" (FALSE) for each answer that doesn't:

C2:C5="A"

The **SUMPRODUCT** function adds the products of the corresponding items in the two Arrays created above.

The result represents the number of students who answered both questions and answered "A" to the second question (column C).

Counting the Number of Excel Files in a List According to File Type and Date Criteria

➤ **Problem:**

In the range A2:B6 are file names and their corresponding creation date.

How could we, for example, count the number of Excel files (".xls") created in April?

➤ **Solution:**

Use the **SUMPRODUCT, MONTH,** and **RIGHT** functions as shown in the following formula:

=SUMPRODUCT((MONTH(B2:B6)=C2)*(RIGHT(A2:A6,3)=C3))

	A	B	C	D
1	**File Name**	**Creation Date**	**Criteria**	**Result**
2	Workbook1.xls	04/02/2005	4	1
3	Document1.doc	01/05/2005	xls	
4	Presentation1.ppt	09/09/2004		
5	Workbook2.xls	01/10/2005		
6	Document2.doc	11/08/2004		
7				
8	**Formula Syntax in cell D2:**			
9	=SUMPRODUCT((MONTH(B2:B6)=C2)*(RIGHT(A2:A6,3)=C3))			
10				

Explanation:

The **MONTH** function returns an Array consisting of the month number (1-12) that corresponds with each creation date in column B (cells B2:B6).

Each month number in that Array is compared with the month criteria in cell C2 (April), creating an Array that consists of "1" (TRUE) for every month number that equals the criteria and "0" (FALSE) for every month number that doesn't.

The **RIGHT** function returns an Array consisting of the three rightmost characters (the file type) of each string in column A (cells A2:A6).

Each string in that Array is compared with the string in C3 ("xls"), and the result is an Array consisting of "1" (TRUE) for every string that matches the criteria and "0" (FALSE) for every string that doesn't.

The **SUMPRODUCT** function adds the products of the corresponding items in the two Arrays created above.

The result is the number of Excel files (ending in "xls") in the range A2:B6 that were created in April (cell C2).

Using Date & Time Criteria to Count Entries in a Combined Date & Time List

➤ **Problem:**

Column A contains date and time values.

We want to count the number of entries with matching date criteria (cell B2) and a time value greater than the one specified in cell C2.

➤ **Solution:**

Use the **SUMPRODUCT, INT,** and **MOD** functions as shown in the following formula:

=SUMPRODUCT((INT(A2:A6)=B2)*(MOD(A2:A6,1)>C2))

	A	B	C	D
1	**Date & Time**	**Date Criteria**	**Time Criteria**	**Result**
2	05/22/2005 13:01:30	05/22/2005	13:02:00	2
3	05/23/2005 13:01:50			
4	05/22/2005 13:05:30			
5	05/25/2005 13:10:30			
6	05/22/2005 13:02:10			
7				
8				
9	**Formula Syntax in cell D2:**			
10	=SUMPRODUCT((INT(A2:A6)=B2)*(MOD(A2:A6,1)>C2))			
11				

Explanation:

The **INT** function rounds down each date and time value in column A (cells A2:A6) to the nearest integer.

Thus, it returns an Array consisting of the date part only of each value in column A.

Each date value in that Array is compared with the criteria date in cell B2, and the result is an Array that consists of "1" (TRUE) for every date that matches the criteria and "0" (FALSE) for every date that doesn't.

The **MOD** function divides each date and time value in column A by 1 and returns the remainder.

Thus, it returns an Array consisting of the time part only of each value in column A.

Each time value in that Array is compared with the time value in cell C2, and the result is an Array that consists of "1" (TRUE) for every time value that is greater than the criteria in cell C2 and "0" (FALSE) for every time that isn't.

The **SUMPRODUCT** function adds the products of the corresponding values in the two Arrays created above.

The result is the number of date and time entries in column A with matching date criteria (cell B2) and a time value greater than the one specified in cell C2.

Counting the Number of Items Sold Every Half Hour

➤ **Problem:**

Columns A:B contain a list of sold items and their matching sale time. Column C contains a list of times, 30 minutes apart.

We want to count the number of items sold in each 30 minute time period.

➤ **Solution:**

To find the number of items sold between 20:00 and 20:30 use the **SUMPRODUCT** function as shown in the following formula:

=SUMPRODUCT(($B$2:$B$5<C3)*($B$2:$B$5>=C2))

	A	B	C	D	E
1	**Item**	**Sale Time**	**Time**	**Result**	
2	Shoes	20:05	20:00	1	
3	T-Shirt	20:30	20:30	2	
4	Jeans	20:50	21:00	1	
5	Sun Glasses	21:00	21:30	0	
6					
7					
8	**Formula Syntax in cell D2:**				
9	=SUMPRODUCT(($B$2:$B$5<C3)*($B$2:$B$5>=C2))				
10					

Explanation:

The following expression returns an Array consisting of "1" (TRUE) for each time value in column B (cells B2:B5) that is earlier than the time value stored in cell C3 (20:30) and "0" (FALSE) for each time value that isn't:

$B$2:$B$5<C3

Similarly, the following expression returns an Array consisting of "1" (TRUE) for each time value in column B that is later than or equal to the time value stored in cell C2 (20:00) and "0" (FALSE) for each time value that isn't:

$B$2:$B$5>=C2

The **SUMPRODUCT** function adds the products of the corresponding items in the two Arrays created above.

The result is the number of time values in column B that are later than 20:00 and earlier than 20:30, which is equivalent to the number of items sold in that 30 minute time period.

Complex Counting Problems

Counting the Number of Times Any of the Numbers in First List Appears within Second List

➤ **Problem:**

Calculating the total number of times any of the numbers in List1 (column A) appear within List2 (column B).

➤ **Solution:**

Use the **SUM** and **COUNTIF** functions as shown in the following *Array formula*:

{=SUM(COUNTIF(B2:B9,A2:A4))}

☞ To apply *Array formula:*

Select the cell, press **<F2>** and simultaneously press **<Ctrl+Shift+Enter>**.

	A	B	C	D
1	**List1**	**List2**	**Result**	
2	1	8	5	
3	3	3		
4	5	2		
5		1		
6		5		
7		7		
8		1		
9		3		
10				
11	**Array Formula in cell C2:**			
12	{=SUM(COUNTIF(B2:B9,A2:A4))}			
13				

Explanation:

The **COUNTIF** function returns an Array consisting of the number of times each value in List1 (cells A2:A4) appears within List2 (cells B2:B9).

The **SUM** function adds the values in that Array.

Thus, it returns the total number of times any of the numbers in List1 appear within List2.

Creating Progressively Incremented Counting Criteria

➢ **Problem:**

Create a new list in column B where the first value is the number of values in List1 (column A) that are smaller than 1, the second value is the number of values in List1 smaller than 2, and so on.

➢ **Solution:**

Use the **COUNTIF** and **ROW** functions as shown in the following formula in the first cell (B2) of the new list, and copy the formula down the column:

=COUNTIF($A$2:$A$6,"<"&ROW()-ROW($B$2)+1)

	A	B	C	D	E
1	**List1**	**Result**			
2	2	0			
3	3	1			
4	4	2			
5	6	3			
6	1	4			
7					
8	**Formula Syntax in cell B2:**				
9	=COUNTIF($A$2:$A$6,"<"&ROW()-ROW($B$2)+1)				
10					

Explanation:

The **ROW** functions in the following expression return the row numbers of the current cell and of the first cell in the result column (cell B2):

ROW()-ROW($B$2)+1

Based on those row numbers, the expression calculates the criteria according to which we would like to count.

Thus, it calculates "1" in the first cell of the result column (row 2), "2" in the second cell (row 3), and so on.

The **COUNTIF** function returns the number of values in List1 (cells A2:A6) that are smaller than the calculated criteria.

Thus, when copied down column B, the formula creates a new list where the first value is the number of values in List1 that are smaller than 1, the second value is the number of values in List1 smaller than 2, and so on.

Counting the Values that Match Criteria in a Filtered List

➤ **Problem:**

Column B shows the answers to the question numbers displayed in column A.

An auto-filter is set for both columns.

We want to create a formula that will count the number of times each possible answer (listed in cells A26:A29) occurs for each of the filtered question numbers.

➤ **Solution:**

Use the **SUMPRODUCT**, **SUBTOTAL**, **OFFSET**, **ROW**, and **MIN** functions as shown in the following formula:

=SUMPRODUCT(($B$2:$B$22=A26)*(SUBTOTAL(3,OFFSET($B$2,ROW($B$2:$B$22)-MIN(ROW($B$2:$B$22)),,))))

Enter the above formula next to the 4 possible answers (cells B26:B29).

	A	B	C	D
1	# Question ▾	Answer ▾		
16	3	D		
17	3	D		
18	3	B		
19	3	D		
20	3	A		
21	3	B		
22	3	B		
23				
24				
25	Answer	Total		
26	A	1		
27	B	3		
28	C	0		
29	D	3		
30				
31				
32	Formula Syntax in B26:			
33	=SUMPRODUCT(($B$2:$B$22=A26)*(SUBTOTAL(3,OFFSET($B$2,ROW($B$2:$B$22)-MIN(ROW($B$2:$B$22)),,))))			
34				

Explanation:

The first **ROW** function in the following expression returns an Array consisting of the row number of each cell in column B (cells B2:B22):

ROW($B$2:$B$22)-MIN(ROW($B$2:$B$22))

The row number of the first cell in the range (cell B2), calculated by the **MIN** function and the second **ROW** function, is subtracted from each row number in that Array.

The **OFFSET** function offsets the reference of cell B2 by as many rows as each number in the above Array.

Thus, the **OFFSET** function returns an Array consisting of the reference of each cell in column B.

The **SUBTOTAL** function returns an Array consisting of the number of values in each cell reference in the **OFFSET** Array.

As the **SUBTOTAL** function ignores hidden cells, the Array consists of "0" for every cell in column B that is currently hidden and "1" for every cell that is currently displayed.

The following expression returns an Array consisting of "1" (TRUE) for each answer in column B (hidden or not) that matches the answer criteria in cell A26 and "0" (FALSE) for each answer that doesn't:

$B$2:$B$22=A26

The **SUMPRODUCT** function adds the products of the corresponding items in the above Array and the **SUBTOTAL** Array.

The result is the number of times the answer specified in cell A26 occurs for the filtered Question number (3).

Creating a Summary Table of a Student Questionnaire

➤ **Problem:**

Columns B:F contain the answers (Y/N) to 5 questions from each of 5 students.

Each row includes the answers of one student.

We want to create a summary table that will show a count of the questions answered Y and N for each student.

➢ **Solution:**

With Student ID in cells H2:H6 and the answer criteria in cells I1:J1, use the **COUNTIF, INDIRECT**, **MATCH,** and **ROW** functions as shown in the following formula:

=COUNTIF(INDIRECT("B"&MATCH($H2,$A$2:$A$6)+ROW($A$2)-1&":F"&MATCH($H2,$A$2:$A$6)+ROW($A$2)-1),I$1)

	A	B	C	D	E	F	G	H	I	J
1	Student ID	Answer1	Answer2	Answer3	Answer4	Answer5		Student ID	Y	N
2	1	N	Y	Y	N	N		1	2	3
3	2	Y	N	Y	Y	Y		2	4	1
4	3	N	N	Y	Y	N		3	2	3
5	4	N	N	N	Y	N		4	1	4
6	5	Y	N	Y	N	Y		5	3	2
7										
8	Formula Syntax in cell I2									
9	=COUNTIF(INDIRECT("B"&MATCH($H2,$A$2:$A$6)+ROW($A$2)-1&":F"&MATCH($H2,$A$2:$A$6)+ROW($A$2)-1),I$1)									
10										

Explanation:

The **MATCH** function in the following expression returns the relative position (row number) within cells A2:A6 of the ID specified in cell H2.

MATCH($H2,$A$2:$A$6)+ROW($A$2)-1

The row number of the first ID in column A (calculated by the **ROW** function) is added to that position and 1 is subtracted from the result.

Thus, the above expression calculates the row number that contains the answers of the student specified in cell H2.

The text "B", the calculated row number, the text ":F", and the calculated row number again (returned by the second occurrence of the above expression in the formula) are all joined into a single string.

That string represents the reference of the range that contains the answers of the student specified in cell H2.

The **INDIRECT** function returns the reference indicated by that string.

Finally, the **COUNTIF** function returns the number of times the answer specified in I1 appears within the reference returned by the **INDIRECT** function.

Thus, it returns the count of questions answered Y (cell I1) by student 1 (cell H2).

In order to complete the summary table and return the results matching each ID/answer combination, copy the formula to range I2:J6 (the references of the cells containing the student ID and answer criteria will update accordingly).

Counting the Number of YES Responses in a Student Questionnaire

> ➤ **Problem:**

Columns B:F contain the answers (Y/N) to 5 questions from each of 7 students.

Each row includes the answers of one student.

We want to count the number of students who gave a certain answer (column H) a specific number of times (column I).

> ➤ **Solution:**

Use the **SUMPRODUCT** and **MMULT** functions as shown in the following *Array formula*:

{=SUMPRODUCT(--(MMULT(--($B$2:$F$8=H2),{1;1;1;1;1})=I2))}

☞ To apply *Array formula:*

Select the cell, press **<F2>** and simultaneously press **<Ctrl+Shift+Enter>**.

	A	B	C	D	E	F	G	H	I	J
1		Answer1	Answer2	Answer3	Answer4	Answer5		Answer	# Times	Result
2	Student1	Y	N	Y	N	N		Y	3	2
3	Student2	N	Y	N	N	Y		N	2	2
4	Student3	Y	Y	Y	Y	N		Y	4	1
5	Student4	N	Y	N	Y	N		N	3	4
6	Student5	Y	Y	N	N	Y				
7	Student6	N	Y	N	Y	Y				
8	Student7	Y	N	N	N	Y				
9										
10										
11	Array Formula Syntax in Cell J2:									
12	{=SUMPRODUCT(--(MMULT(--($B$2:$F$8=H2),{1;1;1;1;1})=I2))}									
13										

Explanation:

The following expression returns an Array consisting of TRUE for every answer in cells B2:F8 that matches the criteria in cell H2 and FALSE for every answer that doesn't:

$B$2:$F$8=H2

The "--" sign converts each TRUE/FALSE in the Array to 1/0 accordingly.

The **MMULT** function returns the matrix product of the Array created above and the following Array:

{1;1;1;1;1}

The result is an Array consisting of the number of times the answer specified in cell H2 appears within each row in range B2:F8.

Each number in that Array, representing a row in cells B2:F8 is compared with the number of times specified in cell I2. The result is an Array consisting of TRUE for each number that matches the criteria in cell I2 and FALSE for every number that doesn't:

The "--" sign converts each TRUE/FALSE in the array to 1/0 accordingly.

Thus, the Array consists of "1" for every student (row) in cells B2:F8 who gave the answer specified in cell H2 as many times as specified in cell I2, and "0" for every student who didn't.

The **SUMPRODUCT** function adds all the values in that Array, and returns the number of students in cells B2:F8 who gave a specific answer (cell H2) a specific number of times (cell I2).

Counting Unique "X" and "O" Occurrences in a Matrix

➢ **Problem:**

Range B2:E6 is a matrix where each cell contains either an "O" or an "X".

We want to count the number of Xs in each column that are unique in their row (i.e. that particular row contains no other "X").

➢ **Solution:**

Use the **SUM**, **MMULT**, **TRANSPOSE**, and **COLUMN** functions as shown in the following *Array formula*:

{=SUM((MMULT(--
($B$2:$E$6="X"),TRANSPOSE(COLUMN(B2:E6))^0)=1)*(B2:B6="X"))}

Enter the above formula in a cell under the first column of your matrix (cell B8), and copy it across to the last column.

☞ To apply *Array formula*:

Select the cell, press **<F2>** and simultaneously press **<Ctrl+Shift+Enter>**.

	A	B	C	D	E	F	G
1							
2		X	O	X	X		
3		X	X	O	X		
4		X	O	O	O		
5		O	X	O	O		
6		O	O	X	O		
7							
8	Result	1	1	1	0		
9			1				
10	Array Formula Syntax in cell B8:						
11	{=SUM((MMULT(--($B$2:$E$6="X"),TRANSPOSE(COLUMN(B2:E6))^0)=1)*(B2:B6="X"))}						
12							

Explanation:

The **MMULT** function, using the **TRANSPOSE** and **COLUMN** functions, returns an Array consisting of the number of "X" occurrences in each row in cells B2:E6.

Each number in that Array is compared with "1", and the result is an Array that consists of "1" (TRUE) for every number that equals 1 and "0" (FALSE) for every number that doesn't.

Hence, the Array consists of "1" for every row in the matrix that includes a unique "X" (i.e. "X" appears only once within the row) and "0" for every row that doesn't.

The following expression returns an additional Array consisting of "1" for every cell in column B that contains "X" and "0" for every cell that doesn't.

B2:B6="X"

The corresponding values in the two Arrays created above are multiplied, and the **SUM** function adds the results.

The number returned by the **SUM** function represents the number of cells in column B that contain an "X" which is unique within the row.

Creating a Counting Grid

➢ **Problem:**

Range A2:B7 contains the letters A to C and a corresponding number from 0 to 5. Each combination can appear any number of times.

Range D3:D6 contains the letters A to D. The numbers 0 to 5 are listed in cells E2:J2.

We want to create a formula that will count the number of rows in the range A2:B7 containing each letter-number combination shown in the range D2:J6.

➢ **Solution:**

Use the **SUMPRODUCT** function as shown in the following formula and enter it in cell E3, then copy the formula to the entire grid (cells E3:J6):

=SUMPRODUCT(($A$2:$A$7=$D3)*($B$2:$B$7=E$2))

	A	B	C	D	E	F	G	H	I	J	K
1	Letter	Number									
2	A	1			0	1	2	3	4	5	
3	A	1		A	0	2	0	1	0	0	
4	A	3		B	0	0	1	0	0	1	
5	B	2		C	1	0	0	0	0	0	
6	B	5		D	0	0	0	0	0	0	
7	C	0									
8											
9	Formula Syntax in cell E3:										
10	=SUMPRODUCT(($A$2:$A$7=$D3)*($B$2:$B$7=E$2))										
11											

Explanation:

The following expression returns an Array consisting of "1" (TRUE) for each letter in column A (cells A2:A7) that is identical to the one in cell D3 and "0" (FALSE) for each letter that isn't:

$A$2:$A$7=$D3

Similarly, the following expression returns an Array consisting of "1" (TRUE) for each number in column B (cells B2:B7) that is equal to the one in cell E2 and "0" (FALSE) for each number that isn't:

$B$2:$B$7=E$2

The **SUMPRODUCT** function adds the products of the corresponding items in the two Arrays created above.

The result represents the number of rows in the range A2:B7 that contain the letter-number combination specified in cells D3 & E2.

In order to complete the counting grid and return the count matching each letter/number combination shown in the range D2:J6, copy the formula to cells E3:J6 (the references of the letter and number criteria will adjust accordingly).

Chapter 7

Summing

About This Chapter

This chapter provides information on the issues and problems involved with summing values, and includes the following sections:

☞ **Summing Techniques & Tips, page 290:** This section covers techniques on summing values at the intersection of ranges, summing values from the same cell address in different sheets, summing from a dynamic range, summing the absolute values in a range, and summing only the subtotals from a range.

☞ **Summing Values Based on Text, Text & Numbers, & Blank Cell Criteria, page 298:** In this section you will find various techniques on summing values from mixed strings (text + numeric values), dealing with spaces in strings, and summing non-blank cells in a range.

☞ **Summing Using Indirect Cell References, page 305:** This section provides summing solutions that use indirect cell references to sum values inside a sheet, across sheets, and from a closed workbook.

☞ **Summing Using One or More Criteria, page 310**: This section provides summing solutions that deal with one or more criteria.

☞ **Summing Last N Values, page 324:** This section contains examples on summing of every Nth value, of the last N number of cells, of the N largest values, and complicated summing of Nth values.

Summing Techniques & Tips

Summing the Values of Cells Occurring at the Intersection of Ranges

➤ **Problem:**

Range A1:B5 contains numbers.

We want a total value of the cells occurring at the intersection of the following ranges:

1. Columns A:B, Row 2:2

2. Column A:A, Row 3:4

3. Columns A:B, Row 1:1 + Columns A:B, Row 5:5

➤ **Solution:**

Use the **SUM** function as shown in the following formulas:

1. =SUM(A:B 2:2)

2. =SUM(A:A 3:4)

3. =SUM(A:B 1:1,5:5)

	A	B	C	D
1	1	6	**Ranges**	**Result**
2	2	7	Columns A:B, Row 2:2	9
3	3	8	Column A:A, Row 3:4	7
4	4	9	Columns A:B, Row 1:1 + Columns A:B, Row 5:5	22
5	5	10		
6				
7	**Formula Syntax in cell D2:**		=SUM(A:B 2:2)	
8	**Formula Syntax in cell D3:**		=SUM(A:A 3:4)	
9	**Formula Syntax in cell D4:**		=SUM(A:B 1:1,5:5)	
10				

Explanation:

To sum the values in cells at the intersection of ranges, leave a space between the argument ranges in the **SUM** function instead of a comma.

Summing Values from Different Sheets for the Same Cell Address

➢ **Problem:**

Summing the values from cell A1 of four successive sheets in the current workbook.

The sheets are named January, February, March, and April.

➢ **Solution:**

1. Select a cell to contain the sum and type =SUM(

2. Select the tab of the first sheet to sum (January).

3. Hold the <**Shift**> key and then select the tab of the last sheet to sum (April).

4. Select the cell to sum (A1).

5. Type) and <**Enter**>.

These actions will create the following formula, which sums the same cell (A1) from all four sheets:

=SUM(January:April!A1)

	A	B	C
1	**Total**	**Formula Syntax in A2**	
2	100	=SUM(January:April!A1)	
3			

Explanation:

The **SUM** function adds all the values in the range "January:April!A1", which consists of cell A1 from sheets "January, "February", "March", and "April".

Creating a Summing Formula that Automatically Adjusts to a Dynamic Range

➢ **Problem:**

List1 (column B) initially consisted of the numbers from cell B2 to cell B7.

In order to calculate their sum the following formula was entered in cell B8:

=SUM(B2:B7)

After performing the above calculation, three more numbers were added to the list, and the formula had to be altered to include those numbers as well.

We want to avoid having to continually make this update by creating a formula that will automatically sum the entire range whenever new values are added.

➢ **Solution:**

Use the **SUM, IF, COUNT,** and **OFFSET** functions as shown in the following formula:

=SUM(B2:B7,(IF(COUNT(B9:B990)>0,OFFSET(B9,0,0,COUNT(B9:B990)), 0)))

	A	B	C	D	E	F	G
1		**List1**					
2		1					
3		2					
4		3					
5		4					
6		5					
7		6					
8	**Result**	41					
9		1					
10		9					
11		10					
12							
13	**Formula Syntax in cell B8:**						
14	=SUM(B2:B7,(IF(COUNT(B9:B990)>0,OFFSET(B9,0,0,COUNT(B9:B990)),0)))						
15							

Explanation:

The **COUNT** function returns the number of numeric values in cells B9:B900, which is the number of numeric values added to List1.

The **OFFSET** function returns the reference of a range that starts at cell B9 and includes as many rows as the number returned by the **COUNT** function.

If any numbers were added to the list (the number returned by the **COUNT** function is greater than 0), the **IF** function returns the reference created by the **OFFSET** function. Else, it returns 0.

The **SUM** function adds the values in cells B2:B7 with the values stored in the range returned by the **IF** function.

Summing the Absolute Values of All Numbers in a Range

➢ **Problem:**

Summing the absolute values of all the numbers in List1 (column A).

➢ **Solution:**

Use the **SUM** and **ABS** functions as shown in the following *Array formula*:

{=SUM(ABS(A2:A8))}

☞ To apply *Array formula:*

Select the cell, press **<F2>** and simultaneously press **<Ctrl+Shift+Enter>**.

	A	B	C	D
1	**List1**	**Result**		
2	-2	44		
3	5			
4	-10			
5	-8			
6	9			
7	3			
8	7			
9				
10	**Array Formula Syntax in cell B2:**			
11	{=SUM(ABS(A2:A8))}			
12				

Explanation:

The **ABS** function returns an Array consisting of the absolute values of all the numbers in List1.

The **SUM** function adds all the numbers in that Array.

Summing Values Using SUBTOTAL Function

➢ **Problem:**

Column A contains three groups of numbers (cells A2:A4, A7:A9, A12:A14).

Cells A5, A10 and A15 contain SUBTOTAL formulas, which total the numbers to each group.

How can we sum the values only while ignoring subtotals?

➢ **Solution:**

Use the **SUBTOTAL** function to sum each group in the range, and then use the **SUBTOTAL** function to sum the values as shown in the following formula:

=SUBTOTAL(9,A:A)

	A	B	C	D	E
1		**Formula Syntax in Column A**		**Formulas:**	**Total**
2	1			**SUM Formula**	36
3	2			**SUBTOTAL Formula**	18
4	3				
5	6	=SUBTOTAL(9,A2:A4)		**Formula Syntax in cell E2:**	
6				=SUM(A:A)	
7	1				
8	2			**Formula Syntax in cell E3:**	
9	3			=SUBTOTAL(9,A:A)	
10	6	=SUBTOTAL(9,A7:A9)			
11					
12	1				
13	2				
14	3				
15	6	=SUBTOTAL(9,A12:A14)			
16					

Explanation:

The **SUBTOTAL** function sum all values in the range except values calculated by the **SUBTOTAL** formulas.

Modifying a SUMPRODUCT function to Return a Sum Rather than a Count

> ## Problem:

Columns B & C list the prices and categories of various items sold.

Column A contains the ID of the salesperson who sold each item.

The following formula was created to count the number of "A" category items that were sold by salesperson "1".

=SUMPRODUCT((A2:A9=1)*(B2:C9="A"))

We want to modify the formula so that it calculates the sum of the prices of all items meeting the above criteria.

> ## Solution:

To cause the **SUMPRODUCT** formula to sum the values from a range instead of counting them, add another argument to the **SUMPRODUCT** formula that contains the range to sum (cells C2:C9):

=SUMPRODUCT((A2:A9=1)*(B2:B9="A")*C2:C9)

	A	B	C	D	E
1	Salesperson ID	Item's Category	Item's Price		Count
2	1	A	$50.00		2
3	2	B	$30.00		
4	1	A	$40.00		
5	3	C	$20.00		Sum
6	2	B	$25.00		90
7	1	C	$35.00		
8	3	A	$65.00		
9	4	B	$28.00		
10					
11	Count Formula Syntax in cell E2:				
12	=SUMPRODUCT((A2:A9=1)*(B2:B9="A"))				
13					
14	Sum Formula Syntax in cell E6:				
15	=SUMPRODUCT((A2:A9=1)*(B2:B9="A")*C2:C9)				
16					

Summing Rounded Numbers

➤ **Problem:**

Cells B2:B4 contain several numbers with two decimal places. Cell B5 contains a **SUM** formula, which adds the values in cells B2:B4.

Cells C2:C4 contain exactly the same numbers as cells B2:B4, but the cells are formatted to display 0 decimal places.

When comparing the result of the **SUM** formula in cell C5 (7) with the apparent sum of the numbers shown above (6), it appears that the sum calculated by the formula is incorrect.

A similar problem occurs in columns D & E. Column E contains the same numbers as those listed in column D, except that they are formatted as thousands.

The result of the **SUM** formula in cell E5, adding cells E2:E4, does not match the apparent sum of those numbers.

➤ **Solution:**

Round all the numbers in cells C2:C4 to the nearest integer prior to summing them.

Use the **SUM** and **ROUND** functions in following *Array formula*:

{=SUM(ROUND(C2:C4,0))}

Round all the numbers in column cells E2:E4 to thousands prior to summing them.

Use the **SUM** and **ROUND** functions in the following *Array formula:*

{=SUM(ROUND(E2:E4,-3))}

☞ To apply *Array formula:*

Select the cell, press <**F2**> and simultaneously press <**Ctrl+Shift+Enter**>.

	A	B	C	D	E
1		List1	List1 (No Decimal Places)	List2	List2 (Thousands)
2		1.11	1	1,252,501	1,253
3		2.22	2	5,235,501	5,236
4		3.33	3	5,232,501	5,233
5	SUM formulas	6.66	7	11,720,503	11,721
6	Formula Syntax in Row 5	=SUM(B2:B4)	=SUM(C2:C4)	=SUM(D2:D4)	=SUM(E2:E4)
7	Corrected SUM		6		11,722
8	Formula Syntax in Row 7		{=SUM(ROUND(C2:C4,0))}		{=SUM(ROUND(E2:E4,-3))}
9	Column Formatting	"0.00"	"0"	"#,##0"	"#,###,"

Explanation:

Excel does not take number formatting into account when performing mathematical calculations.

Instead, it operates on the entire number, using up to 15 significant digits, regardless of how many digits are currently displayed.

Hence, the calculated sum in cell C5 matches the actual values found in the cells, but does not match the numbers displayed.

In order for Excel to sum the numbers as they are displayed (rounded), we must actually round all the numbers prior to summing them, rather than just setting their format to display rounded numbers.

The **ROUND** function in the Array formula entered in cell C7 rounds each of the numbers in cells C2:C4 to 0 decimal places (the nearest integer) and returns the results in a single Array.

The **SUM** function adds all the values in that Array.

Thus, it sums all the numbers in cells C2:C4 after rounding each of them to the nearest integer.

Similarly, the Array formula entered in cells E7 returns the sum of all the numbers in cells E2:E4 after rounding each of them (using the **ROUND** function) to -3 decimal places (thousands).

Summing Values Based on Text, Text & Numbers, & Blank Cell Criteria

Summing Values Based on Text Criteria

> **Problem:**

Each row of columns A & B contains text and a corresponding number.

We want to sum all the numbers in column B corresponding with the text values in column A that meet the following criteria:

1. Text is "Excel".
2. Text starts with "Excel".
3. Text ends with "Excel".
4. Text contains "Excel".
5. Text length is 3 characters.

> **Solution:**

Use the **SUMIF** function as shown in the following formulas:

1. =SUMIF(A2:A7,"Excel",B2:B7)
2. =SUMIF(A2:A7,"Excel*",B2:B7)
3. =SUMIF(A2:A7,"*Excel",B2:B7)
4. =SUMIF(A2:A7,"*Excel*",B2:B7)
5. =SUMIF(A2:A7,"???",B2:B7)

	A	B	C	D	E
1	Text	Number	Criteria	Result	Formula Syntax
2	Excel	1	Text is "Excel"	1	=SUMIF(A2:A7,"Excel",B2:B7)
3	ABC	2	Text starts with "Excel"	10	=SUMIF(A2:A7,"Excel*",B2:B7)
4	Microsoft Excel	3	Text ends with "Excel"	4	=SUMIF(A2:A7,"*Excel",B2:B7)
5	Excel Tip	4	Text contains "Excel"	13	=SUMIF(A2:A7,"*Excel*",B2:B7)
6	Excel Workbook	5	Text length is 3 characters	8	=SUMIF(A2:A7,"???",B2:B7)
7	xyz	6			
8					

Explanation:

The * sign: Any additional characters on the right/left ends of the string are acceptable when searching for the specified criteria.

The ? Sign: Only strings of the same length as the number of "?"s will be returned; any characters are acceptable.

Summing Values from a List Containing Numerical and Textual Substrings

➢ **Problem:**

Listed in columns A & B are file names and their sizes, each of which is one of three types (KB, MB or GB).

We want to sum the totals for each file size type.

➢ **Solution:**

Use the **SUM**, **IF**, **ISNUMBER**, **FIND**, **VALUE**, and **LEFT** functions as shown in the following *Array formula*:

{=SUM(IF(ISNUMBER(FIND(C2,B2:B5)),VALUE(LEFT(B2:B5,FIND(C2,B2:B5)-1)),0))}

☞ To apply *Array formula:*

Select the cell, press **<F2>** and simultaneously press **<Ctrl+Shift+Enter>**.

	A	B	C	D	E	F	G
1	**File name**	**File Size**	**Measure**	**Result**			
2	file1	20MB	MB	420			
3	file2	30KB	KB	30			
4	file3	1.2 GB	GB	1.2			
5	file4	400MB					
6							
7	**Array Formula Syntax in cell D2:**						
8	{=SUM(IF(ISNUMBER(FIND(C2,B2:B5)),VALUE(LEFT(B2:B5,FIND(C2,B2:B5)-1)),0))}						
9							

Explanation:

The **ISNUMBER** and **FIND** functions are used to determine which of the strings in column B contain the measurement type specified in cells C2:C4.

For every string that contains the specified type, the **IF** functions returns the result of the following expression:

VALUE(LEFT(B2:B5,FIND(C2,B2:B5)-1)

The **FIND** function returns the location (character number) of the measurement string within the text in column B.

The **LEFT** function then extracts all the characters in the string up until that location. Thus, extracting the numeric part of the string.

The **VALUE** function converts the numeric part of the string to a number.

The numbers extracted from each string in column B that contains the specified measurement are then put in a single Array which is returned by the **IF** function.

Finally, the **SUM** function adds all the numbers in that Array.

Summing Numerical Substrings

➢ **Problem:**

List1 (column A) contains text values, each of which consists of a number with the letter "T" at the beginning.

We want to extract the numbers from each string and sum them.

➢ **Solution:**

Use the **SUM**, **VALUE**, and **SUBSTITUTE** functions as shown in the following *Array formula*:

{=SUM(VALUE(SUBSTITUTE(A2:A6,"T","")))}

☞ To apply *Array formula*:

Select the cell, press <**F2**> and simultaneously press <**Ctrl+Shift+Enter**>.

	A	B	C	D	E
1	**List1**	**Result**			
2	T1	42			
3	T20				
4	T5				
5	T4				
6	T12				
7					
8	**Array Formula Syntax in cell B2:**				
9	{=SUM(VALUE(SUBSTITUTE(A2:A6,"T","")))}				
10					

Explanation:

The **SUBSTITUTE** function returns an Array of all the strings in column A, with each having had the "T" removed.

The **VALUE** function converts the text values in that Array into numeric values.

The **SUM** function adds all the values.

Summing Values in a Range Containing Redundant Spaces

➤ **Problem:**

The numbers in column A contain redundant spaces.

If we try to calculate a total using the **SUM** function, 0 is returned.

➤ **Solution:**

Use the **SUM**, **VALUE**, and **SUBSTITUTE** functions as shown in the following *Array formula*:

{=SUM(VALUE(SUBSTITUTE(A2:A4," ","")))}

☞ To apply *Array formula:*

Select the cell, press <**F2**> and simultaneously press <**Ctrl+Shift+Enter**>.

	A	B	C
1	**Numbers**	**Result**	
2	3 300	4850	
3	50 0		
4	10 50		
5			
6	**Array Formula Syntax in cell B2:**		
7	{=SUM(VALUE(SUBSTITUTE(A2:A4," ","")))}		
8			

Explanation:

The **SUBSTITUTE** function returns an Array of all the strings in column A after having had all redundant spaces removed.

The **VALUE** function converts the text values in that Array into numeric values.

The **SUM** function adds all the values.

Ignoring Blank Cells Containing Invisible Spaces when Using Array Formulas

➢ **Problem:**

Columns A & B contain the number of points scored by a particular player during each quarter of a game.

An empty cell indicates that no points were scored during that quarter.

When using the following *Array formula* to total the points scored during the 2nd half, #VALUE! is returned.

{=SUM(A2:A5*((B2:B5=3)+(B2:B5=4)))}

➢ **Solution 1:**

Use the **SUM**, **IF**, and **ISNUMBER** functions as shown in the following *Array Formula*:

{=SUM(IF(ISNUMBER(A2:A5),(A2:A5)*((B2:B5=3)+(B2:B5=4))))}

❖ **Note:**

It is most likely that the blank cell in column A is actually not empty, but contains an invisible space.

Using the **ISNUMBER** and **IF** functions overcomes any errors.

☞ To apply *Array formula:*

Select the cell, press **<F2>** and simultaneously press **<Ctrl+Shift+Enter>**.

➤ **Solution 2:**

Use the **SUMIF** function as shown in the following formula:

=SUMIF(B2:B5,3,A2:A5)+SUMIF(B2:B5,4,A2:A5)

	A	B	C	D	E	F	G
1	Points	Quarter		Array Formula Solution1:			10
2	8	1					
3	5	2		SUMIF Formula Solution2:			10
4		3					
5	10	4					
6							
7	Array Formula in cell G1:						
8	{=SUM(IF(ISNUMBER(A2:A5),(A2:A5)*((B2:B5=3)+(B2:B5=4))))}						
9							
10	SUMIF Formula in cell G3:						
11	=SUMIF(B2:B5,3,A2:A5)+SUMIF(B2:B5,4,A2:A5)						
12							

Explanation:

The **ISNUMBER** function returns an Array, which includes a value of "TRUE" for every cell in column A that contains a number and a "FALSE" for every cell that does not contain one.

Based on the **ISNUMBER** results, the **IF** function returns an Array containing the scores stored in all the cells that contain numbers in column A, providing that their corresponding quarter in column B is 3 or 4 (2nd half).

The **SUM** function adds all the scores in that Array.

Summing Values Based on the Criteria of a Non-Empty Adjacent Cell

➢ **Problem:**

Summing each of the numbers in column A (List 1), provided that the adjacent cell in column B (List 2) is not empty.

➢ **Solution 1:**

Use the **SUMIF** function as shown in the following formula:

=SUMIF(B2:B7,"<>",A2:A7)

Explanation:

The **SUMIF** function adds all the values in column A that have non-empty corresponding cells in column B.

➢ **Solution 2:**

Use the **SUMPRODUCT** function as shown in the following formula:

=SUMPRODUCT(A2:A7*(B2:B7<>""))

Explanation:

The following expression creates an Array of TRUE/FALSE results:

B2:B7<>""

The Array includes a "1" (TRUE) for every non-empty cell in column B and a "0" (FALSE) for every empty one.

That Array is then multiplied by another Array, which consists of all the values in column A.

The **SUMPRODUCT** function adds the products of the corresponding values in those two Arrays.

Thus, returning the sum of all the values in column A corresponding to non-empty cells in column B.

	A	B
1	**List 1**	**List 2**
2	20	1
3	10	
4	5	4
5	13	3
6	6	
7	11	8
8		
9	**SUMIF Formula**	49
10	**SUMIF Formula Syntax in cell B9:**	
11	=SUMIF(B2:B7,"<>",A2:A7)	
12		
13	**SUMPRODUCT Formula**	49
14	**SUMPRODUCT Formula in cell B13:**	
15	=SUMPRODUCT(A2:A7*(B2:B7<>""))	
16		

Summing Using Indirect Cell References

Summing Values Using Indirect Cell References

➤ **Problem:**

Numbers Range (A2:C6) contains numbers.

Columns E & F contain pairs of cell references that indicate the beginning and end of parts of Numbers Range that we wish to sum.

We want to create formulas to calculate the sum for each specified sub-range.

➤ **Solution:**

Use the **SUM** and **INDIRECT** functions as shown in the following formula:

=SUM(INDIRECT(E2&":"&F2))

	A	B	C	D	E	F	G
1	Numbers Range				Range Beginning	Range End	Result
2	1	13	20		A2	C2	34
3	5	2	0		A3	C6	98
4	21	7	9				
5	3	17	8				
6	12	4	10				
7							
8	Formula Syntax in cell G2:						
9	=SUM(INDIRECT(E2&":"&F2))						
10							

Explanation:

The cell references in cell E2 (Range Beginning) and cell F2 (Range End) are joined into a single string, with the ":" sign between them.

This creates a text value representing a range reference.

The **INDIRECT** function returns the range reference indicated by that text.

The **SUM** function adds all the values within that range.

Summing Across Multiple Sheets

> ### Problem:

Column A of Sheet1 contains the letters A to D. Column B contains a set of corresponding numbers.

Sheet2 and Sheet3 have a similar layout.

Column A of Total Sheet contains the letters A to D as well.

We want to lookup each of the letters listed in column A of Sheets 1 to 3 and sum the corresponding numbers from column B of all three sheets.

> ### Solution:

Use the **SUMPRODUCT**, **SUMIF**, **INDIRECT**, and **ROW** functions as shown in the following formula:

=SUMPRODUCT(SUMIF(INDIRECT("'Sheet"&ROW(INDIRECT("1:3"))&"'!
$A$1:$A$4"),A1,INDIRECT("'Sheet"&ROW(INDIRECT("1:3"))&"'!$B$1:$B
$4")))

Enter the above formula cell B2 of your Total Sheet, and copy it down the column.

	A	B	C	D	E	F	G	H
1	A	63		**Sheet1**				
2	B	66		Row/Column	A	B		
3	C	69		1	A	11		
4	D	72		2	B	12		
5				3	C	13		
6				4	D	14		
7								
8				**Sheet2**				
9				Row/Column	A	B		
10				1	A	21		
11				2	B	22		
12				3	C	23		
13				4	D	24		
14								
15				**Sheet3**				
16				Row/Column	A	B		
17				1	A	31		
18				2	B	32		
19				3	C	33		
20				4	D	34		
21								
22	**Formula Syntax in cell B1:**							
23	=SUMPRODUCT(SUMIF(INDIRECT("'Sheet"&ROW(INDIRECT("1:3"))&"'!$A$1:$A$4"),A1,INDIRECT("'Sheet"&ROW(INDIRECT("1:3"))&"'!$B$1:$B$4")))							
24								

Explanation:

In the first argument of the **SUMIF** function (range) is an **INDIRECT** function.

Using the **ROW** function and another **INDIRECT** function, it returns an Array containing the references of the range A1:A4 in Sheet1, Sheet2, and Sheet3.

The third argument of the **SUMIF** function (sum_range) is similar to the first one.

In this case, the **INDIRECT** function returns an Array containing the references of the range B1:B4 in Sheet1, Sheet2, and Sheet3.

For each of the three sheets, the **SUMIF** function adds the values in column B for which the corresponding values in column A are identical to the value entered in cell A1. The function then returns an Array consisting of those three sums.

The **SUMPRUDCT** function adds all the values in that Array; thus returning the total sum of the values from all three sheets.

Summing from Closed Workbooks

➢ **Problem:**

The following formula was created to sum a variable number of values in row 3 of Book1, Sheet1, starting at column A:

=SUM(OFFSET('C:\My Documents\[Book1.xls]Sheet1'!$A$3,0,0,1,A2))

However, the formula only works correctly when Book1 is open.

When Book1 is closed, the formula returns #VALUE!.

How can we modify the formula so that it works regardless of whether Workbook1 is open or not?

➢ **Solution:**

Use the **SUM**, **COLUMN**, and **INDIRECT** functions as shown in the following *Array formula*:

{=SUM((COLUMN(INDIRECT("A:Z"))<COLUMN(INDIRECT("A:A"))+A2)*

IF(ISNUMBER('C:\My Documents\[Book1.xls]Sheet1'!$A$3:$Z$3),'C:\My Documents\[Book1.xls]Sheet1'!$A$3:$Z$3))}

☞ To apply *Array formula*:

Select the cell, press <**F2**> and simultaneously press <**Ctrl+Shift+Enter**>.

	A	B	C	D	E	F	G	H	I
1	**Number of Values**	**Result**							
2	4	15							
3	3	9							
4	2	5							
5									
6	**Array Formula Syntax in cell B2:**								
7	{=SUM((COLUMN(INDIRECT("A:Z"))<COLUMN(INDIRECT("A:A"))+A2)* IF(ISNUMBER('C:\My Documents\[Book1.xls]Sheet1'!$A$3:$Z$3),'C:\My Documents\[Book1.xls]Sheet1'!$A$3:$Z$3))}								
8									
9	**Line 3 in Book1, Sheet1**								
10	2	3	4	6	10	7	9		
11									
12	2	3	4	6	10	7	9		
13									
14	2	3	4	6	10	7	9		
15									

Explanation:

The **COLUMN** and **INDIRECT** functions are used to return an Array consisting of a TRUE for every column (A-Z) in Book1, Sheet1, Row 3 to be included in the sum, and a FALSE for every column not to be included.

The results in that Arrays (TRUE/FALSE) are determined based on the number of values to sum, entered in cell A2.

For every column for which TRUE was returned in the above Array, the **IF** function returns the value stored in it, providing that the **ISNUMBER** function determined that the value was a number.

Thus, an Array is created that contains all the numbers to sum.

Finally, the **SUM** function adds all the values in the Array.

Summing Using One or More Criteria

Summing Positive and Negative Numbers Separately

➢ **Problem:**

Calculating separate totals for the negative numbers and the positive numbers in List1 (column A).

➢ **Solution:**

Use the **SUMIF** function as shown in following formulas:

To sum negative numbers:

=SUMIF(A2:A7,"<0")

To sum positive numbers:

=SUMIF(A2:A7,">0")

	A	B	C
1	**List1**	**Negative Sum**	**Positive Sum**
2	-2	-16	10
3	4		
4	5		
5	-6		
6	1		
7	-8		
8			
9	**Negative Sum Formula Syntax in cell B2:**		
10	=SUMIF(A2:A7,"<0")		
11			
12	**Positive Sum Formula Syntax in cell C2:**		
13	=SUMIF(A2:A7,">0")		
14			

Explanation:

The **SUMIF** function adds all the values in column A that meet the specified criteria, that is, smaller or greater than 0.

Sum Total Sales Except for One Specified Item

➤ **Problem:**

Columns A & B contain clothing items and their matching total sales.

We want to create a formula that will sum the sales from column B of all items except the jacket.

➤ **Solution:**

Use the **SUMIF** function as shown in the following formula:

=SUMIF(A2:A6,"<>Jacket",B2:B6)

	A	B	C	D
1	**Items**	**Sales**	**Result**	
2	Shoes	100	175	
3	T-Shirt	20		
4	Jeans	50		
5	Jacket	150		
6	Socks	5		
7				
8	**Formula Syntax in cell C2:**			
9	=SUMIF(A2:A6,"<>Jacket",B2:B6)			
10				

Explanation:

The **SUMIF** function adds all the values (Sales) in column B for which the corresponding Item in column A is not "Jacket".

Summing Corresponding Values in Multiple Columns

➢ **Problem:**

Range A2:G5 contains the scores of four games.

Each row includes the names and scores of the three players who took part in the game specified in column A.

We want to calculate the total number of points scored in all four games by each of the players listed in cells A8:A12.

➢ **Solution:**

Use the **SUMIF** function as shown in the following formula:

=SUMIF($B$2:$F$5,A8,$C$2:$G$5)

	A	B	C	D	E	F	G
1	Game #	Player 1	Player 1 Score	Player 2	Player 2 Score	Player 3	Player 3 Score
2	Game 1	Mike	20	Kate	30	Dan	15
3	Game 2	Kate	25	Mike	35	David	40
4	Game 3	David	45	Dan	25	Kate	50
5	Game 4	Kate	25	John	45	Mike	30
6							
7	Player	Total					
8	Mike	85					
9	Kate	130					
10	David	85					
11	John	45					
12	Dan	40					
13							
14	Formula Syntax in cell B8:						
15	=SUMIF($B$2:$F$5,A8,$C$2:$G$5)						
16							

Explanation:

The **SUMIF** function adds all the values in the range C2:G5 for which the value to the left (cells B2:F5) matches the name specified in cell A8.

Summing Sales Amounts According to Product Category and Customer Name

> ➤ **Problem:**

Columns A:C contain product categories, customer names, and prices paid for various items.

When using the following formula to sum the prices paid by Customer1 on category A products, #NUM! is returned:

=SUMPRODUCT((A:A="A")*(B:B="Customer1"),C:C)

> ➤ **Solution:**

Use the **SUMPRODUCT** function as shown in the following formula:

=SUMPRODUCT((A1:A7="A")*(B1:B7="Customer1"),C1:C7)

> ❖ **Note:**

Summing or counting according to multiple criteria cannot be performed on entire column.

Therefore, in order to use the above formula, the column ranges must be adjusted to specific ranges (i.e. A1:A10, A1:A2000, A1:A65000, etc.).

	A	B	C	D	E
1	**Product Category**	**Customer**	**Price**		
2	A	Customer1	$100.00		
3	B	Customer1	$50.00		
4	C	Customer2	$80.00		
5	A	Customer2	$60.00		
6	C	Customer1	$120.00		
7	A	Customer1	$40.00		
8					
9	**Result**		$140.00		
10					
11	**Formula Syntax in cell B9:**				
12	=SUMPRODUCT((A1:A7="A")*(B1:B7="Customer1"),C1:C7)				
13					

Explanation:

The first argument of the **SUMPRODUCT** formula is an Array returned by the following expression:

(A1:A7="A")*(B1:B7="Customer1")

The Array contains a "1" (TRUE) for all the "A" values in column A (Product Category) that have a corresponding Customer in column B of "Customer1". "0" (FALSE) is returned for all other values in column A.

The second argument is an Array consisting of all the prices in column C.

The **SUMPRODUCT** function adds the products of the corresponding values from those two Arrays.

Thus, totaling the prices of all the "Category A" products purchased by "Customer1".

Summing Total Sales, Based on Quantity & Price

➢ **Problem:**

Calculating the total sales price of all the items listed in column A, based on the amount of items sold (column B), and the price per unit (column C).

➢ **Solution 1:**

Use the **SUMPRODUCT** function as shown in the following formula:

=SUMPRODUCT(B2:B5,C2:C5)

➢ **Solution 2:**

Use the **SUM** function as shown in the following *Array formula*:

{=SUM((B2:B5)*(C2:C5))}

☞ To apply *Array formula:*

Select the cell, press <**F2**> and simultaneously press <**Ctrl+Shift+Enter**>.

	A	B	C	D
1	Item	Amount	Price per Unit	SUMPRODUCT Formula
2	T-Shirt	2	$10.00	$109.00
3	Jeans	1	$30.00	
4	Socks	3	$3.00	Array Formula
5	Shoes	1	$50.00	$109.00
6				
7				
8	Formula Syntax in cell D2:			
9	=SUMPRODUCT(B2:B5,C2:C5)			
10				
11	Array Formula Syntax in cell D5:			
12	{=SUM((B2:B5)*(C2:C5))}			
13				

Explanation

☞ **Explanation to Solution1:**

The **SUMPRODUCT** function adds the products of the corresponding values in cells B2:B5 (Array1) and cells C2:C5 (Array2).

Thus, each Amount is multiplied by its corresponding Price per Unit, and the results are totaled.

☞ **Explanation to Solution 2:**

The following expression returns an Array consisting of the product of each Amount in column B and its corresponding Price in column C.

(B2:B5)*(C2:C5)

The **SUM** function adds all the values in that Array.

Summing Values from Two Ranges, Based on Two Criteria

➤ **Problem:**

Columns A & B contain a list of candy eaten last week and the calories corresponding with each item.

Columns C & D contain the equivalent information regarding fruit and vegetables.

We want a total of the calories gained last week by eating the food items specified in column F.

➤ **Solution 1:**

Use the **SUMPRODUCT** function as shown in either of the following formulas:

=SUMPRODUCT((A2:A7=F2)*(B2:B7))+SUMPRODUCT((C2:C7=F3)*(D2:D7))

=SUMPRODUCT(--(A2:A7=F2),(B2:B7))+SUMPRODUCT(--(C2:C7=F3),(D2:D7))

➤ **Solution 2:**

Use the **SUMIF** function as shown in the following formula:

=SUMIF(A2:A7,F2,B2:B7)+SUMIF(C2:C7,F3,D2:D7)

	A	B	C	D	E	F
1	**Candy**	**Calories**	**Fruit & Vegetables**	**Calories**		**Food Items To Sum**
2	Snickers	350	Tomato	10		Snickers
3	Twix	370	Potato	40		Potato
4	Skittles	250	Apple	30		
5	Snickers	350	Carrot	20		
6	Mars	330	Banana	60		
7	Kit Kat	300	Potato	40		
8						
9	**Formula1:**	780				
10	**Formula2:**	780				
11	**Formula3:**	780				
12						
13	**Formula1 Syntax in cell B9:**					
14	=SUMPRODUCT((A2:A7=F2)*(B2:B7))+SUMPRODUCT((C2:C7=F3)*(D2:D7))					
15						
16	**Formula2 Syntax in cell D10:**					
17	=SUMPRODUCT(--(A2:A7=F2),(B2:B7))+SUMPRODUCT(--(C2:C7=F3),(D2:D7))					
18						
19	**Formula3 Syntax in cell D11:**					
20	=SUMIF(A2:A7,F2,B2:B7)+SUMIF(C2:C7,F3,D2:D7)					
21						

Explanation:

Second Formula:

The first argument of the first **SUMPRODUCT** function is an Array, including a "TRUE" for every value in column A that matches the criteria in cells F2, and a "FALSE" for every value that does not match the criteria.

The "--" sign, entered before the above expression, converts the TRUE and FALSE values in that Array to "1" and "0" accordingly.

The second argument of the first **SUMPRODUCT** function is an Array including all the values in column B (cells B2:B7).

The **SUMPRODUCT** function returns the sum of the products of the corresponding items in those two Arrays (i.e. the sum of all the calorie values that correspond with food items matching the criteria in cell F2).

Similarly, the second **SUMPRODUCT** function in that formula returns the sum of all the calorie values (column D) corresponding with food items in column C that match the criteria in cell F3.

Finally, the two sums are added together.

❖ **Note:**

Putting the "*" operator between the two ranges in the **SUMPRODUCT** function (as done in the first formula) is equivalent to putting the "--" before the first range and separating it from the second range with a comma (as done in the second formula).

Summing How Many Points Scored by a Specified Team in Specified Games

➢ **Problem:**

Listed in columns A:C are the point totals scored by teams A and B in the first four games of the season.

We want to calculate the total number of points scored by Team B in the first two games.

➢ **Solution:**

Use the **SUM** function as shown in the following *Array formula*:

{=SUM((A2:A9="B")*(B2:B9<=2)*C2:C9)}

☞ To apply *Array formula:*

Select the cell, press <**F2**> and simultaneously press <**Ctrl+Shift+Enter**>.

	A	B	C	D
1	Team	Game #	Points	
2	A	1	15	
3	B	1	10	
4	A	2	20	
5	B	2	13	
6	A	3	9	
7	B	3	14	
8	A	4	15	
9	B	4	13	
10				
11	Result	23		
12				
13	**Array Formula Syntax in cell B11:**			
14	{=SUM((A2:A9="B")*(B2:B9<=2)*C2:C9)}			
15				

Explanation:

The following expression returns an Array containing all the scores in column C that correspond with having Team in column A as "B" and Game Number in column B as smaller than or equal to 2:

(A2:A9="B")*(B2:B9<=2)*C2:C9

The **SUM** function adds all the scores in that Array.

Summing Expenses Accumulated to a Specified Month

➢ **Problem:**

Column B contains the expenses for each of the months January to July.

We want to create a formula that will sum the expenses for all the months between January and the month specified in cell D2.

➢ **Solution:**

Use the **SUM**, **OFFSET**, and **MATCH** functions as shown in the following formula:

=SUM(OFFSET(B2,0,0,MATCH(D2,A2:A8,0),1))

	A	B	C	D	E
				Last Month	
1	**Month**	**Total Expenses**		**to Sum**	**Result**
2	Jan	$510.00		May	$2,410.00
3	Feb	$620.00			
4	Mar	$430.00			
5	Apr	$570.00			
6	May	$280.00			
7	June	$300.00			
8	July	$450.00			
9					
10	**Formula Syntax in E2**				
11	=SUM(OFFSET(B2,0,0,MATCH(D2,A2:A8,0),1))				
'12					

Explanation:

The **MATCH** function returns the position (row number) of the month within cells A2:A8 that matches the month entered in cell D2.

The **OFFSET** function returns the reference of a range that starts at cell B2 and includes as many rows as the number returned by the **MATCH** function.

The **SUM** function adds all the values (Total Expenses) in that range.

Calculating Monthly and Accumulated Income, Based on Specified Month

➤ **Problem:**

Cells B3:M5 contain the monthly income from three different sources (listed in cells A3:A5).

Row 1 (cells B1:M1) contains the serial number matching each month in row 2 (cells B2:M2).

Row 6 (cells B6:M6) contains **SUM** formulas, calculating total monthly income.

We want to retrieve the amounts matching each source of income, as well as the total income, for a specified month.

We also want to calculate the accumulated income from each source, up until (and including) that month.

In addition, we want to change the titles above the formulas to include the month name.

➤ **Solution:**

❖ To retrieve income per month, use the **SUMIF** function as shown in the following formula in cell B9:

=SUMIF($B$1:$M$1,$J$8,B3:M3)

❖ To calculate the accumulated income up until the month indicated, use the **SUMIF** function as shown in the following formula in cell C9:

=SUMIF($B$1:$M$1,"<="&$B$10,B3:M3)

❖ To change the titles in cells B8:C8:
Use the **INDEX** function as shown in the following formulas:
To change the title in cell B8:

=INDEX(B2:M2,J8)&" "&"Income"

❖ To change the title in cell C8:

="Accumulated Income Until" &" "& INDEX(B2:M2,J8)

	A	B	C	D	E	F	G	H	I	J	K	L	M
1		1	2	3	4	5	6	7	8	9	10	11	12
2		Jan	Feb	Mar	Apr	May	Jun	Jul	Aug	Sep	Oct	Nov	Dec
3	Income 1	100	200	300	400	500	600	700	800	900	1000	1100	1200
4	Income 2	200	300	400	500	600	700	800	900	1000	1100	1200	1300
5	Income 3	300	400	500	600	700	800	900	1000	1100	1200	1300	1400
6	Total	600	900	1200	1500	1800	2100	2400	2700	3000	3300	3600	3900
7													
8		Jul Income	Accumulated Income Until Jul				Month Number			7			
9	Income 1	700	2800				Formula Syntax in B9:B12						
10	Income 2	800	3500				=SUMIF($B$1:$M$1,$J$8,B3:M3)						
11	Income 3	900	4200				Formula Syntax in C9:C12						
12	Total	2400	10500				=SUMIF($B$1:$M$1,"<="&$J$8,B3:M3)						
13													
14		Formula Syntax in cell B8:					Formula Syntax in cell C8:						
15		=INDEX(B2:M2,J8)&" "&"Income"					="Accumulated Income Until" &" "& INDEX(B2:M2,J8)						
16													

Explanation:

☞ **Income per Month Formula:**

The **SUMIF** function adds all the values in cells B3:M3 (Income1 amounts) which have corresponding month number that match the one entered in cell J8.

Thus, the Income1 amount for the specified month is returned.

☞ **Accumulated Income Formula:**

The **SUMIF** function adds all the values in cells B3:M3 (Income1 amounts) which have corresponding month numbers smaller than or equal to the one entered in cell J8.

Thus, the accumulated sum of Income1 amounts up until the specified month is returned.

☞ **Title (cell B8) Formula:**

The **INDEX** function returns the value in cells B2:M2 that is stored in the position specified in cell J8.

Summing Annual Expenses by Respective Quarters

> ➤ **Problem:**

The range A2:B9 contains a list of dates with corresponding expenses.

We want to create a total of the expenses paid during each quarter.

> ➤ **Solution:**

Use the **SUM**, **ROUNDUP**, and **MONTH** functions as shown in the following *Array formula*:

{=SUM((C2=ROUNDUP(MONTH($A$2:$A$9)/3,0))*$B$2:$B$9)}

> ☞ To apply *Array formula:*
>
> Select the cell, press **<F2>** and simultaneously press **<Ctrl+Shift+Enter>**.

	A	B	C	D	E	F
1	**Date**	**Expense**	**Quarter Number**	**Result**		
2	05/01/2005	$200	1	$350		
3	20/03/2005	$150	2	$430		
4	11/04/2005	$30	3	$255		
5	11/06/2005	$400	4	$200		
6	22/08/2005	$35				
7	16/09/2005	$220				
8	02/11/2005	$120				
9	03/12/2005	$80				
10						
11	**Array Formula Syntax in cell D2:**					
12	{=SUM((C2=ROUNDUP(MONTH($A$2:$A$9)/3,0))*$B$2:$B$9)}					
13						

Explanation:

The **MONTH** function returns an Array which contains the month number matching each date in column A.

The **ROUNDUP** function divides each of those month numbers by 3 and rounds it up to the nearest integer (0 decimal places).

Thus, an Array is returned that contains the quarter number matching each date in column A.

The quarter number in cell C2 is compared with that Array, returning an Array of TRUE/FALSE results.

"1" (TRUE) is returned for every quarter number in the Array that matches the number in cell C2 and "0" (FALSE) is returned for every value that does not match it.

That Array of 1/0 results is then multiplied by another Array, including the values in column B (Expenses).

Thus, a new Array is created that contains the expenses corresponding to all the dates matching the desired quarter number.

Finally, the **SUM** function adds all the values (Expenses) in that Array.

Summing the Number of Hours an Employee Worked During a Two Week Period

➢ **Problem:**

Columns A & B contain the number of hours worked by each ID this week.

Columns D & E contain the equivalent information for last week.

We want a total of the hours worked by a specified ID over the entire period.

➢ **Solution:**

Use the **SUMIF** function as shown as shown in the following formula:

=SUMIF(A3:A7,B10,B3:B7)+SUMIF(D3:D7,B10,E3:E7)

	A	B	C	D	E	F
1	This Week			Last Week		
2	ID	Hours Worked		ID	Hours Worked	
3	1	5		1	10	
4	2	7		4	6	
5	3	10		6	8	
6	4	12		3	5	
7	5	4		8	9	
8						
9						
10	ID	4				
11	Total Hours	18				
12						
13	Formula Syntax in cell B11:					
14	=SUMIF(A3:A7,B10,B3:B7)+SUMIF(D3:D7,B10,E3:E7)					
15						

Explanation:

The first **SUMIF** function adds all the values in column B (Hours Worked) that have corresponding IDs (in column A) that match the one entered in cell B10.

The second **SUMIF** function does the same thing for the Hours Worked in column E and IDs in column D.

The two sums are then added together, creating a total of the hours worked in both weeks.

Summing Last N Values

Summing Groups of Every N Values in a Row

➤ **Problem:**

Cells in the range B2:M2 contain numerical values, and the row above contains matching serial numbers.

We want to subdivide the values into batches of three and calculate the sum of each batch.

> ➤ **Solution 1:**

Use the **SUM** and **INDEX** functions as shown in the following formula:

=SUM(INDEX($B$2:$M$2,3*A6-2):INDEX($B$2:$M$2,3*A6))

> ➤ **Solution 2:**

Use the **SUM** and **OFFSET** functions as shown in the following formula:

=SUM(OFFSET($B$2:$D$2,0,3*(A6-1)))

	A	B	C	D	E	F	G	H	I	J	K	L	M
1	Serial #	1	2	3	4	5	6	7	8	9	10	11	12
2	Values	5	6	7	3	2	3	4	5	0	2	1	9
3													
4													
5	Batch #	INDEX Formula	OFFSET Formula										
6	1	18	18										
7	2	8	8										
8	3	9	9										
9	4	12	12										
10													
11	INDEX Formula Syntax in cell B6:												
12	=SUM(INDEX($B$2:$M$2,3*A6-2):INDEX($B$2:$M$2,3*A6))												
13													
14	OFFSET Formula Syntax in cell C6:												
15	=SUM(OFFSET($B$2:$D$2,0,3*(A6-1)))												
16													

Explanation:

☞ **Explanation to Solution 1:**

The first **INDEX** function uses the batch number in cell A6 to calculate the position (column number) of the first cell of that batch.

Based on that position, it returns the reference of the first cell of the batch.

Similarly, the second **INDEX** function returns the reference of the last cell of the batch.

The ":" sign between the two **INDEX** functions creates a reference of the range containing the desired batch.

The **SUM** function adds all the values in that range.

☞ **Explanation to Solution 2:**

The **OFFSET** function offsets the range reference of the first batch (cells B2:D2) by as many columns as calculated by the following expression:

3*(A6-1)

Thus, it returns the reference of the range containing the desired batch.

The **SUM** function adds all the values in that range.

Summing the Last N Values in a Column

➤ **Problem:**

Calculating the sum of the last n numbers in List1 (column A) for each value of N in column B.

➤ **Solution:**

Use the **SUM**, **OFFSET**, and **COUNTA** functions as shown in the following formula:

=SUM(OFFSET($A$2,COUNTA($A$2:$A$7)-1,0,-B2))

	A	B	C	D
1	List1	Number of Values	Result	
2	10	2	14	
3	3	3	21	
4	5	4	26	
5	7	5	29	
6	12	6	39	
7	2			
8				
9	Formula Syntax in cell C2:			
10	=SUM(OFFSET($A$2,COUNTA($A$2:$A$7)-1,0,-B2))			
11				

Explanation:

The **COUNTA** function returns the number of values in column A.

The **OFFSET** function offsets the given reference (cell A2) down as many rows as the number calculated by the **COUNTA** function minus 1, and creates the reference of a range that ends at that point (the cell containing the last value in List1) and includes as many rows as the number entered in cell B2.

The **SUM** function adds all the values in that range.

Summing the N Largest Values in a Range

> **Problem:**

Summing the n largest values in List1 (column A) for each value of N in column B.

> **Solution:**

Use the **SUM**, **LARGE**, **ROW**, and **INDIRECT** functions as shown in the following *Array formula*:

{=SUM(LARGE($A$2:$A$11,ROW(INDIRECT("1 :"&B2))))}

☞ To apply *Array formula:*

Select the cell, press **<F2>** and simultaneously press **<Ctrl+Shift+Enter>**.

	A	B	C	D	E
1	List1	Values to Sum	Result		
2	10	5	43		
3	5	4	37		
4	2	3	30		
5	7	2	22		
6	3	1	12		
7	1				
8	6				
9	12				
10	4				
11	8				
12					
13	Array Formula Syntax in cell C2:				
14	{=SUM(LARGE($A$2:$A$11,ROW(INDIRECT("1:"&B2))))}				
15					

Explanation:

The text value "1:" and the number of values to sum (cell B2) are joined into a single text value, representing a reference of the rows from "1" to the number in cell B2.

The **INDIRECT** function returns the reference indicated by that text.

The **ROW** function returns an Array consisting of the row numbers of each row included in that reference.

The **LARGE** function uses each of those row numbers as a value for kth and returns an Array consisting of the kth largest number in column A for each value of K.

The **SUM** function adds all the values in that Array.

Creating a List in which Each Number is the Sum of the Previous N Numbers

➤ Problem:

We want to create a sequence of numbers where each member of the sequence is the sum of the previous N number of values.

➤ **Solution:**

Use the **SUM, OFFSET, INDIRECT, ADDRESS, ROW,** and **COLUMN**
functions as shown in the following formula:

=SUM(OFFSET(INDIRECT(ADDRESS(ROW(),COLUMN())),0,-1,1,-2))

	A	B	C	D	E	F	G	H	I	J
1										
2	1	1	2	3	5	8	13	21	34	55
3										
4	1	1	2	4	7	13	24	44	81	149
5										
6	**Summing two last values, Formula Syntax in cells C2:J2**									
7	=SUM(OFFSET(INDIRECT(ADDRESS(ROW(),COLUMN())),0,-1,1,-2))									
8										
9	**Summing three last values, Formula Syntax in cell D4:J4**									
10	=SUM(OFFSET(INDIRECT(ADDRESS(ROW(),COLUMN())),0,-1,1,-3))									
11										

Explanation:

The **ADDRESS** function, using the **ROW**() and **COLUMN**() functions,
returns a text value representing the reference of the current cell.

The **INDIRECT** function returns the reference indicated by that text value.

The **OFFSET** function returns the reference of a range that consists of the
two cells located to the right of that reference (current cell).

The **SUM** function adds the values in that range.

The last two arguments of the **OFFSET** function delineate the size of the
range (height& width).

When the range width of the **OFFSET** function is -2, the above formula
adds the previous 2 numbers to form the current number.

When the width is -3, the formula sums the previous 3 numbers, and so
on.

Chapter 8

List

About This Chapter

This chapter provides information on the issues and problems involved
with the use of List formulas, and includes the following sections:

☞ **Sorting, Reversing, & Retrieving Values, page 332:** This section
contains formulas for sorting values in ascending/ descending order,
and for reversing and shuffling values in lists.

☞ **Creating a New List Using Criteria, page 338:** This section contains
various formulas for creating a new list by retrieving unique values,
by ignoring blank values, and by checking for values that are in
sequence.

☞ **Identifying Duplicate Values, page 348:** This section covers formulas
for identifying duplicate values in a list.

☞ **Transposing a List, page 352**: This section contains formulas that
transpose values from rows to columns and vice versa.

Sorting, Reversing, & Retrieving Values

Sorting Numbers in Ascending or Descending Order

➢ **Problem:**

List1 (column A) contains a range of unsorted numbers.

We want to create two new lists of the same numbers: one sorted in ascending order, and the other in descending order.

➢ **Solution:**

❖ To sort in ascending order, use the **SMALL** and **ROW** functions as shown in the following formula (in cell B2):

=SMALL($A$2:$A$5,ROW()-ROW($B$2)+1)

❖ To sort in descending order, use the **LARGE** and **ROW** functions as shown in the following formula (in cell C2):

=LARGE($A$2:$A$5,ROW()-ROW($C$2)+1)

	A	B	C
1	**List1**	**List1 Ascending**	**List1 Descending**
2	4	1	8
3	3	3	4
4	8	4	3
5	1	8	1
6			
7	**Formula Syntax in cell B2:**		
8	=SMALL($A$2:$A$5,ROW()-ROW($B$2)+1)		
9			
10	**Formula Syntax in cell C2:**		
11	=LARGE($A$2:$A$5,ROW()-ROW($C$2)+1)		
12			

Explanation:

☞ **Sort Ascending Formula (cell B2):**

The **ROW** functions in the following expression return the row numbers of the current cell and the first cell in the result column (cell $B$2):

ROW()-ROW($B$2)

The result of this expression represents the number of values that have been retrieved from List1 so far.

The **SMALL** function returns the kth smallest number in List1, where kth is the number calculated by the above expression, plus 1.

Thus, it returns the smallest number in List1 that has not yet been retrieved; resulting in an ascending list of numbers.

☞ **Sort Descending Formula (cell C2):**

The **ROW** functions·in the following expression return the row numbers of the current cell and the first cell in the result column (cell $C$2):

ROW()-ROW($C$2)

The result of this expression represents the number of values that have been retrieved from List1 so far.

The **LARGE** function returns the kth largest number in List1, where kth is the number calculated by the above expression, plus 1.

Thus, it returns the largest number in List1 that has not yet been retrieved; resulting in a descending list of numbers.

Sorting Numbers Based on Their Frequency within a List

➤ **Problem:**

We want to create a list in column B that consists of each unique value from List1 (column A).

The values are to be sorted in descending order according to their frequency of occurrence in List1 (i.e. the most frequent number in List1 will appear first, followed by the second most frequent number, and so on).

➢ **Solution:**

Enter the **MODE** function as shown in the following formula (in cell B2):

=MODE(A2:A15)

Then, use the **MODE**, **IF**, and **COUNTIF** functions as shown in the following *Array formula* in cell B3 and copy it down the column until the #N/A error is returned:

{=MODE(IF(COUNTIF($B$2:B2,$A$2:$A$15)=0,$A$2:$A$15))}

☞ To apply *Array formula:*

Select the cell, press <**F2**> and simultaneously press <**Ctrl+Shift+Enter**>.

	A	B	C	D	E	F
1	**List1**	**Result**				
2	5	8				
3	5	9				
4	8	2				
5	8	5				
6	8	#N/A				
7	8					
8	8					
9	2					
10	2					
11	2					
12	9					
13	9					
14	9					
15	9					
16						
17	**Formula Syntax in cell B2:**					
18	=MODE(A2:A15)					
19						
20	**Array Formula Syntax in cell B3 and copied down column B:**					
21	{=MODE(IF(COUNTIF($B$2:B2,$A$2:$A$15)=0,$A$2:$A$15))}					
22						

Explanation:

☞ **First Formula (cell B2):**

The **MODE** function returns the most common number in List1.

☞ **Second Formula (cells B3:B6):**

The **COUNTIF** function returns an Array consisting of the number of times each value in List1 (cells A2:A15) matches one of the values currently in column B (i.e. cells $B$2:B2).

A count of 0 represents a number in List1 that does not yet appear in column B.

Any other count represents a number in List1 that has already been added to column B.

The **IF** function returns an Array consisting of the values in List1 corresponding to each zero returned by the **COUNTIF** function, i.e. all the numbers in List1 that have not yet been added to column B.

The **MODE** function returns the most common number in that Array.

Thus, the second most frequent number in List1 now appears in cell B3.

Similarly, the third most frequent number will appear in cell B4, and so on.

Reversing the Order of Values in a List

➢ **Problem:**

We want to rearrange the contents of the list in column A in reverse order.

➢ **Solution:**

Use the **OFFSET**, **COUNTA**, and **ROW** functions as shown in the following formula:

=OFFSET($A$2,COUNTA($A$2:$A$6)-ROW()+1,0))

	A	B	C	D
1	**List**	**Result**		
2	1	5		
3	2	4		
4	3	3		
5	4	2		
6	5	1		
7				
8	**Formula Syntax in cell B2:**			
9	=OFFSET($A$2,COUNTA($A$2:$A$6)-ROW()+1,0)			
10				

Explanation:

The **COUNTA** function returns the number of values (non-blank cells) in cells A2:A6.

The **ROW** function returns the row number of the current cell.

The calculated row number is then subtracted from the number of values, and 1 is added to the result.

The **OFFSET** function offsets the reference of the first cell in the list (cell $A$2) as many rows as the number calculated above.

Thus, the contents of the list are copied in reverse order.

Shuffling a List of Values

➤ **Problem:**

List1 (column B) contains a range of alphabetically sorted letters.

We want to create a randomly shuffled list of the same letters in column C.

➤ **Solution:**

Enter the **RAND** function as shown in each of the corresponding cells in column A:

=RAND()

In column C, use the **VLOOKUP**, **LARGE**, and **ROW** functions as shown in the following formula:

=VLOOKUP(LARGE($A$2:$A$9,ROW()-
ROW($C$2)+1),$A$2:$B$9,2,FALSE)

The list will reshuffle with each recalculation (<**F9**> key).

	A	B	C	D
1	**Random Numbers**	**List1**	**Shuffled List**	
2	0.294027342	A	G	
3	0.850399196	B	B	
4	0.520558944	C	D	
5	0.630015243	D	C	
6	0.337647388	E	E	
7	0.2196904	F	A	
8	0.944411605	G	F	
9	0.072461297	H	H	
10				
11	Formula Syntax In Column A:			
12	=RAND()			
13				
14	Formula Syntax in cell C2:			
15	=VLOOKUP(LARGE($A$2:$A$9,ROW()-ROW($C$2)+1),$A$2:$B$9,2,FALSE)			
16				

Explanation:

☞ **First Formula (Column A):**

The **RAND** function returns a random number between 0 and 1.

☞ **Second Formula (Column C):**

The **ROW** functions return the row numbers of the current cell and of the first cell in the shuffled list (cell C2):

Subtracting these numbers represents the number of letters that have currently been retrieved from List1 (cells B2:B9).

The **LARGE** function returns the kth largest random number from cells A2:A9, where kth is the number calculated by the **ROW** expression, plus 1.

Thus, in the first cell of the shuffled list (cell C2), the **LARGE** function returns the largest random number, in the second cell (cell C3), it returns the second largest random number, and so on.

The **VLOOKUP** function looks up column A for the number returned by the **LARGE** function, and retrieves the corresponding value from the second column (column B).

As the random values in column A change with each recalculation (<**F9**> key), the order of the letters in the shuffled list will also change accordingly.

Creating a New List Using Criteria

Retrieving Unique Values from a List

➢ **Problem:**

Column A contains a list of values, each of which may appear more than once.

We want to create a list in column B in which each value from column A may only appear once.

➢ **Solution:**

Use the **INDEX**, **MATCH**, and **COUNTIF** functions as shown in the following *Array formula*:

{=INDEX($A$2:$A$8,MATCH(0,COUNTIF($B$2:B2,$A$2:$A$8),0))}

❖ **Note:**

The first cell in the unique list (column B) must remain empty.

The formula should be entered in the second cell and copied down until the #N/A error is returned.

☞ To apply *Array formula*:

Select the cell, press **<F2>** and simultaneously press **<Ctrl+Shift+Enter>**.

	A	B	C	D	E	F
1	**List**	**Distinct List**				
2	Red					
3	Blue	Red				
4	Green	Blue				
5	Yellow	Green				
6	Green	Yellow				
7	Blue	#N/A				
8	Blue	#N/A				
9						
10	**Array Formula Syntax in cell B3:**					
11	{=INDEX($A$2:$A$8,MATCH(0,COUNTIF($B$2:B2,$A$2:$A$8),0))}					
12						

Explanation:

The **COUNTIF** function returns an Array consisting of the number of times each value in the list (cells A2:A8) matches one of the values currently in column B (i.e. cells $B$2:B2).

A count of 0 represents a value in the list that does not yet appear in column B.

Any other count represents a value in the list that has already been added to column B

The **MATCH** function returns the position of the first 0 within that Array.

The **INDEX** function returns the value stored in the same position in the list.

Thus, the first value in the list that does not already appear in column B is now added.

When the formula is copied to the other cells, the reference of the result column (cells $B$2:B2) changes to include all the cells in column B above the current cell.

Retrieving List Values that Do Not Appear in a Second List

➤ **Problem:**

We want to create a new list consisting of the values from List1 (column A) that are not common to List2 (column B) as well.

➤ **Solution:**

Use the **INDEX**, **SMALL**, **IF**, **COUNTIF**, and **ROW** functions as shown in the following *Array formula*:

{=INDEX($A$2:$A$7,SMALL(IF(COUNTIF($B$2:$B$7,$A$2:$A$7)=0,ROW($A$2:$A$7),1000),ROW()-ROW($C$2)+1)-ROW($C$2)+1)}

Enter the formula in cell C2 and copy it down the column until the #REF! error is returned.

☞ To apply *Array formula*:

Select the cell, press <**F2**> and simultaneously press <**Ctrl+Shift+Enter**>.

	A	B	C	D	E
1	**List1**	**List2**	**Result**		
2	4	3	8		
3	8	9	7		
4	6	12	2		
5	7	4	#REF!		
6	2	6			
7	12	1			
8					
9	**Array Formula Syntax in cell C2:**				
10	{=INDEX($A$2:$A$7,SMALL(IF(COUNTIF($B$2:$B$7,$A$2:$A$7)=0,ROW($A$2:$A$7),1000),ROW()-ROW($C$2)+1)-ROW($C$2)+1)}				
11					

Explanation:

The **COUNTIF** function returns an Array consisting of the number of times each value in List1 (cells A2:A7) matches one of the values in List2 (cells B2:B7).

The **IF** function returns an Array consisting of the row number (calculated by the **ROW** function) of each value in List1 for which the **COUNTIF** function returned a count of 0 (i.e. values that don't exist in List2), and the number 1000 for every other value.

The **ROW** functions in the following expression return the row numbers of the current cell and the first cell in the result column (cell $C$2):

ROW()-ROW($C$2)

The result of this expression represents the number of values that have been retrieved from List1 so far.

The **SMALL** function returns the kth smallest number in the Array returned by the **IF** function, where kth is the number calculated by the above expression, plus 1.

Thus, it returns the row number of the first value in List1 that is not common to List2 and has not yet been retrieved.

The row number of the first cell in the result column (cells $C$2) is then subtracted from the row number returned by the **SMALL** function, and 1 is added to the result.

The result of that calculation represents the position within List1 of the first value that does not appear in List2 and that has not yet been retrieved.

The **INDEX** function returns the value stored in that position in List1.

Thus, a list is created of all the values in List1 that are not common to List2.

Retrieving Values that are Common to Two Lists

➢ **Problem:**

We want to create a new list consisting of the values that are common to both List1 (column A) and List2 (Column B).

➢ **Solution:**

Use the **INDEX**, **SMALL**, **IF**, **COUNTIF**, and **ROW** functions as shown in the following *Array formula*:

{=INDEX($A$2:$A$9,SMALL(IF(COUNTIF($B$2:$B$9,$A$2:$A$9)>0,ROW($A$2:$A$9),1000),ROW()-ROW($D$2)+1)-ROW($D$2)+1)}

Enter the formula in cell D2 and copy it down the column until the #REF! error is returned.

☞ To apply *Array formula*:

Select the cell, press **<F2>** and simultaneously press **<Ctrl+Shift+Enter>**.

	A	B	C	D	E
1	**List1**	**List2**		**Common Values**	
2	1	4		6	
3	8	9		2	
4	6	11		4	
5	10	2		#REF!	
6	2	5			
7	4	0			
8	12	7			
9	15	6			
10					
11	**Array Formula Syntax in cell D2:**				
12	{=INDEX($A$2:$A$9,SMALL(IF(COUNTIF($B$2:$B$9,$A$2:$A$9)>0,ROW($A$2:$A$9),1000),ROW()-ROW($D$2)+1)-ROW($D$2)+1)}				

Explanation:

The **COUNTIF** function returns an Array consisting of the number of times each value in List1 (cells A2:A9) matches one of the values in List2 (cells B2:B9).

The **IF** function returns an Array consisting of the row number (calculated by the **ROW** function) of each value in List1 for which the **COUNTIF** function returned a count greater than 0 (i.e. the value exists in List2), and the number 1000 for every other value.

The **ROW** functions in the following expression return the row numbers of the current cell and the first cell the result column (cell $D$2):

ROW()-ROW($D$2)

The result of this expression represents the number of common values that have been retrieved so far.

The **SMALL** function returns the kth smallest number in the Array returned by the **IF** function, where kth is the number calculated by the above expression, plus 1.

Thus, it returns the row number of the first value in List1 that also exists in List2 and has not yet been retrieved.

The row number of the first cell in the result column (cell $D$2) is then subtracted from the row number returned by the **SMALL** function, and 1 is added to the result.

The result of that calculation represents the position within List1 of the first common value that has not yet been retrieved.

The **INDEX** function returns the value stored in that position in List1.

Thus, a list is created of all the values in List1 that also appear in List2.

Creating a List of All Non-Blank Cells in a Column

➤ **Problem:**

List1 (column A) contains values as well as blank cells.

We want to create a new list in column B that consists of just the values from List1.

➤ **Solution:**

Use the **INDEX**, **SMALL**, **IF**, and **ROW** functions as shown in the following *Array formula*:

{=INDEX($A$2:$A$11,SMALL(IF($A$2:$A$11<>"
",ROW($A$2:$A$11),1000),ROW()-ROW($B$2)+1)-ROW($B$2)+1)}

Enter the formula in cell B2, and copy it down the column, until the #REF! error is returned.

☞ To apply *Array formula:*

Select the cell, press **<F2>** and simultaneously press **<Ctrl+Shift+Enter>**.

	A	B	C	D	E
1	**List1**	**Result**			
2	1	1			
3	2	2			
4		4			
5	4	6			
6		7			
7	6	10			
8	7	#REF!			
9					
10					
11	10				
12					
13	**Formula Syntax in cell B2:**				
14	{=INDEX($A$2:$A$11,SMALL(IF($A$2:$A$11<>"",ROW ($A$2:$A$11),1000),ROW()-ROW($B$2)+1)- ROW($B$2)+1)}				
15					

Explanation:

The **IF** function returns an Array consisting of the row number (calculated by the **ROW** function) of each non-blank cell in List1 and the number 1000 for each blank cell.

The **ROW** functions in the following expression return the row numbers of the current cell and the first cell in the result column (cell $B$2):

ROW()-ROW($B$2)

The result of that calculation represents the position within List1 of the first non-blank cell that has not yet been retrieved.

The **SMALL** function returns the kth smallest number in the Array returned by the **IF** function, where kth is the number calculated by the above expression, plus 1.

Thus, it returns the row number of the first non-blank cell in List1 that has not yet been retrieved.

The row number of the first cell in the result column (cell $B$2) is then subtracted from the row number returned by the **SMALL** function, and 1 is added to the result.

The result of that calculation represents the position of the first non-blank cell that has not yet been retrieved from List1.

The **INDEX** function returns the value that is stored in that position in List1.

Thus, a list of all the non-blank cells in List1 is created.

Retrieving Values from a List that are Greater than a Specified Number

➢ **Problem:**

We want to retrieve all the numbers from List1 (column A) that are greater than the number specified in cell B2.

➢ **Solution:**

Use the **INDEX**, **SMALL**, **IF**, and **ROW** functions as shown in the following *Array formula*:

{=INDEX($A$2:$A$8,SMALL(IF($A$2:$A$8>$B$2,ROW($A$2:$A$8)-ROW($C$2)+1,100),ROW()-ROW($C$2)+1))}

Enter the formula in cell C2 and then copy it down the column until the #REF! error is returned.

☞ To apply *Array formula:*

Select the cell, press **<F2>** and simultaneously press **<Ctrl+Shift+Enter>**.

	A	B	C	D	E	F
1	**List1**	**Criteria**	**Result**			
2	5	6	12			
3	12		7			
4	2		8			
5	7		#REF!			
6	1					
7	4					
8	8					
9						
10	**Array Formula Syntax in cell C2:**					
11	{=INDEX($A$2:$A$8,SMALL(IF($A$2:$A$8>$B$2,ROW($A$2:$A$8) -ROW($C$2)+1,100),ROW()-ROW($C$2)+1))}					
12						

Explanation:

The **IF** function returns an Array consisting of the row number (calculated by the **ROW** function) of each value in List1 that is greater than the number in cell B2, and the number 100 for each value that isn't.

The **ROW** functions in the following expression return the row numbers of the current cell and the first cell in the result column (cell $C$2):

ROW()-ROW($C$2)

The result of this expression represents the number of values that have been retrieved from List1 so far.

The **SMALL** function returns the kth smallest number in the Array returned by the **IF** function, where kth is the number calculated by the above expression, plus 1.

Thus, it returns the row number of the first value in List1 that is greater than the number in cell B2 and has not yet been retrieved.

The row number of the first cell in the result column (cell $C$2) is then subtracted from the row number returned by the **SMALL** function, and 1 is added to the result.

The result of that calculation represents the position within List1 of the first value that is greater than the number in cell B2 and that has not yet been retrieved.

The **INDEX** function returns the value stored in that position in List1.

Thus, a list is created of all the values in List1 that are greater than the number in cell B2.

Checking for Sequences within a Sorted List

> **Problem:**

List1 (column A) is a series of numbers that has been sorted in ascending order.

We want to create a formula that will check whether each number is part of a consecutive sequence.

> **Solution:**

Use the **IF** and **OR** functions as shown in the following formula:

=IF(OR((A2+1=A3),(A2-1=A1)),"Sequential","Not Sequential")

	A	B	C	D	E
1	**List1**	**Result**			
2	1	Sequential			
3	2	Sequential			
4	4	Not Sequential			
5	6	Sequential			
6	7	Sequential			
7	9	Not Sequential			
8	11	Sequential			
9	12	Sequential			
10					
11	**Formula Syntax in cell B2:**				
12	=IF(OR((A2+1=A3),(A2-1=A1)),"Sequential","Not Sequential")				
13					

Explanation:

The **OR** function returns TRUE if the number in cell A2 plus 1 equals the number succeeding it (cell A3), or if the number in cell A2 minus 1 equals the number preceding it (cell A1).

Thus, TRUE is returned if the number in cell A2 is sequential to either of its immediate neighbors.

If TRUE is returned, the **IF** function returns the string "Sequential". Otherwise, it returns "Not Sequential".

Identifying Duplicate Values

Checking for Duplicate Values within a Range

➤ **Problem:**

Columns A & B contain two lists of values.

We want to create a formula that will check whether there is any duplication of values within either list (blank cells are to be ignored).

> ### Solution:

Use the **IF**, **COUNTA**, **SUMPRODUCT**, and **COUNTIF** functions as shown in the following formula:

=IF(COUNTA(A2:A7)=SUMPRODUCT((A2:A7<>" ")/COUNTIF(A2:A7,A2:A7&"")),"No Duplicates","Duplicates")

The formula will return "Duplicates" if the list contains duplicate values, otherwise it will return "No Duplicates".

	A	B	C	D
1	List1	List2		
2	1	1		
3	2			
4	3	B		
5	A	2		
6		3		
7	1	4		
8				
9	Result List1	Duplicates		
10	Result List2	No Duplicates		
11				
12	Formula Syntax in cell B9:			
13	=IF(COUNTA(A2:A7)=SUMPRODUCT((A2:A7<>"")/COUNTIF (A2:A7,A2:A7&"")),"No Duplicates","Duplicates")			
14				
15	Formula Syntax in cell B10:			
16	=IF(COUNTA(B2:B7)=SUMPRODUCT((B2:B7<>"")/COUNTIF (B2:B7,B2:B7&"")),"No Duplicates","Duplicates")			
17				

Explanation:

The **SUMPRODUCT** function (using the **COUNTIF** function) returns the number of unique values in List1.

The **COUNTA** function returns the total number of values (non-blank cells) in List1.

These two results are then compared. If they are equal, the **IF** function returns the string "No Duplicates". Otherwise, it returns "Duplicates".

Identifying Duplicate Rows within a Range

➤ **Problem:**

The range A2:C6 contains a list of items with their matching categories and prices.

Any rows containing identical entries are duplicate records.

We want to identify each duplicate record in the range.

➤ **Solution:**

Use the **SUMPRODUCT** function as shown in the following formula:

=SUMPRODUCT((B2=$B$2:$B$6)*(A2=$A$2:$A$6)*(C2=$C$2:$C$6))>1

	A	B	C	D	E	F	G
1	Item	Category	Price	Result			
2	T-Shirt	A	8	FALSE			
3	Jeans	B	5	FALSE			
4	T-Shirt	A	5	TRUE			
5	T-Shirt	C	8	FALSE			
6	T-Shirt	A	5	TRUE			
7							
8	**Formula Syntax in cell D2:**						
9	=SUMPRODUCT((B2=$B$2:$B$6)*(A2=$A$2:$A$6)*(C2=$C$2:$C$6))>1						
10							

Explanation:

The following expression returns an Array consisting of "1" (TRUE) for every value in cells B2:B6 that equals the value in cell B2 and "0" (FALSE) for every value that doesn't:

B2=$B$2:$B$6

Similar expressions are used regarding columns A & C and the values entered in cells A2 & C2.

The **SUMPRODUCT** function adds the products of the corresponding values in all three Arrays.

Thus, a count is returned of all the rows in range A2:C6 that contain the three values stored in cells A2:C2.

If that count is larger than 1 (i.e. the same combination of values appears in more than one row), TRUE is returned. Otherwise, FALSE is returned.

Determining and Indicating the Number of Times Each Value Has Been Entered in a List

➤ **Problem:**

We want to create a formula to determine the total number of times each value in List1 (column A) has been entered. The formula should also provide a textual indication of the calculated frequency.

➤ **Solution:**

Use the **IF** and **COUNTIF** functions as shown in the following formula:

=IF(COUNTIF($A$2:$A$8,A2)=1,"Unique",
COUNTIF($A$2:$A$8,A2)&" Duplicates")

	A	B	C	D
1	**List1**	**Result**		
2	1	3 Duplicates		
3	2	2 Duplicates		
4	4	Unique		
5	1	3 Duplicates		
6	3	Unique		
7	2	2 Duplicates		
8	1	3 Duplicates		
9				
10	**Formula Syntax in cell B2:**			
11	=IF(COUNTIF($A$2:$A$8,A2)=1,"Unique", COUNTIF($A$2:$A$8,A2)&" Duplicates")			
12				

Explanation:

The **COUNTIF** function returns the number of values in List1 (cells A2:A8) that are equal to the one entered in cell A2.

If that number is equal to 1, the **IF** function returns the string "Unique".

Otherwise, it returns a string composed of the result of the **COUNTIF** function and the text "Duplicates".

Transposing a List

Transposing an Entire Range of Data into a Single Column

➢ Problem:

Transposing all the values from Data Range (cells B3:E5) into a single column.

➢ Solution:

❖ To process the values in Data Range from left to right (i.e. row by row):

Use the **OFFSET**, **INT**, **ROW**, and **MOD** functions as shown in the formula in cell H3:

=OFFSET($B$3,INT((ROW()-ROW($H$3))/4),MOD(ROW()-ROW($H$3),4))

❖ To process the values in Data Range from top to bottom (i.e. column by column):

Use the **OFFSET**, **MOD**, **ROW**, and **INT** functions as shown in the following formula in cell I3:

=OFFSET($B$3,MOD(ROW()-ROW($I$3),3),INT((ROW()-ROW($I$3))/3))

	A	B	C	D	E	F	G	H	I
1									
2				Data Range				Data Range Left to Right	Data Range Top to Bottom
3		2	3	4	10			2	2
4		1	7	8	12			3	1
5		9	5	6	20			4	9
6								10	3
7								1	7
8								7	5
9								8	4
10	Left to Right Formula Syntax in cell H3:							12	8
11	=OFFSET($B$3,INT((ROW()-ROW($H$3))/4),MOD(ROW()-ROW($H$3),4))							9	6
12								5	10
13	Top to Bottom Formula Syntax in cell I3:							6	12
14	=OFFSET($B$3,MOD(ROW()-ROW($I$3),3),INT((ROW()-ROW($I$3))/3))							20	20
15									

Explanation:

☞ **Left to Right Formula (cell H3):**

The **ROW** functions in the following expression return the row numbers of the current cell and the first cell in the result column (cell $H$3):

ROW()-ROW($H$3)

The result of this expression represents the number of values that have been retrieved from Data Range so far, and is used to calculate the row_num and column_num arguments of the **OFFSET** function.

row_num:

The number calculated by the **ROW** functions is divided by 4 (the number of values in each row of Data Range), and the **INT** function rounds the result to the nearest integer. The result represents the number of full rows in Data Range that have been retrieved so far.

column_num:

The **MOD** function divides the number calculated by the **ROW** functions by 3 (the number of values in each column of Data Range), and returns the remainder. The result represents the number of values retrieved so far from the row that is currently being processed.

The **OFFSET** function offsets the reference of the first cell in Data Range (cell B3) by as many rows and columns as the numbers calculated by the **INT** and **MOD** functions.

Thus, each of the values in the first row is processed, and then the values in the second row, and so on.

☞ **Top to Bottom Formula (cell I3):**

The **ROW** functions in the following expression return the row numbers of the current cell and the first cell in the result column ($I$3):

ROW()-ROW($I$3)

The result of this expression represents the number of values that have been retrieved from Data Range so far, and is used to calculate the row_num and column_num arguments of the **OFFSET** function.

row_num:

The number calculated by the **ROW** functions is divided by 3 (the number of values in each column of Data Range), and the **INT** function rounds the result to the nearest integer. The result represents the number of full columns in Data Range that have been retrieved so far.

column_num:

The **MOD** function divides the number calculated by the **ROW** functions by 4 (the number of values in each row of Data Range), and returns the remainder. The result represents the number of values retrieved so far from the column that is currently being processed.

The **OFFSET** function offsets the reference of the first cell in Data Range (cell B3) by as many rows and columns as the numbers calculated by the **INT** and **MOD** functions.

Thus, each of the values in the first column is processed, then the values in the second column, and so on.

Transposing a Column into Successive Rows of a Specified Length

> ### Problem:

Transposing List1 (column A) into successive three-cell rows.

> ### Solution:

Use the **OFFSET**, **ROW**, and **COLUMN** functions as shown in the following formula in cell C2:

=OFFSET($A$2,(ROW()-ROW($C$2)+1)*3-3+COLUMN()-COLUMN($C$2),0)

Copy the formula across to D2 & E2, and then copy all three cells down columns C:E.

	A	B	C	D	E	F	G	H
1	List1			Result				
2	A		A	B	C			
3	B		D	E	F			
4	C		G	H	I			
5	D		J	K	L			
6	E							
7	F							
8	G							
9	H		Formula Syntax in cell C2:					
10	I		=OFFSET($A$2,(ROW()-ROW($C$2)+1)*3-3+COLUMN()-COLUMN($C$2),0)					
11	J							
12	K							
13	L							
14								

Explanation:

The **ROW** and **COLUMN** functions return the row and column numbers of the current cell and the first cell in the result range (cell C2).

Those numbers are used to calculate the position of the current cell within the result range.

Based on that position and the number of cells to be transposed into each row (3), the formula calculates the number of values that have been retrieved from List1 so far (i.e. if the current cell was cell D2, the result would be 1).

The **OFFSET** function offsets the reference "$A$2" (the first cell in List1) as many rows as the number calculated above.

Transposing a Range in Ascending Order

➤ **Problem:**

Columns A & B contain a list of client payments, and the dates they were made.

We want to transpose the data from columns A & B (cells A2:B6) into rows 1 & 2 (E1:I2). In doing so, the payments are to be sorted from earliest to latest.

➤ **Solution:**

Use the **SMALL** and **COLUMN** functions as shown in the following formula and enter the formula in cells E1:I1 :

=SMALL($A$2:$A$6,COLUMN()-COLUMN($E$1)+1)

Then, use the **INDEX** and **MATCH** functions as shown in the following formula and enter the formula in cells E2:I2:

=INDEX($B$2:$B$6,MATCH(E1,$A$2:$A$6,0))

	A	B	C	D	E	F	G	H	I
1	**Pay Date**	**Payment**		**Pay Date**	12/20/2004	01/10/2005	03/05/2005	05/14/2005	07/08/2005
2	03/05/2005	$2,500		**Payment**	$2,050	$3,000	$2,500	$1,750	$1,800
3	01/10/2005	$3,000							
4	07/08/2005	$1,800							
5	12/20/2004	$2,050							
6	05/14/2005	$1,750							
7									
8	**Formula Syntax in E1:I1**								
9	=SMALL($A$2:$A$6,COLUMN()-COLUMN($E$1)+1)								
10									
11	**Formula Syntax in E2:I2**								
12	=INDEX($B$2:$B$6,MATCH(E1,$A$2:$A$6,0))								
13									

Explanation:

☞ **Pay Date Formula (cells E1:I1):**

The **COLUMN** functions in the following expression return the column numbers of the current cell and the first cell in the result row (cell $E$1):

COLUMN()-COLUMN($E$1)

The result of this expression represents the number of pay dates that have been retrieved from cells A2:A6 so far.

The **SMALL** function returns the kth earliest date in cells A2:A6, where kth is the number calculated by the above expression, plus 1.

Thus, it returns the earliest pay date that has not yet been retrieved; resulting in an ascending list of dates in row 1.

☞ **Payment Formula (cells E2:I2):**

The **MATCH** function returns the position (row number) within cells A2:A6 of the date returned into E1.

The **INDEX** function returns the payment stored at the same position within cells B2:B6.

Thus, the payment matching each date in row 1 is returned into row 2.

Transposing Values from Columns into Rows, and Vice Versa

➤ **Problem:**

Transposing the values in List1 (cells A2:A5) into a row, and the values in List2 (cells B10:F10) into a column.

➤ **Solution 1: To transpose from a Column into a Row.**

To transpose the values in Column A (List1) into a Row:

Using the **INDEX** and **COLUMN** functions, enter the following formula in cell C2, and then copy it across the next 3 cells in the row:

=INDEX($A$2:$A$5,COLUMN()-COLUMN($C$2)+1)

Alternative solution:

Select cells C2:F2 and enter the **TRANSPOSE** function as shown in the following *Array formula*:

{=TRANSPOSE(A2:A5)}

➢ **Solution 2: To transpose from a Row into a Column.**

To transpose the values in Row 10 (List2) into a Column:

Using the **INDEX** and **ROW** functions, enter the following formula in cell H10, and then copy it down to the next 4 cells in the column:

=INDEX($B$10:$F$10,ROW()-ROW($H$10)+1)

Alternative solution:

Select cells H10:H14 and enter the **TRANSPOSE** function as shown in the following *Array formula*:

{=TRANSPOSE(B10:F10)}

☞ To apply *Array formula:*

Select the cell, press <**F2**> and simultaneously press <**Ctrl+Shift+Enter**>.

	A	B	C	D	E	F	G	H
1	List1		Transposed List1 From Row to Column					
2	1		1	2	3	4		
3	2							
4	3		INDEX Formula Syntax in cell C2:					
5	4		=INDEX($A$2:$A$5,COLUMN()-COLUMN($C$2)+1)					
6			TRANSPOSE Array Formula			{=TRANSPOSE(A2:A5)}		
7								
8								
9								Transposed List2
10	List2	5	6	7	8	9		5
11								6
12	INDEX Formula Syntax in cell H10:							7
13	=INDEX($B$10:$F$10,ROW()-ROW($H$10)+1)							8
14	TRANSPOSE Array Formula		{=TRANSPOSE(B10:F10)}					9
15								

Explanation:

☞ **Transposing from a Column into a Row:**

INDEX and **COLUMN** Formula:

The **COLUMN** functions in the following expression return the column numbers of the current cell and of the first cell in the result row (cell $C$2).

COLUMN()-COLUMN($C$2)+1

The result of that expression represents the position (serial number) of the value to be retrieved from List1 (cells A2:A5).

The **INDEX** function returns the value stored in that position in List1.

When the formula is copied to the next cell, the result of the above expression increases by 1 (with respect to the column number of the current cell), therefore, the formula returns the next value in List1.

☞ **TRANSPOSE Array Formula:**

The **TRANSPOSE** function returns an Array that is the transposed version of the Array representing List1 (cells A2:A5).

As the values in List1 are arranged in a column, the values in the Array returned by the **TRANSPOSE** function are arranged in a row.

That Array is returned into cells C2:F2 (selected on entering the formula).

☞ **Transposing from a Row into a Column:**

INDEX and **ROW** Formula:

The ROW functions in the following expression return the row numbers of the current cell and of the first cell in the result column (cell $H$10).

ROW()-ROW($H$10)+1

The result of that expression represents the position (serial number) of the value to be retrieved from List2 (cells B10:F10).

The **INDEX** function returns the value stored in that position in List2.

When the formula is copied to the next cell, the result of the above expression increases by 1 (with respect to the row number of the current cell), therefore, the formula returns the next value in List2.

☞ **TRANSPOSE Array Formula:**

The **TRANSPOSE** function returns an Array that is the transposed version of the Array representing List2 (cells B10:F10).

As the values in List2 are arranged in a row, the values in the Array returned by the **TRANSPOSE** function are arranged in a column.

That Array is returned into cells H10:H14 (selected on entering the formula).

Chapter 9

Miscellaneous Calculation & Math

About This Chapter

This chapter deals with formulas used for complex mathematical calculations and other miscellaneous calculations using various functions. It includes the following sections:

- ☞ **Averaging Values, page 363:** This section contains simple averaging calculations.

- ☞ **Averaging Using Criteria, page 365:** This section contains many examples that use criteria to calculate averages. For example, finding the average of list price and sale price, averaging sales by salesperson, averaging values from a dynamic range, averaging every Nth value, and more.

- ☞ **Finding Minimum / Maximum Values, page 382:** This section covers formulas dealing with minimum/maximum values in a list.

- ☞ **Rounding Values, page 390**: This section contains various formulas dealing with rounding of currency values, sales tax, numerical substrings, and more.

- ☞ **Ranking Values, page 398**: This section provides examples of formulas dealing with ranking lists of numbers, ranking values in a dynamic list, and calculating commissions based on sales ranking.

- ☞ **Random Calculation, page 402**: This section contains examples of formulas that deal with random calculations.

☞ **Miscellaneous Calculation, page 407**: This section contains solutions to many issues that are not allocated to other sections.

☞ **Converting Units, page 426**: In this section few examples using the **CONVERT** function to convert measurements of distance, temperature and units.

Averaging Values

Calculating Average Annual Growth

➢ **Problem:**

Columns A & B show annual profits for a number of years.

We want to calculate the average rate at which profits grew each year.

➢ **Solution:**

Use the **AVERAGE** function in the following *Array formula*:

{=AVERAGE((B3:B5-B2:B4)/B2:B4)}

☞ To apply *Array formula*:

Select the cell, press **<F2>** and simultaneously press **<Ctrl+Shift+Enter>**.

	A	B	C
1	**Year**	**Profit**	**Result**
2	2001	$80,000	65.87%
3	2002	$120,000	
4	2003	$280,000	
5	2004	$320,000	
6			
7	**Formula Syntax in cell C2:**		
8	{=AVERAGE((B3:B5-B2:B4)/B2:B4)}		
9			

Explanation:

An annual growth rate is calculated by subtracting last year's profit from this year's profit, and dividing the result by last year's profit.

The following expression returns an Array consisting of the difference between each profit in the years 2002-2004 (cells B3:B5) and the profit in the previous year (cells B2:B4):

B3:B5-B2:B4

Each difference in that Array is then divided by the corresponding profit in cells B2:B4.

Thus, an Array consisting of the annual growth rate for each year (2002-2004) is returned.

The **AVERAGE** function returns the average of all the values in that Array.

Thus, it returns the average rate at which profits grew each year.

Calculating the Average Growth of a Child

➢ **Problem:**

A child's height has been measured once a year.

Columns A & B show the results of these measurements for a period of six years.

We want to use these figures to calculate the average number of centimeters the child grew each year.

➢ **Solution:**

Use the **AVERAGE** function in the following *Array formula*:

{=AVERAGE(B3:B7-B2:B6)}

☞ To apply *Array formula:*

Select the cell, press <**F2**> and simultaneously press <**Ctrl+Shift+Enter**>.

	A	B	C
1	Age	Height (Cm)	Result
2	7	120	7.60
3	8	128	
4	9	134	
5	10	143	
6	11	150	
7	12	158	
8			
9	Formula Syntax in cell C2:		
10	{=AVERAGE(B3:B7-B2:B6)}		
11			

Explanation:

The following expression calculates the difference between each of the cells B3:B7 and the cell above it (cells B2:B6):

B3:B7-B2:B6

Thus, creating an Array containing the number of centimeters the child grew each year.

The **AVERAGE** function returns the average of all the values in that Array, which is the average number of centimeters the child grew each year.

Averaging Using Criteria

Calculating the Average for Numbers Meeting Specified Criteria

➢ **Problem:**

We want to calculate the average of all prices in column A that are higher than 200.

➢ **Solution:**

Use the **IF** and **AVERAGE** functions in the following *Array formula*:

{=AVERAGE(IF(A2:A7>B2,A2:A7))}

☞ To apply *Array formula:*

Select the cell, press <**F2**> and simultaneously press <**Ctrl+Shift+Enter**>.

	A	B	C	D
1	**Prices**	**Criteria**	**Result**	
2	500	200	330	
3	150			
4	40			
5	230			
6	110			
7	260			
8				
9	**Array Formula Syntax in cell C2:**			
10	{=AVERAGE(IF(A2:A7>B2,A2:A7))}			
11				

Explanation:

The following expression returns an Array consisting of TRUE for every value in column A that is greater than the value in cell B2, and FALSE for every value that isn't:

A2:A7>B2

The **IF** function returns an Array consisting of the values in column A (cells A2:A7) for which TRUE was returned by the above expression.

Thus, an Array is returned consisting of the prices in column A that are higher than the criteria in cell B2.

The **AVERAGE** function returns the average of all the values in that Array.

Calculating the Average Difference between List Price and Sale Price

➢ **Problem:**

Column A contains the list prices for a range of items. Their matching sale prices are shown in column B.

We want to calculate the average of the differences between the list and sale price and average difference in percentage.

➢ **Solution 1:**

To calculate the average difference in dollar amount, use the **AVERAGE** function in the following *Array Formula*:

{=AVERAGE(A2:A5-B2:B5)}

➢ **Solution 2:**

To calculate the average difference in dollar amount, use the **SUM** and **COUNT** functions in the following formula:

=(SUM(A2:A5)-SUM(B2:B5))/COUNT(A2:A5)

➢ **Solution 3:**

To calculate the average difference in percentage, use the **AVERAGE** function in the following *Array formula:*

{=AVERAGE((A2:A5/B2:B5-1)*100)}

☞ To apply *Array formula:*

Select the cell, press **<F2>** and simultaneously press **<Ctrl+Shift+Enter>**.

	A	B	C	D	E
1	**List Price**	**Sale Price**			
2	200	150			
3	120	100			
4	300	270			
5	50	50			
6					
7		**Result**	**Formula Syntax in cells B8, B9, B10:**		
8	Average Difference	25	{=AVERAGE(A2:A5-B2:B5)}		
9	Average Difference	25	=(SUM(A2:A5)-SUM(B2:B5))/COUNT(A2:A5)		
10	Average Difference (%)	16.111111	{=AVERAGE((A2:A5/B2:B5-1)*100)}		
11					

Explanation:

☞ **Explanation to Solution 1:**

The following expression returns an Array consisting of the difference between each value in cells A2:A5 (List Price) and the corresponding value in cells B2:B5 (Sale Price):

A2:A5-B2:B5

The **AVERAGE** function returns the average of all the values in that Array.

Thus, calculating the average difference between List Price and Sale Price.

☞ **Explanation to Solution 2:**

The first **SUM** function adds all the values in cells A2:A5 (List Prices).

The second **SUM** function adds all the values in cells B2:B5 (Sale Prices).

The sum of the Sale Prices is then subtracted from the sum of the List Prices, returning the total difference between all List Prices and all Sale Prices.

Finally, that difference is divided by the total number of prices in cells A2:A5 (returned by the **COUNT** function), returning the average difference between List Price and Sale Price.

☞ **Explanation to Solution 3:**

The following expression divides each value in cells A2:A5 (List Price) by the corresponding value in cells B2:B5 (Sale Price) and subtracts 1 from each result:

A2:A5/B2:B5-1

Thus, an Array is created that consists of the difference rate between each List Price and its corresponding Sale Price.

Each value in that Array is then multiplied by 100 to convert the rates to percentages.

The **AVERAGE** function returns the average of all the values in the Array.

Thus, calculating the average difference in percentage between List Price and Sale Price.

Finding Specified Items in a List and Averaging their Associated Values

➢ **Problem:**

We want to look up List1 (column A) for each of the values in column C. For each lookup, we want to calculate the average of all the numbers from List2 (column B) that correspond to matches in List1.

➤ **Solution:**

Use the **AVERAGE** and **IF** functions in the following *Array formula*:

{=AVERAGE(IF($A$2:$A$7=C2,$B$2:$B$7))}

☞ To apply *Array formula:*

Select the cell, press <**F2**> and simultaneously press <**Ctrl+Shift+Enter**>.

	A	B	C	D
1	List1	List2	Value to Look For	Result
2	A	20	A	11
3	B	2	B	3
4	A	5	C	1
5	B	4		
6	C	1		
7	A	8		
8				
9	Array Formula Syntax in cell D2:			
10	{=AVERAGE(IF($A$2:$A$7=C2,$B$2:$B$7))}			
11				

Explanation:

The **IF** function returns an Array consisting of all the numbers in List2 (cells B2:B7) that have corresponding values in List1 (cells A2:A7) that are equal to the value in cell C2.

The **AVERAGE** function returns the average of the numbers in that Array.

Excluding Exceptional Values when Calculating an Average

➤ **Problem:**

List1 (column A) contains 10 numbers, two of which (0 & 500) are significantly smaller or greater than the remainder.

If included in an average calculation, these exceptional values would disproportionately influence the result.

We, therefore, need a way of calculating an average that more accurately reflects the general spread of data.

➤ **Solution:**

Use the **TRIMMEAN** function as shown in the following formula:

=TRIMMEAN(A2:A11,0.2)

	A	B
1	**List1**	**Result**
2	100	104.5
3	105	
4	0	
5	102	
6	101	
7	500	
8	110	
9	106	
10	104	
11	108	
12		
13	**Formula Syntax in cell B2:**	
14	=TRIMMEAN(A2:A11,0.2)	
15		

Explanation:

The **TRIMMEAN** function returns the mean of the interior of a data set.

The first argument of this function is the data set to average.

The second argument is the percentage of top and bottom values to be excluded from the calculation.

Thus, the above **TRIMMEAN** function will average the middle 80% of the values in cells A2:A11; excluding both the top 10% (500) and the bottom 10% (0).

Calculating an Average, Only Including Prices on Which There Was no Discount

➢ **Problem:**

Calculating the average of the prices from column B, but only including those on which there was no discount (as shown in column A).

➢ **Solution 1:**

Use the **AVERAGE** and **IF** functions as shown in the following *Array Formula*:

{=AVERAGE(IF(A2:A6="No",B2:B6))}

☞ To apply *Array formula:*

Select the cell, press **<F2>** and simultaneously press **<Ctrl+Shift+Enter>**.

➢ **Solution 2:**

Use the **SUMIF** and **COUNTIF** functions as shown in the following formula:

=SUMIF(A2:A6,"No",B2:B6)/COUNTIF(A2:A6,"No")

	A	B	C	D
1	**Discount**	**Price**		
2	No	$50		
3	Yes	$100		
4	No	$80		
5	Yes	$200		
6	Yes	$120		
7				
8	**Result- Array Formula**	$65		
9	**Array Formula Syntax in cell B8:**			
10	{=AVERAGE(IF(A2:A6="No",B2:B6))}			
11				
12	**Result**	$65		
13	**Formula Syntax in cell B12:**			
14	=SUMIF(A2:A6,"No",B2:B6)/COUNTIF(A2:A6,"No")			
15				

Explanation:

☞ **Explanation to Solution 1:**

The **IF** function returns an Array consisting of all the values (Prices) in cells B2:B6 for which the corresponding string in cells A2:A6 is "No".

The **AVERAGE** function returns the average of all the values in that Array.

Thus, calculating the average of all the prices in column B on which there is no discount.

☞ **Explanation to Solution 2:**

The **SUMIF** function adds all the values in cells B2:B6 for which the corresponding strings in cells A2:A6 are "No".

Similarly, the **COUNTIF** function returns the number of values in cells B2:B6 for which the corresponding strings in cells A2:A6 are "No".

The sum calculated by the SUMIF function is then divided by the count returned by the **COUNTIF** function, returning the average of all the values in cells B2:B6 for which the corresponding strings in A2:A6 are "No".

Thus, calculating the average of all the prices in column B on which there is no discount.

Averaging Sales Totals by Day of the Week

➢ **Problem:**

Columns A & B contain dates and their matching sales totals.

We want to determine which day of the week corresponds with each date in column A, and then calculate an average sales figure for each day of the week over the whole period. That is, we want an average sales total for all of the Mondays, one for all the Tuesdays, and so on.

> ➤ **Solution:**

Use the **AVERAGE**, **IF**, and **WEEKDAY** functions in the following *Array formula:*

{=AVERAGE(IF(WEEKDAY(A2)=WEEKDAY($A$2:$A$16),$C$2:$C$16)}

☞ To apply *Array formula:*

Select the cell, press **<F2>** and simultaneously press **<Ctrl+Shift+Enter>**.

	A	B	C	D
				Average Sales Total per
1	**Date**	**Day of the Week**	**Sales Total**	**Weekday**
2	06/05/2005	Sunday	$2,000	$2,100
3	06/06/2005	Monday	$1,500	$1,575
4	06/07/2005	Tuesday	$1,200	$1,200
5	06/08/2005	Wednesday	$800	$1,100
6	06/09/2005	Thursday	$2,200	$2,075
7	06/10/2005	Friday	$3,000	$2,625
8	06/11/2005	Saturday	$0	$0
9	06/12/2005	Sunday	$1,800	$2,100
10	06/13/2005	Monday	$1,650	$1,575
11	06/14/2005	Tuesday	$1,200	$1,200
12	06/15/2005	Wednesday	$1,400	$1,100
13	06/16/2005	Thursday	$1,950	$2,075
14	06/17/2005	Friday	$2,250	$2,625
15	06/18/2005	Saturday	$0	$0
16	06/19/2005	Sunday	$2,500	$2,100
17				
18	**Array Formula Syntax in cell D2:**			
19	{=AVERAGE(IF(WEEKDAY(A2)=WEEKDAY($A$2:$A$16),$C$2:$C$16)}			
20				

Explanation:

The first **WEEKDAY** function in the following expression returns a serial number (1-7) that represents the day of the week corresponding with the date in cell A2:

WEEKDAY(A2)=WEEKDAY($A$2:$A$16)

Similarly, the second **WEEKDAY** function in that expression returns an Array of numbers, representing the day of the week corresponding with each date in cells A2:A16.

The result of the above expression is an Array consisting of TRUE for every date in cells A2:A16 that has a corresponding day of the week equal to that of the date in cell A2, and FALSE for every date that doesn't.

For each of the TRUE values in that Array, the **IF** function returns the corresponding value from column C (Sales Total).

Thus, an Array is created consisting of the sales totals for all the dates in column A that have the same day of the week as the date in cell A2.

The **AVERAGE** function returns the average of the values in that Array.

Averaging Values that Correspond with the X Largest Values in a Dynamic Range

➢ **Problem:**

Column A contains dates of recent basketball games.

Column B contains the number of points scored by a particular player during each game.

Whenever a new game is played, the relevant dates and scores are added to the sheet.

We want to create formulas that will average the most recent X number of scores for each value for X listed in column D. The formulas should automatically update whenever new data is added.

➢ **Solution:**

Use the **AVERAGE**, **IF**, and **LARGE** functions in the following *Array formula*:

{=AVERAGE(IF($A$2:$A$65000>=LARGE($A$2:$A$65000,D2),$B$2:$B$65000))}

☞ To apply *Array formula*:

Select the cell, press <**F2**> and simultaneously press <**Ctrl+Shift+Enter**>.

	A	B	C	D	E
1	Date of Game	Score		# Games to Average	Averaged Score
2	04/03/2005	18		2	15
3	04/10/2005	15		4	12.5
4	04/17/2005	10		6	13
5	04/24/2005	22		8	13.5
6	05/01/2005	8			
7	05/08/2005	12			
8	05/15/2005	16			
9	05/22/2005	12			
10	05/29/2005	8			
11	06/05/2005	10			
12	06/12/2005	20			
13					
14			Array Formula Syntax in cell E2:		
15			{=AVERAGE(IF($A$2:$A$65000>=LARGE($A$2:$A$65000,D2),$B$2:$B$65000))}		

Explanation:

The **LARGE** function returns the K largest number in column A (the kth most recent date), where kth is the Number of Games to Average in cell D2.

The **IF** function returns an Array consisting of all the scores in column B that have a corresponding date in column A later than or equal to the one returned by the **LARGE** function.

Thus, an Array is returned that contains the scores of the kth most recent games.

The **AVERAGE** function returns the average of the values in that Array.

Calculating the Average of a Range of Numbers, Excluding the Minimal Value

➢ **Problem:**

We want to identify the minimum value from the range A2:B5, and then perform an average calculation of the remaining numbers.

➢ **Solution:**

Use the **SUM, MIN,** and **COUNT** functions in the following formula:

=(SUM(A2:B5)-MIN(A2:B5))/(COUNT(A2:B5)-1)

	A	B	C	D	E
1	**Numbers**			**Result**	
2	20	1		14.43	
3	5	25			
4	13	16			
5	14	8			
6					
7	**Formula Syntax in cell D2:**				
8	=(SUM(A2:B5)-MIN(A2:B5))/(COUNT(A2:B5)-1)				
9					

Explanation:

The **SUM** function adds all the values in range A2:B5.

The **MIN** function returns the minimum number in that range.

As the minimum value is to be excluded in the calculation, the number returned by the **MIN** function is subtracted from the sum returned by the **SUM** function.

The result is then divided by the number of values in the range (calculated by the **COUNT** function) minus 1 (because the minimum value is excluded from the sum).

Thus, the formula returns the average of all the numbers in range A2:B5 except for the minimum.

Calculating the Average of Every Nth Value

➢ **Problem:**

Calculating the average of the values from every 4th line in a list.

➢ **Solution:**

Use the **AVERAGE**, **IF**, **MOD**, and **ROW** functions in the following *Array formula*:

{=AVERAGE(IF((MOD(ROW($B$2:$B$10)-
ROW($B$2)+1,C2))=0,$B$2:$B$10))}

☞ To apply *Array formula*:

Select the cell, press <**F2**> and simultaneously press
<**Ctrl+Shift+Enter**>.

	A	B	C	D	E	F
1	**Serial Number**	**Value**	**N Value**			
2	1	20	4			
3	2	40				
4	3	50	**Result**			
5	4	30	20			
6	5	8				
7	6	400				
8	7	35				
9	8	10				
10	9	100				
11						
12	**Array Formula Syntax in cell C5:**					
13	{=AVERAGE(IF((MOD(ROW($B$2:$B$10)-ROW($B$2)+1,C2))=0,$B$2:$B$10))}					
14						

Explanation:

The first **ROW** function in the following expression returns the row number of each cell in cells B2:B10:

ROW($B$2:$B$10)-ROW($B$2)+1

The second **ROW** function returns the row number of the first cell in the list (cell B2).

Those row numbers are used by the above expression to calculate an Array of serial numbers matching each cell in cells B2:B10.

The **MOD** function divides each of the serial numbers in the Array by the N value in cell C2 (4), and returns an Array consisting of the remainder of each calculation.

The **IF** function returns an Array consisting of all the values in cells B2:B10 that have serial numbers that are divisible by N (i.e. the remainder returned by the **MOD** function is 0).

The **AVERAGE** function returns the average of all the values in that Array, i.e. the average of the values from every nth (4th) line in the list.

Calculating the Average of Every Nth Value, Excluding Zeros

➢ **Problem:**

For each value of n found in column C, we want to calculate the average of every nth cell from List1. We also want to exclude any zeros from the calculation.

➢ **Solution:**

Use the **AVERAGE, IF, MOD,** and **ROW** functions as shown in the following *Array formula*:

{=AVERAGE(IF((MOD(ROW($A$2:$A$13)-
ROW($A$2)+1,C2)=0)*($A$2:$A$13<>0),$A$2:$A$13))}

☞ To apply *Array formula*:

Select the cell, press **<F2>** and simultaneously press **<Ctrl+Shift+Enter>**.

	A	B	C	D	E
1	**List1**		**N Value**	**Result**	
2	5		3	12	
3	10		5	15	
4	2				
5	12				
6	0				
7	9				
8	20				
9	6				
10	0				
11	15				
12	8				
13	25				
14					
15	**Formula Syntax in cell D2:**				
16	{=AVERAGE(IF((MOD(ROW($A$2:$A$13)-ROW($A$2)+1,C2)=0)*($A$2:$A$13<>0),$A$2:$A$13))}				
17					

Explanation:

The first **ROW** function in the following expression returns the row number of each cell in List1 (cells A2:A13):

ROW($A$2:$A$13)-ROW($A$2)+1

The second **ROW** function returns the row number of the first cell in the list (cell A2).

Those row numbers are used by the above expression to calculate an Array of serial numbers matching each cell in List1.

The **MOD** function divides each of the serial numbers in that Array by the N value in cell C2, and returns an Array consisting of the remainder of each calculation.

The following expression returns an additional Array consisting of TRUE for every value in List1 that is not equal to 0 and FALSE for every other value:

$A$2:$A$13<>0

The **IF** function returns an Array consisting of the values in List1 for which TRUE was returned by the above expression (non-zeros) and for which the serial numbers (calculated above) were divisible by N (i.e. the remainder returned by the **MOD** function is 0).

The **AVERAGE** function returns the average of all the values in that Array.

Thus, an average is calculated for every nth cell in List1, excluding zeros.

Calculating the Average Value in Every Nth Column, Excluding Zeros

> ## Problem:

Row 2 contains numeric values, with their matching serial numbers shown in row 1.

We want to calculate an average of the values from every 3rd column, excluding zeros from the calculation.

> ## Solution:

Use the **AVERAGE, IF, MOD, COLUMN,** and **CELL** functions in the following *Array formula*:

{=AVERAGE(IF((MOD(COLUMN(B2:K2)-CELL("col",B2)+1,E4)=0)*(B2:K2<>0),B2:K2))}

☞ To apply *Array formula:*

Select the cell, press **<F2>** and simultaneously press **<Ctrl+Shift+Enter>**.

	A	B	C	D	E	F	G	H	I	J	K
1	Serial Number	1	2	3	4	5	6	7	8	9	10
2	Value	20	12	6	4	10	50	30	2	0	18
3											
4	Array Formula	28		N Value	3						
5											
6	Array Formula Syntax in cell B4:										
7	{=AVERAGE(IF((MOD(COLUMN(B2:K2)-CELL("col",B2)+1,E4)=0)*(B2:K2<>0),B2:K2))}										
8											

Explanation:

The **COLUMN** function in the following expression returns the column number of each numeric value in row 2 (cells B2:K2):

COLUMN(B2:K2)-CELL("col",B2)+1,

The **CELL** function returns the column number (specified by using the string "col" as the first argument of the function) of the first numeric value in the row (cell B2).

Those column numbers are used by the above expression to calculate an Array of serial numbers matching each numeric value in row 2.

The **MOD** function divides each of the serial numbers in that Array by the N value in cell E4, and returns an Array consisting of the remainder of each calculation.

The following expression returns an additional Array consisting of TRUE for every numeric value in row 2 that is not equal to 0 and FALSE for every other value:

B2:K2<>0

The **IF** function returns an Array consisting of the values in row 2 for which TRUE was returned by the above expression (non-zeros) and for which the serial numbers (calculated above) were divisible by N (i.e. the remainder returned by the **MOD** function is 0).

The **AVERAGE** function returns the average of all the values in that Array.

Thus, an average is calculated for every nth value in row 2, excluding zeros.

Finding Minimum / Maximum Values

Finding the Minimum Value in a Referenced Range

➢ **Problem:**

Column A contains a list of numbers.

We want to find the minimum value in the range between row 2 (first value in the list) and each row number specified in column B.

➢ **Solution:**

Use the **MIN** and **INDIRECT** functions in the following formula:

=MIN(INDIRECT("$A$2:A"&B2))

	A	B	C
1	**List1**	**Row Number**	**Result**
2	100	2	100
3	25	3	25
4	400	4	25
5	30	5	25
6	2	6	2
7	30	7	2
8			
9	**Formula Syntax in cell C2:**		
10	=MIN(INDIRECT("$A$2:A"&B2))		
11			

Explanation:

The text "$A$2:A" and the row number stored in cell B2 are joined into a single string.

The **INDIRECT** function returns the reference indicated by that string, which is the reference of the range in column A that is between row 2 (first value in the list) and the row number specified in cell B2.

The **MIN** function returns the minimum value in that range.

Calculating the Lowest Common Multiple (LCM)

➢ **Problem:**

Calculating the lowest common multiple of each pair of numbers in columns A & B.

➢ **Solution 1:**

Use the **MAX**, **LEFT**, **TEXT**, and **MIN** functions in the following formula:

=MAX(A2:B2)*LEFT(TEXT(MIN(A2:B2)/MAX(A2:B2),"0000000/0000000"),7)

➢ **Solution 2:**

Use the **LCM** function in the following formula:

=LCM(A2:B2)

	A	B	C	D	E	F
1	**Num1**	**Num2**	**Regular Formula**	**LCM Formula**		
2	2	3	6	6		
3	10	12	60	60		
4	34	52	884	884		
5	107	33	3531	3531		
6	6	8	24	24		
7						
8	**Regular Formula Syntax in cell C2:**					
9	=MAX(A2:B2)*LEFT(TEXT(MIN(A2:B2)/MAX(A2:B2),"0000000/0000000"),7)					
10						
11	**LCM Formula Syntax in cell D2:**					
12	=LCM(A2:B2)					
13						

Explanation:

☞ **Explanation to Solution 1:**

The **MIN** function returns the minimum value in cells A2:B2, i.e. the smaller number of that pair.

Similarly, the **MAX** function (the second one in the formula) returns the larger number of the pair.

The smaller number is then divided by the larger number. The **TEXT** function formats the result as "0000000/0000000", and converts it to text.

The result of the **TEXT** function is a string representing the reduced fraction created by the above calculation.

Hence, the string "0000002/0000003" is returned for the values in cells A2:B2, "0000005/0000006" is returned for the values in cells A3:B3, and so on.

The **LEFT** function returns the 7 leftmost characters of that string, i.e. the numerator of the reduced fraction.

Finally, the larger number in cells A2:B2 (returned by the first **MAX** function in the formula) is multiplied by the number represented by the result of the **LEFT** function.

The result of that calculation is the lowest common multiple of the numbers in cells A2:B2.

☞ **Explanation to Solution 2:**

The **LCM** function returns the least common multiple of the numbers in cells A2:B2.

 Analysis ToolPak Add-In:

The **LCM** function is included in the Analysis ToolPak Add-In. To install the Analysis ToolPak Add-in: Select *Tools → Add-Ins → Analysis ToolPak*, Click OK.

Returning the Nth Largest / Smallest Values in a Range

➢ **Problem:**

Finding variously ranked numbers in List1. For example, the second largest number, the third smallest number, and so on.

➢ **Solution:**

Use the **LARGE** and **SMALL** functions in the following formulas:

To find 2nd largest number enter:

=LARGE(A2:A8,2)

To find 3rd smallest number enter:

=SMALL(A2:A8,3)

	A	B	C	D
1	**List1**		**Result**	**Formula Syntax in column C**
2	20	2nd largest number	50	=LARGE(A2:A8,2)
3	10	4th largest number	15	=LARGE(A2:A8,4)
4	50			
5	5		**Result**	
6	80	3rd smallest number	10	=SMALL(A2:A8,3)
7	4	5th smallest number	20	=SMALL(A2:A8,5)
8	15			
9				

Explanation:

The **LARGE** and **SMALL** functions return the kth largest/smallest number in a data set.

The first argument of those functions is the data set (range reference/ Array).

The second argument is the number to be used as K.

Finding the Largest Number among Those Meeting Specified Criteria

➤ **Problem:**

Column A contains 5-digit numbers.

We want to find the largest number from the list whose first two digits are "11".

➤ **Solution:**

Use the **MAX**, **LEFT,** and **TEXT** functions in the following *Array formula*:

{=MAX((LEFT(A2:A6,2)=TEXT(C2,"@"))*A2:A6)}

☞ To apply *Array formula:*

Select the cell, press <**F2**> and simultaneously press <**Ctrl+Shift+Enter**>.

	A	B	C	D
1	**Numbers**		**Criteria**	
2	11509		11	
3	14204			
4	11703		**Array Formula**	
5	22908		11703	
6	11305			
7				
8	**Array Formula Syntax in cell C5:**			
9	{=MAX((LEFT(A2:A6,2)=TEXT(C2,"@"))*A2:A6)}			
10				

Explanation:

The **LEFT** function extracts the two leftmost characters of each string in cells A2:A6 (the first two digits).

The **TEXT** function formats the number in cell C2 as "@" and converts it to text.

The text, representing the criteria in cell C2, is then compared with the two first digits of each string in column A (extracted by the **LEFT** function).

Thus, an Array is returned consisting of "1" (TRUE) for each number in column A which has its first two digits the same as the digits in cell C2, and "0" for each that doesn't.

Each value in that Array is multiplied by the number it represents in column A.

Thus, an Array is returned containing all the numbers in column A that meet the criteria (first two digits are the same as the digits in cell C2) and zeros for of all the numbers that don't.

The **MAX** function returns the largest value in that Array, which is the largest number in column A that has "11" as its first two digits.

Finding the Score that Was the Nth Highest for a Specified Team

➤ **Problem:**

Range A2:C6 shows the respective teams and scores for a group of players.

We want to create a formula that will retrieve the second highest score from column C that matches each team listed in column E.

➤ **Solution:**

Use the **LARGE** function in the following *Array formula*:

{=LARGE(($B$2:$B$6=E2)*($C$2:$C$6),2)}

☞ To apply *Array formula:*

Select the cell, press **<F2>** and simultaneously press **<Ctrl+Shift+Enter>**.

	A	B	C	D	E	F
1	**Player**	**Team**	**Score**		**Team**	**Result**
2	Jerry	Team1	22		Team1	17
3	Mark	Team2	18		Team2	18
4	Michael	Team1	10			
5	Anthony	Team1	17			
6	David	Team2	21			
7						
8	**Array Formula Syntax in cell F2:**					
9	{=LARGE(($B$2:$B$6=E2)*($C$2:$C$6),2)}					
10						

Explanation:

The following expression returns an Array consisting of "1" (TRUE) for each team name in cell B2:B6 that equals the team criteria in cell E2 and "0" (FALSE) for each team name that doesn't.

$B$2:$B$6=E2

Each value in that Array, representing a team name in column B, is then multiplied by the corresponding score from column C.

Thus returning an Array containing all the Scores of the Team specified in cell E2, and zeros for the scores of all other teams.

The **LARGE** function returns the 2nd largest number in that Array, which is the 2nd highest score by the team specified in cell E2.

Finding the Largest Value from Two Different Lists, Subject to Specified Criteria

➤ **Problem:**

Columns A & B contain two lists of numbers.

We want to create a formula that will return the maximum value from either list, providing that the following two conditions are satisfied:

❖ Numbers from List1 must be larger than 3.

❖ Numbers from List2 must be larger than 20.

If the maximum value found does not meet the above criteria, the formula should look for the next largest number until finding the largest number matching criteria.

➢ **Solution:**

Use the **MAX** functions in the following *Array Formula*:

{=MAX(MAX((A2:A5>C2)*A2:A5),MAX((B2:B5>C3)*B2:B5))}

☞ To apply *Array formula:*

Select the cell, press **<F2>** and simultaneously press **<Ctrl+Shift+Enter>**.

	A	B	C	D	E	F
1	**List1**	**List2**	**Criteria**	**Result**		
2	3	20	3	22		
3	5	22	20			
4	1	14				
5	2	4				
6						
7	**Array Formula in cell D2:**					
8	{=MAX(MAX((A2:A5>C2)*A2:A5),MAX((B2:B5>C3)*B2:B5))}					
9						

Explanation:

The following expression returns an Array consisting of "1" (TRUE) for each number in List1 that is greater than the criteria in cell C2 and "0" (FALSE) for each number that isn't:

A2:A5>C2

Each value in that Array is then multiplied by the number it represents in List1.

Thus returning an Array consisting of all the numbers in List1 that meet the criteria in cell C2 and zeros for the ones that don't.

The **MAX** function (the second one in the formula) returns the maximum value in that Array, which is the largest number in List1 that is greater than the criteria in cell C2.

Similarly, the third **MAX** function in the formula returns the largest number in List2 that is greater than the criteria in cell C3.

The first **MAX** function in the formula returns the larger of the two numbers returned by the second and third **MAX** functions.

Rounding Values

Rounding Prices to the Nearest Nickel, Dime, Quarter and Dollar

➢ **Problem:**

Rounding the prices in column A to the nearest nickel (5 cents), dime (10 cents), quarter (25 cents), and dollar.

➢ **Solution:**

Use the **ROUND** function in the following formulas:

Nearest Nickel Formula =ROUND(A2*20,0)/20

Nearest Dime Formula =ROUND(A2*10,0)/10

Nearest Quarter Formula =ROUND(A2*4,0)/4

Nearest Dollar Formula =ROUND(A2,0)

	A	B	C	D	E
1	**Prices**	**Nearest Nickel**	**Nearest Dime**	**Nearest Quarter**	**Nearest Dollar**
2	$13.13	$13.15	$13.10	$13.25	$13.00
3	$4.46	$4.45	$4.50	$4.50	$4.00
4	$22.64	$22.65	$22.60	$22.75	$23.00
5					
6	Nearest Nickel Formula in cell B2:	=ROUND(A2*20,0)/20			
7	Nearest Dime Formula in cell C2:	=ROUND(A2*10,0)/10			
8	Nearest Quarter Formula in cell D2:	=ROUND(A2*4,0)/4			
9	Nearest Dollar Formula in cell E2:	=ROUND(A2,0)			
10					

Explanation:

Nearest Nickel Formula:

The price in cell A2 is multiplied by 20 (representing the number of nickels in a dollar).

The **ROUND** function rounds the result of the calculation to the nearest integer (0 decimal places).

Finally, the number returned by the **ROUND** function is divided by 20 (representing the number of nickels in a dollar).

Thus, the formula rounds the price in cell A2 to the nearest nickel.

Dividing an Amount into Equal Payments While Avoiding Division / Rounding Errors

➢ **Problem:**

The price in cell B1 must be divided accurately into 5 similar payments.

When simply dividing the price $48.04 by 5 and rounding the result to two decimal places, we get individual payments of $9.61.

However, this would add up to a total payment of $48.05, which is not the exact amount we started with.

Therefore, we want to calculate 5 similar numbers that add up to the total amount.

➢ **Solution:**

Step 1: Calculate the first payment by dividing the price by 5 and rounding the result.

Use the **ROUND** function in the following formula:

=ROUND(B1/5,2)

Step 2: Calculate each remaining payment.

Use the **ROUND**, **SUM**, and **ROW** functions in the following formula:

=ROUND(($B$1-SUM($B$2:B2))/(5-ROW()+ROW($B$2)),2)

	A	B	C	D	E	F	G	H
1	Total Price	$48.04		Formula Syntax in column B:				
2	Payment 1	$9.61		=ROUND(B1/5,2)				
3	Payment 2	$9.61		=ROUND(($B$1-SUM($B$2:B2))/(5-ROW()+ROW($B$2)),2)				
4	Payment 3	$9.61		=ROUND(($B$1-SUM($B$2:B3))/(5-ROW()+ROW($B$2)),2)				
5	Payment 4	$9.61		=ROUND(($B$1-SUM($B$2:B4))/(5-ROW()+ROW($B$2)),2)				
6	Payment 5	$9.60		=ROUND(($B$1-SUM($B$2:B5))/(5-ROW()+ROW($B$2)),2)				
7								

Explanation:

In order to find the 5 similar payments, we have to calculate each payment by dividing the current price (original price - payments already calculated) by the number of remaining payments (those not yet calculated).

☞ **First Payment Formula:**

The price in cell B1 is divided by 5 (the total number of payments).

The **ROUND** function rounds the result to 2 decimal places.

☞ **Formula for Each Remaining Payment:**

The **SUM** function adds all the values in the range between cell $B$2 (the first payment) and the cell above the current one in column B (range $B$2:B2).

Thus, it calculates the sum of all the payments already calculated.

That sum is then subtracted from the original price in cell B1, returning the current price.

The current price is then divided by the number of remaining payments, calculated by subtracting the row number of the current cell (returned by the first **ROW** function) from the total number of payments (5) and adding the row number of the first payment (calculated by the second **ROW** function).

Finally, the **ROUND** function rounds the result of that calculation to 2 decimal places.

Rounding the Calculation of Retail Price and Sales Tax

> ➤ **Problem:**

Calculating the retail price and sales tax (7.75 percent) for each price in column A.

> ➤ **Solution:**

To calculate Retail Price use the **ROUND** function in the following formula:

=ROUND(A2/(1+7.75%),2)

To calculate Sales Tax use the **ROUND** function in the following formula:

=ROUND(7.75%*B2,2)

	A	B	C
1	**Total Price**	**Retail Price**	**Sales Tax**
2	$20.00	$18.56	$1.44
3	$15.00	$13.92	$1.08
4	$100.00	$92.81	$7.19
5	$250.00	$232.02	$17.98
6	$60.00	$55.68	$4.32
7			
8	**Formula Syntax in cell B2:**		
9	=ROUND(A2/(1+7.75%),2)		
10			
11	**Formula Syntax in cell C2:**		
12	=ROUND(7.75%*B2,2)		
13			

Explanation:

☞ **Retail Price Formula:**

The Total Price in cell A2 is divided by 107.75% (1+7.75%).

The result of that calculation is the Retail Price (excluding Sales Tax) for the Total Price in cell A2.

The **ROUND** function rounds the result to 2 decimal places.

☞ **Sales Tax Formula:**

The Retail Price in cell B2, calculated by the first formula, is multiplied by 7.75%.

The result of that calculation is the Sales Tax for the Total Price in cell A2.

The **ROUND** function rounds the result to 2 decimal places.

Rounding Up / Down to the Nearest Multiple of a Specific Number

➤ **Problem:**

Rounding the numbers in List1 (column A) to the nearest multiple of 50. We want to round both up and down.

➤ **Solution:**

To round up, use the **CEILING** function in the following formula:

=CEILING(A2,50)

To round down, use the **FLOOR** function in the following formula:

=FLOOR(A2,50)

	A	B	C
1	**List1**	**CEILING Formula**	**FIOOR Formula**
2	20	50	0
3	60	100	50
4	110	150	100
5	190	200	150
6	250	250	250
7	1023	1050	1000
8			
9	**CEILING Formula Syntax in cell B2:**		
10	=CEILING(A2,50)		
11			
12	**FIOOR Formula Syntax in cell C2:**		
13	=FLOOR(A2,50)		
14			

Explanation:

☞ **CEILING Formula:**

The **CEILING** function rounds the number in cell A2 up to the nearest multiple of 50.

☞ **FLOOR Formula:**

The **FLOOR** function rounds the number in A2 down to the nearest multiple of 50.

Rounding Numbers that Meet Specified Criteria

➤ **Problem:**

Rounding all the numbers in column A to zero decimal places, except for those that have "5" in the first decimal place.

➤ **Solution:**

Use the **IF**, **MOD**, and **ROUND** functions in the following formula:

=IF(MOD(A2,1)=0.5,A2,ROUND(A2,0))

	A	B	C	D
1	**Number**	**Result**		
2	6.6	7		
3	4.5	4.5		
4	3.3	3		
5	2.4	2		
6				
7	**Formula Syntax in cell B2:**			
8	=IF(MOD(A2,1)=0.5,A2,ROUND(A2,0))			
9				

Explanation:

The **MOD** function divides the number in cell A2 by 1 and returns the remainder.

If that remainder is 0.5 (the number in cell A2 has "5" in the first decimal place), the **IF** function returns the original number from A2.

Otherwise, the **IF** function returns the result of the **ROUND** function, rounding the number in cell A2 to the nearest integer (0 decimal places).

Rounding Numerical Substrings

➤ **Problem:**

Rounding the numbers in the string stored in cell A2 (12.34567<>3.4567) to 3 decimal places.

➤ **Solution:**

Use the **ROUND**, **LEFT**, **FIND**, and **MID** functions in the following formula:

=ROUND(LEFT(A2,FIND("<>",A2)-1),3)&"<>"&ROUND(MID(A2,FIND("<>",A2)+2,255),3)

	A	B	C	D	E	F
1	**Original String**	**Rounded String**				
2	12.34567<>3.4567	12.346<>3.457				
3						
4	**Formula Syntax in cell B2:**					
5	=ROUND(LEFT(A2,FIND("<>",A2)-1),3)&"<>"&ROUND(MID(A2,FIND("<>",A2)+2,255),3)					
6						

Explanation:

The **FIND** function returns the relative position (character number) of the text "<>" within the string in cell A2.

The **LEFT** function extracts all the characters in cell A2 that are to the left of that position (up to the position returned by the **FIND** function minus 1).

Thus returning the left number of the string in cell A2.

The **ROUND** function (the first one in the above formula) rounds that number to 3 decimal places.

The **MID** function extracts all the characters in cell A2 that are to right of "<>" sign (starting at the position returned by the **FIND** function plus 2).

The number 255, used as the third argument of the **MID** function, is for the maximum number of characters that Excel can hold in one string.

Thus, the **MID** function returns the right number of the string in cell A2.

The **ROUND** function (the second one in the above formula) rounds that number to 3 decimal places.

Finally, the number returned by the first **ROUND** function is joined with the text "<>" and with the number returned by the second **ROUND** function.

Hence, the formula creates a new string which incorporates the rounded version of the numbers from the original string.

Rounding a Value to Make It Divisible by a Specified Number

➢ **Problem:**

Rounding up each number in column A to the nearest value that makes it divisible by the corresponding number in column B.

➢ **Solution:**

Use the **ROUNDUP** function in the following formula:

=ROUNDUP(A2/B2,0)*B2

	A	B	C
1	**Num1**	**Num2**	**Result**
2	123.45	0.2	123.6
3	12	5	15
4	111	30	120
5	3456.78	0.01	3456.78
6			
7	**Formula Syntax in cell C2:**		
8	=ROUNDUP(A2/B2,0)*B2		
9			

Explanation:

The number stored in cell A2 is divided by the corresponding number in cell B2.

The **ROUNDUP** function rounds the result up to the nearest integer (0 decimal places).

The number returned by the **ROUNDUP** function is then multiplied by the number in cell B2.

Thus, the formula rounds the number in cell A2 up to the nearest value that makes it divisible by cell B2.

Ranking Values

Ranking a List of Numbers

> **Problem:**

Columns A & B list the names of the players who took part in the last game and their respective scores.

We want to rank all the scores, in both descending and ascending order.

> **Solution:**

❖ To rank the scores in descending order (labeling the highest score as 1), use the **RANK** function in the following formula:

=RANK(B2,$B$2:$B$9,0)

❖ To rank the scores in ascending order (labeling the lowest score as 1), use the **RANK** function in the following formula:

=RANK(B2,$B$2:$B$9,1)

	A	B	C	D
1	**Player**	**Score**	**Rank (1 for Highest Score)**	**Rank (1 for Lowest Score)**
2	Mike	12	4	5
3	John	15	3	6
4	Dan	8	5	4
5	Adam	2	8	1
6	Ron	4	6	3
7	David	20	1	8
8	Anthony	16	2	7
9	Ben	3	7	2
10				
11	**Formula Syntax in cell C2:**		**Formula Syntax in cell D2:**	
12	=RANK(B2,$B$2:$B$9,0)		=RANK(B2,$B$2:$B$9,1)	
13				

Explanation:

The **RANK** function returns the rank of the number stored in cell B2 within the list of numbers in cells B2:B9.

The third argument of the **RANK** function represents the order by which the numbers in the list are ranked.

0 or omitted represents a descending order (labeling the largest number as 1), and 1 represents an ascending order (labeling the smallest number as 1).

Ranking Numbers in a Dynamic List

> ### Problem:

Range A4:A8 contains a list of numbers that is frequently changed by the addition or removal of numbers. Consequently, the current rank of each number is constantly changing.

We want to create a formula that will automatically update the rankings in column B upon the addition or removal of numbers in column A.

> ### Solution:

Use the **RANK**, **OFFSET**, and **COUNTA** functions in the following formula:

=RANK(A4,OFFSET($A$4,0,0,COUNTA($A$4:$A$9),1))

	A	B	C	D	E	F	G	H
1	Original List:							
2								
3	Number	Rank	Formula Syntax in cell B4:					
4	500	3	=RANK(A4,OFFSET($A$4,0,0,COUNTA($A$4:$A$9),1))					
5	800	1						
6	400	4						
7	300	5						
8	600	2						
9								
10	List after adding and removing							
11								
12	Number	Rank	Formula Syntax in cell B13:					
13	500	6	=RANK(A13,OFFSET($A$13,0,0,COUNTA($A$13:$A$20),1),0)					
14	800	4						
15	400	7						
16	300	8						
17	600	5						
18	900	3						
19	1200	2						
20	1500	1						
21								

Explanation:

The **COUNTA** function returns the number of values (non-blank cells) in cells A4:A9.

The **OFFSET** function returns the reference of a range that starts at cell A4 (the first cell in the list) and includes as many rows as the number calculated by the **COUNTA** function.

That reference represents the range that currently includes numbers to rank.

As the result of the **COUNTA** function changes upon the removal or addition of numbers to and from the list, the reference returned by the **OFFSET** function will update accordingly to exclude/include only those cells in the range.

The **RANK** function returns the rank of the number stored in cell A4 within the range returned by the **OFFSET** function (labeling the largest number as 1).

Hence, the rankings in column B will be automatically updated upon the addition or removal of numbers in column A.

Calculating Commissions Based on Sales Rank

➤ **Problem:**

Columns A & B list the sales totals and IDs of five salespersons. We want to calculate each person's commission based on ranking in total sales, as per the following scheme:

Highest sales total - 15%

2nd highest total - 12%

3rd highest total - 10%

4th highest total - 8%

5th highest total - 5%

➤ **Solution:**

Use the **CHOOSE** and **RANK** functions in the following formula:

=CHOOSE(RANK(B2,$B$2:$B$6),15%,12%,10%,8%,5%)*B2

	A	B	C	D	E
1	Salesperson ID	Total Sales	Rank	Result	
2	1	$3,200	3	$320	
3	2	$1,500	4	$120	
4	3	$5,000	1	$750	
5	4	$4,300	2	$516	
6	5	$1,000	5	$50	
7					
8	Formula Syntax in cell C2:				
9	=RANK(B2,$B$2:$B$6)				
10					
11	Formula Syntax in cell D2:				
12	=CHOOSE(RANK(B2,$B$2:$B$6),15%,12%,10%,8%,5%)*B2				
13					

Explanation:

The **RANK** function returns the rank of the Sales Total in cell B2 within the totals listed in cells B2:B6 (labeling the highest total as 1).

The **CHOOSE** function returns the nth member of the list of percentages in the formula (15%,12%,10%,8%,5%) where N is the number returned by the **RANK** function.

Thus, it returns the percentage that matches the ranking of the total in cell B2, based on the scheme listed above.

Finally, the percentage returned by the **CHOOSE** function is multiplied by the total in cell B2.

The result is the commission for that total.

Random Calculation

Selecting a Set of Random Numbers, Avoiding Duplicates

➤ **Problem:**

Selecting a set of 5 random numbers between 1 and 10, without getting duplicates.

➤ **Solution:**

In Data Range (A1:C11):

Step 1: Enter **RAND** function in column A:

=RAND()

Step 2: Enter the following **RANK** formula in column B:

=RANK(A2,$A$2:$A$11)

Step 3: Enter the numbers 1-10 in column C.

In Lottery Range (A14:B19):

In column B, use the **VLOOKUP** and **ROW** functions in the following formula:

=VLOOKUP((ROW()-ROW($A$19)+1),$B$2:$C$12,2,FALSE)

As a result, 5 unique random numbers between 1 and 10 will be displayed in column B.

The numbers will change with each recalculation (press the **<F9>** key).

	A	B	C	D
1	**Random Number**	**Rank of Random Number**	**Numbers to Select**	**Formula Syntax in columns A, B**
2	0.359933926	8	1	
3	0.409537778	7	2	**In Column A:**
4	0.907417292	1	3	=RAND()
5	0.535407564	3	4	
6	0.452485543	5	5	**In Column B:**
7	0.722560415	2	6	=RANK(A2,$A$2:$A$11)
8	0.343407819	9	7	
9	0.451436817	6	8	
10	0.287480548	10	9	
11	0.462850071	4	10	
12				
13	**Lottery Range**			
14		**Numbers Selected**		
15	**Num1**	3		
16	**Num2**	6		
17	**Num3**	4		
18	**Num4**	10		
19	**Num5**	5		
20				
21		**Formula Syntax in cell B15:**		
22		=VLOOKUP((ROW()-ROW($A$15)+1),$B$1:$C$11,2,FALSE)		
23				

Adjusting Values Returned by the RAND Function

➢ **Problem:**

Retrieving two random numbers between 0 and 30, ensuring that the first number (Num1) is always greater than the second one (Num2).

➢ **Solution:**

Step 1: To retrieve Num1, use the **INT** and **RAND** functions in the following formula in cell A2:

=INT(RAND()*30)+1

This ensures an upper limit of 30 for the number generated.

Step 2: To retrieve Num2, use the **INT** and **RAND** functions in the following formula in cell B2:

=INT(RAND()*A2)

This ensures the number generated is smaller than Num1.

	A	B
1	**Num1**	**Num2**
2	27	12
3		
4	**Formula Syntax in cell A2:**	
5	=INT(RAND()*30)+1	
6		
7	**Formula Syntax in cell B2:**	
8	=INT(RAND()*A2)	
9		

Explanation:

☞ **First Formula (Num1 in cell A2):**

The **RAND** function returns a random number.

That number is multiplied by 30 and the **INT** function rounds down the result to the nearest integer.

1 is then is added to the result of the **INT** function.

Thus, the formula generates a random number between 1 and 30.

☞ **Second Formula (Num2 in cell B2):**

The **RAND** function returns a random number.

That number is multiplied by the number returned into cell A2 (Num1, calculated by the first formula) and the **INT** function rounds down the result to the nearest integer.

Thus, the formula generates a random number between 0 and Num1-1.

❖ **Note:**

Num1 and Num2 will automatically change upon recalculation (<**F9**> key).

Randomly Selecting a Value from a Range

➢ **Problem:**

Randomly selecting one of the letters from the range A1:C4.

➢ **Solution:**

Use the **INDEX** and **RANDBETWEEN** functions in the following formula:

=INDEX(A1:C4,RANDBETWEEN(1,4),RANDBETWEEN(1,3))

	A	B	C	D	E	F
1	A	E	I		**Result**	
2	B	F	J		D	
3	C	G	K			
4	D	H	L			
5						
6	**Formula Syntax in cell E2:**					
7	=INDEX(A1:C4,RANDBETWEEN(1,4),RANDBETWEEN(1,3))					
8						

Explanation:

The first **RANDBETWEEN** function returns a random number between 1 and 4 (the number of rows in range A1:C4).

The second **RANDBETWEEN** function returns a random number between 1 and 3 (the number of columns in range A1:C4).

The **INDEX** function uses those numbers as row and column numbers. The function then returns the value that is stored at the intersection of that row and column in range A1:C4.

Thus, the formula randomly selects one of the letters from range A1:C4.

❖ **Note:**

The value retrieved by the formula will automatically change upon recalculation (<**F9**> key).

 Analysis ToolPak Add-In:

The **RANDBETWEEN** function is included in the Analysis ToolPak Add-In. To install the Analysis ToolPak Add-in: Select *Tools* → *Add-Ins* → *Analysis ToolPak*, Click OK.

Random Selection from a List

➢ **Problem:**

Randomly selecting one of the values from the list in column A.

➢ **Solution:**

Use the **INDEX**, **ROUND**, **RAND**, and **COUNTA** functions in the following formula:

=INDEX(A2:A7,ROUND(RAND()*COUNTA(A2:A7),0))

❖ **Note:**

The value returned by the formula will change with each recalculation (<**F9**> key).

	A	B	C	D
1	**List1**	**Result**		
2	10	2		
3	2			
4	1			
5	3			
6	6			
7	5			
8				
9	**Formula Syntax in cell B2:**			
10	=INDEX(A2:A7,ROUND(RAND()*COUNTA(A2:A7),0))			
11				

Explanation:

The **COUNTA** function returns the number of values (non-blank cells) in List1 (cells A2:A7).

The **RAND** function returns a random number between 0 and 1.

Those two numbers are multiplied together and the result rounded to the nearest integer (0 decimal places) by the **ROUND** function.

Thus, a random number is returned that is between 0 and the number of values in List1, which represents a random position (row number) in List1.

The **INDEX** function returns the value that is stored in that random position.

Hence, it returns a random number from the list.

Miscellaneous Calculation

Creating a Dynamic Inventory List Based on Daily Sales

➢ **Problem:**

Columns A & B contain a log of all the sales from a particular day.

Each row consists of the name of an item and the quantity sold.

Columns D & E show the initial inventory for all items.

We want to create formulas in column F that will calculate the current inventory of each item. The formulas should update upon every sale added to the log.

➤ **Solution:**

Use the **SUMIF** function in the following formula:

=E2-SUMIF($A:$A,D2,$B:$B)

	A	B	C	D	E	F
1	**Item**	**Quantity Sold**		**Item**	**Initial Inventory**	**Current Inventory**
2	A	1		A	100	89
3	B	2		B	150	138
4	A	2		C	80	75
5	C	3		D	50	41
6	B	4				
7	A	2				
8	A	5			**Formula Syntax in cell F2:**	
9	B	3			=E2-SUMIF($A:$A,D2,$B:$B)	
10	C	2				
11	D	5				
12	A	1				
13	B	3				
14	D	4				
15						

Explanation:

The **SUMIF** function adds all the values in column B (Quantity Sold) for which the corresponding value in column A (Item) equals the value in cell D2.

Thus, it returns the total quantity sold for the item listed in cell D2.

That total is then subtracted from the Initial Inventory in cell E2, returning the Current Inventory of the item shown in cell D2.

Calculating Net Sale Price According to Text Criteria

> ## Problem:

Columns A & B contain the full price of various items along with a matching category.

The letter "D" in the category name indicates a 20% discount on the full price for that item.

We want to create a formula that calculates the appropriate sales price for each item.

> ## Solution:

Use the **IF, ISERROR,** and **FIND** functions in the following formula:

=IF(ISERROR(FIND("D",B2)),A2,80%*A2)

	A	B	C
1	**Full Price**	**Category**	**Price To Pay**
2	$100.00	SD	$80.00
3	$80.00	D	$64.00
4	$150.00	N	$150.00
5	$50.00	RD	$40.00
6			
7	**Formula Syntax in cell C2:**		
8	=IF(ISERROR(FIND("D",B2)),A2,80%*A2)		
9			

Explanation:

The **FIND** function returns the position (character number) of the character "D" within the text stored in cell B2. If that character does not appear in cell B2, it returns the #VALUE! error.

The **ISERROR** function determines whether or not the result of the **FIND** function is an error and returns TRUE/FALSE accordingly.

If TRUE is returned (the letter "D" does not appear in the category name in cell B2), the **IF** function returns the full price in cell A2.

Otherwise (the letter "D" appears in the category name in cell B2), it returns 80% of that price (20% discount).

Thus, it returns the appropriate sales price for the full price in cell A2, based on the category name in cell B2.

Calculating the Proportion of Characters from One String that Appears in another String

➤ **Problem:**

Calculating the percentage of the characters from each string in column B that appear within the corresponding string in column A.

➤ **Solution:**

Use the **SUM, ISNUMBER, FIND, MID, ROW, INDIRECT**, and **LEN** functions as shown in the following *Array Formula*:

{=SUM(--
ISNUMBER(FIND(MID(B2,ROW(INDIRECT("1:"&LEN(B2))),1),A2)))/LEN(B
2)}

☞ To apply *Array formula:*

Select the cell, press **<F2>** and simultaneously press **<Ctrl+Shift+Enter>**.

	A	B	C	D	E
1	**String1**	**String2**	**Result**		
2	abc	abcd	75%		
3	agce	ac	100%		
4	cba	ab	100%		
5	xyz	w	0%		
6	x	Excel	20%		
7					
8	**Array Formula Syntax in cell C2:**				
9	{=SUM(-- ISNUMBER(FIND(MID(B2,ROW(INDIRECT("1:"&LEN(B2))), 1),A2)))/LEN(B2)}				
10					

Explanation:

The **ROW** and **INDIRECT** functions are used to create an Array of all the numbers between 1 and the number representing the length of the string in cell B2 (calculated by the **LEN** function).

The **MID** function uses that Array to create a new Array consisting of all the characters in cell B2.

The **FIND** function returns an Array containing the relative positions of each character extracted by the **MID** function within the string in cell A2.

If the character is not found within that string, the function returns an error.

The **ISNUMBER** returns an Array consisting of a "1" (TRUE) for every value in that Array that is a number (i.e. represents a character found within A2), and a "0" (FALSE) for every value that is not a number.

The **SUM** function adds the values in that Array; thus returning a count of the characters in B2 that also appear within cell A2.

Finally, that count is divided by the length of cell B2 (calculated by the **LEN** function), returning the percentage of characters in cell B2 that also appear within cell A2.

Calculating the Remaining Credit after Each Purchase

➢ **Problem:**

Calculating the credit that remains after each purchase is made.

Once the credit limit (stored in cell B1) is exceeded, zero is to be returned for all further purchases.

➢ **Solution:**

Use the **MAX** and **SUM** functions in the following formula:

=MAX(0,$B$1-SUM($A$4:A4))

	A	B
1	**Credit Limit**	$150.00
2		
3	**Purchases**	**Remaining Credit**
4	$20.00	$130.00
5	$50.00	$80.00
6	$100.00	$0.00
7	$40.00	$0.00
8		
9	Formula Syntax in cell B4:	
10	=MAX(0,$B$1-SUM($A$4:A4))	
11		

Explanation:

The **SUM** function adds all the values in the range $A$4:A4, which includes all the cells in column A between the first cell ($A$4) and the cell in the current row.

Thus, it calculates a running total of all the Purchases up to the current row.

That total is then subtracted from the Credit Limit in cell B1.

The result represents the remaining credit after the purchase listed in the current row.

The **MAX** function returns the largest number in a data set that consists of zero (the first argument of the function) and the remaining credit calculated above (the second argument of the function).

Thus, it returns the remaining credit only until the credit limit is exceeded.

Once the credit limit is exceeded (the calculated remaining credit is smaller than 0), zero is returned.

Calculating Total Annual Payment Based on Cumulative Monthly Payments

➤ **Problem:**

Column A is a list of several different payments that are due each month. Column B indicates the date that each payment is no longer required.

We want to calculate the total amounts that need to be paid during each year listed in column C.

➤ **Solution:**

Use the **SUM**, **YEAR**, and **MONTH** functions in the following *Array formula*:

{=SUM((YEAR($B$2:$B$6)>C2)*12*$A$2:$A$6+(YEAR($B$2:$B$6)=C2)* MONTH($B$2:$B$6)*$A$2:$A$6)}

☞ To apply *Array formula*:

Select the cell, press **<F2>** and simultaneously press **<Ctrl+Shift+Enter>**.

	A	B	C	D
1	**Monthly Payment**	**Date**	**Year**	**Result**
2	$500	12/31/2004	2004	$21,200
3	$200	10/31/2005	2005	$14,600
4	$700	05/31/2007	2006	$11,200
5	$100	02/29/2004	2007	$3,500
6	$350	08/31/2006		
7				
8	**Array Formula Syntax in cell D2:**			
9	{=SUM((YEAR($B$2:$B$6)>C2)*12*$A$2:$A$6+(YEAR($B$2:$B$6)= C2)*MONTH($B$2:$B$6)*$A$2:$A$6)}			
10				

Explanation:

The **YEAR** function returns the year number of each date in cells B2:B6.

The following expression returns an Array consisting of "1" (TRUE) for each date in column B that has a year number greater than the one in cell C2, and "0" (FALSE) for each date that doesn't:

YEAR($B$2:$B$6)>C2

Each value in that Array, representing a date in column B, is then multiplied by the corresponding monthly payment from column A and by 12 (to calculate a yearly payment).

Thus, an Array is returned that consists of the yearly amounts matching the payments in column A that need to be paid for the entire year.

The following expression returns an Array consisting of "1" (TRUE) for each date in column B that has a year number (calculated by the **YEAR** function) equal to the one in C2, and "0" (FALSE) for each date that doesn't:

YEAR($B$2:$B$6)=C2

Each value in that Array, representing a date in column B, is then multiplied by the corresponding monthly payment from column A and by the month number of that date (returned by the **MONTH** function).

Thus, an Array is returned that consists of the cumulative amounts of the payments in column A that needs to be paid for part of the year.

The **SUM** function adds the values in both Arrays.

Thus, it calculates the total amount that needs to be paid during the year shown in cell C2.

Placing the Previous Payment Date beside Each Pay Date in a List

➤ **Problem:**

Columns A & B contain Client ID's and their recent payment dates.

We want to add the date of the previous payment from the same client next to each entry.

> ➤ **Solution:**

Use the **INDEX**, **MATCH**, **MIN**, and **IF** functions in the following *Array formula*:

{=INDEX($B$2:$B$10,MATCH(MIN(IF(((B2-$B$2:$B$10)>0)*(A2=$A$2:$A$10),(B2-$B$2:$B$10))),B2-$B$2:$B$10,0))}

Enter the formula in cell C2, and drag down the column.

If a previous payment date does not exist for a particular client, the date of the current pay date will be displayed in both columns.

☞ To apply *Array formula:*

Select the cell, press **<F2>** and simultaneously press **<Ctrl+Shift+Enter>**.

	A	B	C
1	**Client ID**	**Pay Dates**	**Previous Pay Date**
2	1	05/13/2005	01/08/2005
3	1	06/12/2005	05/13/2005
4	2	04/20/2005	02/14/2005
5	3	12/15/2004	12/15/2004
6	1	07/11/2005	06/12/2005
7	2	02/14/2005	02/14/2005
8	1	01/08/2005	01/08/2005
9	3	05/05/2005	12/15/2004
10	1	09/09/2005	07/11/2005
11			
12	**Array Formula Syntax in cell C2:**		
13	{=INDEX($B$2:$B$10,MATCH(MIN(IF(((B2-$B$2:$B$10)>0)*(A2=$A$2:$A$10),(B2-$B$2:$B$10))),B2-$B$2:$B$10,0))}		
14			

Explanation:

The following expression returns an Array of the differences between the date in cell B2 and each date in cells B2:B10:

B2-$B$2:$B$10

For each date in cells B2:B10 for which that difference is greater than 0 (eliminating the difference between the date in cell B2 and itself), and for which the corresponding ID (column A) equals the one in cell A2, the **IF** function returns the difference calculated above.

Thus, it returns an Array of the differences between the date in cell B2 and each of the pay dates corresponding to the same client ID (cell A2).

The **MIN** function returns the smallest difference in that Array, which is the difference between the date in cell B2 and the date of the previous payment made by the client in cell A2.

The **MATCH** function returns the position of that difference within the Array of differences calculated above (by the expression: B2-B2:B10).

The **INDEX** function returns the date stored in the corresponding position in column B.

Thus, it returns the date of the previous payment made by the client in cell A2.

Restricting the Automatic Recalculation of Volatile Functions

➢ **Problem:**

When using volatile functions, such as **NOW** and **RANDBETWEEN**, the results change whenever changes are made to the worksheet.

Can we restrict the automatic recalculation so that the results will change only on demand?

➢ **Solution 1:**

Use the **IF** and **RANDBETWEEN** functions as shown in the following formula in cell B2:

=IF(A2,RANDBETWEEN(2,12),B2)

Thus, NOW() will automatically recalculate only when the corresponding value in column A is TRUE.

To stop the result from changing, alter the value in column A to FALSE, and the last value calculated will remain unchanged upon recalculation.

➢ **Solution 2:**

To allow iteration calculations:

Select *Tools* → *Options*, check the *Iteration* box, and press OK.

In column A, next to your original formula, enter either TRUE to enable automatic recalculation or FALSE to disable it.

In place of your original formula in B3 (=NOW()), use the **IF** and **NOW** functions as shown in the following formula:

=IF(A3,NOW(),B3)

	A	B
1	**Allow Recalculation**	**Result**
2	FALSE	4
3	TRUE	16:16:53
4		
5	**Formula Stntax in cell B2:**	
6	=IF(A2,RANDBETWEEN(2,12),B2)	
7		
8	**Formula Stntax in cell B3:**	
9	=IF(A3,NOW(),B3)	
10		

Analysis ToolPak Add-In:

The **RANDBETWEEN** function is included in the Analysis ToolPak Add-In. To install the Analysis ToolPak Add-in: Select *Tools* → *Add-Ins* → *Analysis ToolPak*, Click OK.

Calculating the Percentage of Cells in a Range that Contain a Specified String

➢ **Problem:**

We want to create a formula that searches List1 (cells A2:A9) for each string in column B and returns the percentage of cells containing that string.

➢ **Solution:**

Use the **COUNTIF** and **COUNTA** functions in the following formula, and then apply percentage formatting to the cells:

=COUNTIF($A$2:$A$9,B2)/COUNTA($A$2:$A$9)

	A	B	C	D
1	**List1**	**String**	**Percentage**	
2	Excel	Word	13%	
3	Word	Excel	38%	
4	Excel	Access	25%	
5	Access	Outlook	13%	
6	Outlook	PowerPoint	0%	
7	Access			
8	Excel			
9	PhotoShop			
10				
11	**Formula Syntax in cell C2:**			
12	=COUNTIF($A$2:$A$9,B2)/COUNTA($A$2:$A$9)			
13				

Explanation:

The **COUNTIF** function returns the number of strings in List1 (cells A2:A9) that are identical to the string stored in cell B2.

The result is then divided by the total number of strings in List1, as calculated by the **COUNTA** function (returns the number of non-blank cells in cells A2:A9).

Thus, the formula calculates the percentage of strings in List1 that are identical to the one in cell B2.

Calculating the Absolute Difference between Each List Value and the Minimum Value in the List

> ## Problem:

For each value in List1 (column A), we want to calculate the absolute difference between it and the minimum value in the list.

> ## Solution:

Use the **ABS** and **MIN** functions in the following formula:

=ABS(MIN($A$2:$A$8)-A2)

	A	B	C
1	**List1**	**Result**	
2	-1	11	
3	-8	4	
4	-12	0	
5	-4	8	
6	-10	2	
7	-2	10	
8	-5	7	
9			
10	Formula Syntax in cell B2:		
11	=ABS(MIN($A$2:$A$8)-A2)		
12			

Explanation:

The **MIN** function returns the minimum value in List1 (cells A2:A8).

The number stored in cell A2 is then subtracted from the minimum, returning the difference between them.

The **ABS** function returns the absolute value of the result, which is the absolute difference between the number in cell A2 and the minimum value in the list.

Determining Divisibility

➤ **Problem:**

Determining whether each of the numbers listed in column A is divisible by the corresponding number in column B.

➤ **Solution:**

Use the **IF** and **MOD** functions in the following formula:

=IF(MOD(A2,B2)=0,"Divisible","Non-Divisible")

	A	B	C	D
1	**Num1**	**Num2**	**Result**	
2	20	3	Non-Divisible	
3	10	5	Divisible	
4	132	8	Non-Divisible	
5	216	6	Divisible	
6	1170	9	Divisible	
7	12345	3	Divisible	
8				
9	**Formula Syntax in cell C2:**			
10	=IF(MOD(A2,B2)=0,"Divisible","Non-Divisible")			
11				

Explanation:

The **MOD** function divides the number stored in cell A2 by the corresponding number in cell B2 and returns the remainder.

If the remainder equals 0, the **IF** function returns the text "Divisible". Otherwise, it returns "Non-Divisible".

Multiplying Values from Two Matrixes that Occupy Corresponding Addresses

➤ **Problem:**

Matrix1 (cells A3:D6) and Matrix2 (cells F3:I6) have a similar structure.

Range A8:C11 contains pairs of index values, representing columns and rows for both matrixes.

We want to create a formula to multiply the corresponding values from each matrix that are stored in the positions indicated by each pair of index values.

➤ **Solution:**

Use the **INDEX**, **OFFSET**, and **MATCH** functions in the following formula:

=INDEX(OFFSET($A$3:$D$6,1,1,3,3)*OFFSET($F$3:$I$6,1,1,3,3), MATCH(B9,$F$3:$F$6,0)-1,MATCH(A9,$A$3:$D$3,0)-1)

	A	B	C	D	E	F	G	H	I
1	Matrix1					Matrix2			
2									
3		X	Y	Z			X	Y	Z
4	1	5	6	7		1	4	5	6
5	2	8	9	10		2	7	8	9
6	3	11	12	13		3	10	11	12
7									
8	Column	Row	Result						
9	X	3	110						
10	Y	2	72						
11	Z	1	42						
12									
13	Formula Syntax in cell C9:								
14	=INDEX(OFFSET($A$3:$D$6,1,1,3,3)*OFFSET($F$3:$I$6,1,1,3,3), MATCH(B9,$F$3:$F$6,0)-1,MATCH(A9,$A$3:$D$3,0)-1)								
15									

Explanation:

The first **OFFSET** function in the above formula offsets the reference of the first cell in Matrix1 (cell A3) by 1 column and 1 row and returns an Array of the values included in a range that starts at that offset reference (cell B4) and spreads over 3 rows and 3 columns (cells B4:D6).

Thus, it returns an Array consisting of all the values in Matrix1 (without the index row and column).

Similarly, the second **OFFSET** function returns an Array consisting of all the values in Matrix2 (without the index row and column).

The two Arrays returned by the **OFFSET** functions are then multiplied, creating an Array of the products of each pair of corresponding values in Matrix1 and Matrix2. The structure of that Array is identical to the structure of Matrix1 and Matrix2.

The first **MATCH** function returns the position (row number) of the value stored in cell B9 (row index value) within cells F3:F6 (the index column of Matrix2).

The second **MATCH** function returns the position (column number) of the value stored in cell A9 (column index value) within cells A3:D3 (the index row of Matrix1).

The two numbers returned by the **MATCH** functions represent the position (row and column) of the corresponding values in Matrix1 and Matrix2 for which the product should be returned.

Finally, the **INDEX** function returns the value stored in that position within the Array of products created above.

Thus, it returns the product of the corresponding values from each matrix that are stored in the position indicated by the pair of index values in cells A9:B9.

Converting Decimal Fractions to Fractions of a Specified Number

➢ **Problem:**

Converting the decimal fractions in List1 to fractions of four, where each quarter is the equivalent of one decimal unit (tenth).

➢ **Solution 1:**

Use the **INT** function as shown in the following formula:

=INT(A2)+((A2-INT(A2))*4)/10

➢ **Solution 2:**

Use the **DOLLARFR** function as shown in the following formula:

=DOLLARFR(A2,4)

	A	B	C
1	List1	INT Formula	DOLLARFR Formula
2	0.25	0.1	0.1
3	0.75	0.3	0.3
4	2.5	2.2	2.2
5	10.625	10.25	10.25
6			
7	INT Formula Syntax in cell B2:		
8	=INT(A2)+((A2-INT(A2))*4)/10		
9			
10	DOLLARFR Formula Syntax in cell C2:		
11	=DOLLARFR(A2,4)		
12			

Explanation:

☞ **INT Formula:**

The **INT** function in the following expression rounds down the decimal fraction in cell A2 to the nearest integer.

((A2-INT(A2))*4)

The number returned by the **INT** function (the integer part of the fraction in cell A2) is then subtracted from the number in cell A2 and the result (the non-integer part of the number in cell A2) is multiplied by 4 (the fraction to which the number in cell A2 should be converted).

The result of the above expression is divided by 10 (the fraction from which the number in cell A2 should be converted) and added with the number returned by the **INT** function (the integer part of cell A2).

Thus, the decimal fraction in cell A2 is converted to fractions of four, where each quarter is the equivalent of one decimal unit (tenth).

☞ **DOLLARFR Formula:**

The **DOLLARFR** function converts the decimal number in cell A2 to a fraction of 4.

 Analysis ToolPak Add-In:

The **DOLLARFR** function is included in the Analysis ToolPak Add-In. To install the Analysis ToolPak Add-in: Select *Tools → Add-Ins → Analysis ToolPak*, Click OK.

Simplifying Formulas by Defining Names for Often-Repeated Parts

➢ **Problem:**

The following formula searches column A for each of the serial numbers listed in column C.

It then analyses the corresponding number from column B: for numbers less than or equal to 40, 10 is added; and for numbers greater than or equal to 90, 10 is subtracted. Other numbers are returned as is.

=IF(VLOOKUP($C2,$A$2:$B$5,2,FALSE)>=90,VLOOKUP($C2,$A$2:$B$5,2, FALSE)-
10,IF(VLOOKUP($C2,$A$2:$B$5,2,FALSE)<=40,VLOOKUP($C2,$A$2:$B$5, 2,FALSE)+10,VLOOKUP($C2,$A$2:$B$5,2,FALSE)))

As can be seen, the underlined **VLOOKUP** part of the formula is repeated a number of times, thus creating a long and very complicated formula.

To make our spreadsheet easier to understand, we would like to simplify the formula.

➢ **Solution:**

Step1: Define a name for the repeated part of the formula:

Select a cell → *Insert → Name → Define* → type the name "value" in the *Names in workbooks* text box → and enter the following formula in the *Refers to* box:

=VLOOKUP($C2,$A$2:$B$5,2,FALSE)

Step 2: Enter the following formula in cell D2, and copy it down the column:

=IF(value>=90,value-10,IF(value<=40,value+10,value))

	A	B	C	D	E	F
1	**Serial Num**	**Value**	**Serial Num to Look**	**Result**		
2	1	100	4	40		
3	2	80	2	80		
4	3	40	1	90		
5	4	30	3	50		
6						
7	**Formula Syntax in "Refers to" text box in the Define Name Dialog box:**					
8	=VLOOKUP($C2,$A$2:$B$5,2,FALSE)					
9						
10	**Formula Syntax in cell D2:**					
11	=IF(value>=90,value-10,IF(value<=40,value+10,value))					
12						

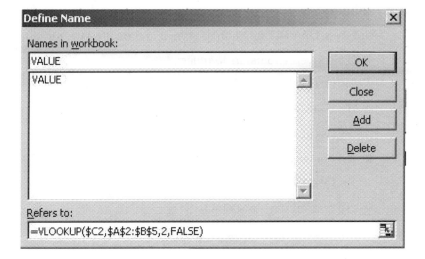

Explanation:

The **VLOOKUP** function, defined as "value" in the above formula, looks up the first column of range A2:B5 (column A) for the serial number entered in cell C2. It then returns the corresponding value from the second column (column B).

If that value is larger than or equal to 90, the **IF** function subtracts 10 from it, and returns the result.

If the value returned by **VLOOKUP** function is smaller than or equal to 40, the **IF** function adds 10 to it and returns the result.

Otherwise, it returns the exact value retrieved by the **VLOOKUP** function.

Converting Units

> ## Problem:

Column A contains 4 pairs of numbers, which represent kilometers, degrees Celsius, milligrams, and days.

We want to convert the quantities to their equivalents in miles, degrees Fahrenheit, kilograms, and seconds respectively.

> ## Solution:

Use the **CONVERT** function as shown in the following formulas:

❖ To convert kilometers to miles:

=CONVERT(A2,"km","mi")

❖ To convert Celsius to Fahrenheit:

=CONVERT(A6,"C","F")

❖ To convert milligrams to kilograms:

=CONVERT(A10,"mg","kg")

❖ To convert days to seconds:

=CONVERT(A14,"day","sec")

	A	B	C
1	**Km**	**Mile**	**Formula Syntax in Column B**
2	1.5	0.932056788	=CONVERT(A2,"km","mi")
3	12.87475	8	=CONVERT(A3,"km","mi")
4			
5	**Celsius**	**Fahrenheit**	
6	23	73.4	=CONVERT(A6,"C","F")
7	0	32	=CONVERT(A7,"C","F")
8			
9	**Mg**	**Kg**	
10	80	0.00008	=CONVERT(A10,"mg","kg")
11	50000	0.05	=CONVERT(A11,"mg","kg")
12			
13	**Day**	**Second**	
14	1	86400	=CONVERT(A14,"day","sec")
15	2.8	241920	=CONVERT(A15,"day","sec")

Analysis ToolPak Add-In:

The **CONVERT** function is included in the Analysis ToolPak Add-In. To install the Analysis ToolPak Add-in: Select *Tools → Add-Ins → Analysis ToolPak*, Click OK.

Chapter 10

Income Tax & Financial

About This Chapter

This chapter contains formulas for calculating Income Tax, various financial calculations, and Amortization Tables. It includes the following sections:

☞ **Calculating Income Tax, page 430:** This section contains an example on how to calculate income tax using a Taxable Income Brackets Table.

☞ **Financial Formulas, page 432:** This section contains various financial formulas that calculate monthly repayments of a loan, interest payments, Canadian mortgages, and more.

☞ **Amortization Tables, page 434:** This section deals with three amortization tables: regular, with a grace period, and with random loan payments.

Calculating Income Tax

Calculating Total Income Tax

> ➤ **Problem:**
>
> We want to use variable-rate Taxable Income Brackets to calculate a person's total income tax.

	A	B	C	D
1	IRS Taxable Income Brackets for 2004 (Single)			
2				
3	**Bracket**	**Tax Rate**	**Accumulated Income Tax**	**Formulas in column C**
4	$0	0%		
5	$7,150	10%	$715	=A5*B5
6	$29,050	15%	$4,000	=(A6-A5)*B6+C5
7	$70,350	25%	$14,325	=(A7-A6)*B7+C6
8	$146,750	28%	$35,717	=(A8-A7)*B8+C7
9	$319,100	33%	$92,593	=(A9-A8)*B9+C8
10	Over $319,100	35%		
11				

> ➤ **Solution:**
>
> Use the **INDEX**, **MATCH**, and **LOOKUP** functions as shown in the following formula:
>
> =INDEX(TaxTable,MATCH(C13,Bracket),3)+(INDEX(TaxTable,
>
> MATCH(C13,Bracket)+1,2))*(C13-LOOKUP(C13,Bracket))

11					
12	**Example:**				
13	**Taxable Income is:**		**$25,000**		
14	**Result - Calculated Income Tax:**		**$3,393**		
15					
16	**FORMULA in cell C14:**				
17	=INDEX(TaxTable,MATCH(C13,Bracket),3)+(INDEX(TaxTable,MATCH(C13,Bracket)+1,2))*(C13-LOOKUP(C13,Bracket))				
18					
19	**Formula Break Down and explanation:**				
20					
21	**Names Defined:**				
22	Bracket	=$A$4:$A$10			
23	TaxTable	=$A$4:$C$10			
24					
25	**FORMULAS used:**		**FORMULAS in column B (from cell B26):**		
26	Step 1:	2	=MATCH(C13,Bracket)		
27	Step 2:	$7,150	=LOOKUP(C13,Bracket)		
28	Step 3:	$17,850	=(C13-LOOKUP(C13,Bracket))		
29	Step 4:	$2,678	=B28*(INDEX(TaxTable,B26+1,2))		
30	Step 5:	$3,393	=INDEX(TaxTable,MATCH(C13,Bracket),3)+B29		
31					

Explanation to Formulas used (see rows 26:30 in the screenshot):

Step 1: Find the row number of the highest tax bracket below taxable income.

Step 2: Find the $ amount of the highest tax bracket below taxable income.

Step 3: Calculate the difference between taxable income and the highest tax bracket below taxable income.

Step 4: Calculate the tax for the difference between taxable income and the highest tax bracket below taxable income.

Step 5: Add the accumulated tax for the highest tax bracket below taxable income + the tax calculated on the in step 4.

Financial Formulas

Using Financial Functions

➢ **Problem:**

The range B2:G6 contains some of the following parameters for a number of different loans (each occupying a separate column):

Principal, interest rate, total number of payments, and monthly payment.

Based on those details, we want to calculate the following:

1. Monthly payment for the loan detailed in column B.

2. Principal payments in the first month, first year, and last year for the loan detailed in column C.

3. Total number of payments for the loan detailed in column D.

4. Interest rate for the loan detailed in column E.

5. Present value of the loan detailed in column F.

6. First month's interest payment for the loan detailed in column G.

➢ **Solution:**

Use the formulas as shown in the screenshot.

	A	B	C	D	E	F	G
1	**Functions**	**PMT**	**PPMT**	**NPER**	**RATE**	**PV**	**IPMT**
2							
3	Principal	100,000	100,000	100,000	100,000	113,922	75,000
4	Interest Rate	10%	10%	10%	83%	12%	12%
5	Total No. of Payments	36	36	36	36	48	48
6	Monthly Payment	3,227	3,227	3,227	3,227	3,000	
7	Total Years						
8	Principal First Month		-2,393				
9	Principal First Year		-33,057				
10	Principal Last Year		-33,610				
11	Interest First Month						750
12	Function Syntax	=PMT(B4/12,B5,-B3)		=NPER(D4/12,D6,-D3)		=PV(F4/12,F5,F6)*-1	
13					=RATE(E5,-E6,E3)*100		=IPMT(G4/12,1,G5/12,-G3)
14	Principal First Month		=PPMT(C4/12,1,C5,C3)				
15	Principal First Year		=PPMT(C4/12,1,C5/12,C3)				
16	Principal Last Year		=PPMT(C4/12,3,C5/12,C3)				

Calculating Canadian Mortgage Payments

➤ **Problem:**

The following **PMT** formula calculates the monthly payment for a $100,000 mortgage, repaid over a period of 20 years, at 8% annual interest:

=PMT(8%/12,12*20,100000,0,0)

As Canadian interest rates are calculated semi-annually, rather than annually, the above formula will not calculate the payments correctly.

How can we modify the above PMT formula to calculate monthly payments for Canadian mortgages?

➤ **Solution:**

With interest rate in column A, period (years) in column B, and mortgage sum in column C, use the **PMT** function as shown in the following formula:

=PMT((A2/2+1)^(2/12)-1,12*B2,C2,0,0)

	A	B	C	D
1	Interest Rate	Period (Years)	Mortgage Sum	Result
2	8.0%	20	$150,000	$1,242.54
3	4.0%	10	$50,000	$505.44
4	3.2%	15	$120,000	$839.06
5	6.8%	8	$80,000	$1,079.01
6				
7	**Formula Syntax in cell D2:**			
8	=PMT((A2/2+1)^(2/12)-1,12*B2,C2,0,0)			
9				

Amortization Tables

Creating an Amortization Schedule

➤ **Problem:**

Listed in cells C3:C5 are the principal, interest rate, and number of payments for a loan.

Range B3:B5 contains a list of the Names defined for each of the cells in cells C3:C5.

We want to create an amortization schedule based on the data in cells B3:C5.

➤ **Solution:**

Use the formulas as shown in the screenshot.

	A	B	C	D	E	F	G
1		**Data**			**Results**		**Formula Syntax**
2		Cell Name					
3	Principal	Loan	100,000	Monthly Payment		3,321	=PMT(Int/12,NumPay,-Loan)
4	Interest rate	Int	12%	Total Interest Paid		19,572	=SUM(D:D)
5	No. of payments	NumPay	36	Total Principal Paid		100,000	=SUM(E:E)
6							
7	Formula in cell B16		=IF(ROWS($B$16:B16)>NumPay,0,ROWS($B$16:B16))				
8	Formula in cell C16		=Loan				
9	Formula in cell C17		=IF(B17=0,0,G16)				
10	Formula in cell D16		=IF(B16=0,0,IPMT(Int/12,B16,NumPay,-Loan))				
11	Formula in cell E16		=IF(B16=0,0,PPMT(Int/12,B16,NumPay,-Loan))				
12	Formula in cell F16		=D16+E16				
13	Formula in cell G16		=IF(B16=0,0,Loan-SUM($E$16:E16))				
14							
15	**Return Date**	**Payment Number**	**Principal Balance at the Beginning of Month**	**Interest**	**Principal**	**Monthly Payment**	**Principal Balance End of Month**
16	1/1/2005	1	100,000	1,000	2,321	3,321	97,679
17	2/1/2005	2	97,679	977	2,345	3,321	95,334
18	3/1/2005	3	95,334	953	2,368	3,321	92,966
19	4/1/2005	4	92,966	930	2,392	3,321	90,574
20	5/1/2005	5	90,574	906	2,416	3,321	88,158
21	6/1/2005	6	88,158	882	2,440	3,321	85,719
22	7/1/2005	7	85,719	857	2,464	3,321	83,254
23	8/1/2005	8	83,254	833	2,489	3,321	80,765
24	9/1/2005	9	80,765	808	2,514	3,321	78,252
25	10/1/2005	10	78,252	783	2,539	3,321	75,713

Creating an Amortization Schedule with a Grace Period

> ➤ **Problem:**

Listed in cells C2:C5 are the principal, interest rate, number of payments, and grace period (in months) for a loan.

We want to create an amortization schedule based on the data in cells C2:C5.

> ➤ **Solution:**

Use the formulas as shown in the screenshot.

	A	B	C	D	E	F	G
1		Data				Results		Formula Syntax
2	Principal		100,000	Monthly Payment		3,227	=PMT(C3/12,C4,-C2)
3	Interest rate		10%	Total Interest Paid		21,162	=SUM(D:D)
4	No. of Payments		36	Total Principal Paid		100,000	=SUM(E:E)
5	Grace Period		7	Total grace period+ numbers of payments		42	=IF(C5=0,C4,C4+(C5-1))
6							
7	Formula in cell C14		=C2				
8	Formula in cell D14		=IF(B14<=$F$5,C14*($C$3/12),0)				
9	Formula in cell E14		=IF(B14<$C$5,0,IF(B14<=$F$5,$F$2-D14,0))				
10	Formula in cell F14		=D14+E14				
11	Formula in cell G14		=IF(B14<=$F$5,C14-E14,0)				
12							
13	Return Date	Payment Number	Principal Balance at the Beginning of Month	Interest	Principal	Monthly Payment	Principal Balance End of Month
14	1/10/2000	1	100,000.00	833.33	0.00	833.33	100,000.00
15	1/11/2000	2	100,000.00	833.33	0.00	833.33	100,000.00
16	1/12/2000	3	100,000.00	833.33	0.00	833.33	100,000.00
17	1/1/2001	4	100,000.00	833.33	0.00	833.33	100,000.00
18	1/2/2001	5	100,000.00	833.33	0.00	833.33	100,000.00
19	1/3/2001	6	100,000.00	833.33	0.00	833.33	100,000.00
20	1/4/2001	7	100,000.00	833.33	2,393.39	3,226.72	97,606.61
21	1/5/2001	8	97,606.61	813.39	2,413.33	3,226.72	95,193.28
22	1/6/2001	9	95,193.28	793.28	2,433.44	3,226.72	92,759.84
23	1/7/2001	10	92,759.84	773.00	2,453.72	3,226.72	90,306.12

Creating an Amortization Schedule for Random Loan Payments

➢ **Problem:**

Listed in cells C3:C5 is a loan's principal, the date it was received, and its interest rate.

Range B3:B5 contains a list of the Names defined for each of the cells in cells C3:C5.

Listed in cells A15:B17 are the return dates of the loan, and the principal paid on each payment.

We want to create an amortization schedule for the random payments in column A, based on the data in cells B3:C5.

➢ **Solution:**

Use the formulas as shown in the screenshot.

	A	B	C	D	E	F	G
1		**Data**			**Results**		**Formula Syntax**
2		Cell Name				Total	
3	Principal	Loan	$100,000	Total Interest paid		$424	=SUM(E15:E20)
4	Date Loan received	Date	01/15/2005	Total Principal paid		$22,076	=SUM(F15:F19)
5	Interest Rate	Int	12%				
6							
7	Formula in cell C15		=Loan				
8	Formula in cell C16		=IF(G15=0,0,G15)				
9	Formula in cell D15		=IF(B15=0,0,IF(A15<Date,"please ck return date",A15-Date))				
10	Formula in cell E15		=IF(A15<Date,0,B15*D15/365*Int)				
11	Formula in cell F15		=IF(E15=0,0,B15-E15)				
12	Formula in cell G15		=IF(E15=0,0,C15-F15)				
13							
14	**Return Date**	**Principal Paid**	**Beginning Principal Balance**	**No. of Days**	**Interest**	**Principal Return**	**Ending Principal Balance**
15	02/15/2005	$10,000	$100,000	31	$102	$9,898	$90,102
16	03/20/2005	$7,500	$90,102	64	$158	$7,342	$82,760
17	04/25/2005	$5,000	$82,760	100	$164	$4,836	$77,924
18			$77,924	0	$0	$0	$0
19			$0	0	$0	$0	$0

Appendix

List of Functions

ABS

Returns the absolute value of a number.

Function syntax: number

Appears in topic: (page number) 109, 174, 293, 419

ADDRESS

Creates a cell address as text, given specified row and column numbers.

Function syntax:
row_num,column_num,abs_num,a1,sheet_text

Appears in topic: (page number) 66, 160, 328

AND

Returns TRUE if all its arguments are TRUE; returns FALSE if one or more arguments is FALSE.

Function syntax: logical1,logical2, …

Appears in topic: (page number) 63, 73, 221, 222, 223, 224, 229

AVERAGE

Calculates the average arithmetic mean of the values in the list of arguments.

Function syntax: value1,value2,…

Appears in topic: (page number) 227, 230, 246, 363, 364, 365, 366, 368, 371, 372, 374, 377, 378, 380

CEILING

Returns number rounded up, away from zero, to the nearest multiple of significance.

Function syntax: number,significance

Appears in topic: (page number) 121, 95, 394

CELL

Returns information about the formatting, location, or contents of the upper-left cell in a reference.

Function syntax: info_type,reference

Appears in topic: (page number) 380

CHAR

Returns the character specified by a number.

Function syntax: number

Appears in topic: (page number) 56, 64, 186

CHOOSE

Uses index_num to return a value from the list of value arguments.

Function syntax: index_num,value1,value2,...

Appears in topic: (page number) 94, 98, 140, 216, 401

CODE

Returns a numeric code for the first character in a text string.

Function syntax: text

Appears in topic: (page number) 56, 64

COLUMN

Returns the column number of the given reference.

Function syntax: reference

Appears in topic: (page number) 66, 166, 177, 206, 207, 208, 261, 285, 308, 328, 355, 356, 357, 380

CONCATENATE

Joins several text strings into one text string.

Function syntax: text1,text2,...

Appears in topic: (page number) 35

CONVERT

Converts a number from one measurement system to another.

Function syntax: number,from_unit,to_unit

Appears in topic: (page number) 426

COUNT

Counts the number of cells that contain numbers and numbers within the list of arguments.

Function syntax: value1,value2, ...

Appears in topic: (page number) 123, 242, 251, 292, 366, 376

COUNTA

Counts the number of cells that are not empty and the values within the list of arguments.

Function syntax: value1,value2, ...

Appears in topic: (page number) 178, 242, 251, 252, 326, 335, 348, 399, 406, 418

COUNTBLANK

Counts empty cells in a specified range of cells.

Function syntax: range

Appears in topic: (page number) 40, 242

COUNTIF

Counts the number of cells within a range that meet the given criteria.

Function syntax: range,criteria

Appears in topic: (page number) 29, 85, 123, 143, 181, 184, 223, 242, 242, 244, 246, 247, 251, 257, 260, 264, 266, 271, 277, 278, 281, 333, 338, 340, 342, 348, 351, 371, 418

DATE

Returns the serial number that represents a particular date.

Function syntax: year,month,day

Appears in topic: (page number) 72, 74, 75, 81, 84, 85, 89, 90, 92, 99, 127, 154, 257

DATEDIF

Calculates the number of days, months, or years between two dates.

Function syntax: start_date,end_date,unit

Appears in topic: (page number) 73

DATEVALUE

Returns the serial number of the date represented by date_text

Function syntax: date_text

Appears in topic: (page number) 72

DAY

Returns the day of a date, represented by a serial number.

Function syntax: serial_number

Appears in topic: (page number) 73, 89, 92, 99, 154

DOLLARDE

Converts a dollar price expressed as a fraction into a dollar price expressed as a decimal number.

Function syntax: fractional_dollar,fraction

Appears in topic: (page number) 115, 422

EOMONTH

Returns the serial number for the last day of the month that is the indicated number of months before or after start_date.

Function syntax: start_date,months

Appears in topic: (page number) 75, 154

EXACT

Compares two text strings and returns TRUE if they are exactly the same, FALSE otherwise.

Function syntax: text1,text2

Appears in topic: (page number) 59, 186

FIND

FIND finds one text string (find_text) within another text string (within_text), and returns the number of the starting position of find_text, from the first character of within_text.

Function syntax: find_text,within_text,start_num

Appears in topic: (page number) 47, 48, 49, 50, 53, 54, 55, 61, 65, 113, 128, 299, 396, 409, 410

FLOOR

Rounds number down, toward zero, to the nearest multiple of significance.

Function syntax: number,significance

Appears in topic: (page number) 119, 120, 394

FREQUENCY

Calculates how often values occur within a range of values, and then returns a vertical array of numbers.

Function syntax: data_array,bins_array

Appears in topic: (page number) 244

HLOOKUP

Searches for a value in the top row of a table or an array of values, and then returns a value in the same column from a row you specify in the table or array.

Function syntax:
lookup_value,table_array,row_index_num,range_lookup

Appears in topic: (page number) 177

HOUR

Returns the hour of a time value.

Function syntax: serial_number

Appears in topic: (page number) 114, 120

IF

Returns one value if a condition you specify evaluates to TRUE and another value if it evaluates to FALSE.

Function syntax: logical_test,value_if_true,value_if_false

Appears in topic: (page number) 33, 35, 37, 39, 40, 51, 55, 58, 59, 63, 66, 67, 68, 79, 80, 100, 102, 109, 111, 125, 140, 149, 151, 161, 168, 174, 175, 177, 180, 189, 190, 204, 206, 207, 216, 218, 221, 224, 225, 226, 227, 229, 230, 234, 237, 238, 244, 247, 250, 258, 268, 277, 292, 299, 302, 333, 340, 342, 344, 345, 347, 348, 351, 365, 368, 371, 372, 374, 377, 378, 380, 395, 409, 414, 416, 420, 434, 435, 436

INDEX

Returns the value of a specified cell or array of cells within array.

Function syntax: array,row_num,column_num

Appears in topic: (page number) 132, 170, 170, 172, 173, 174, 177, 179, 183, 184, 186, 189, 193, 194, 195, 196, 198, 199, 200, 201, 203, 206, 207, 208, 210, 320, 324, 338, 340, 342, 344, 345, 356, 357, 405, 406, 414, 421, 430

INDIRECT

Returns the reference specified by a text string.

Function syntax: ref_text,a1

Appears in topic: (page number) 45, 160, 161, 162, 163, 164, 165, 166, 167, 264, 281, 305, 306, 308, 327, 328, 382, 410

INT

Rounds a number down to the nearest integer.

Function syntax: number

Appears in topic: (page number) 73, 97, 103, 131, 275, 352, 404, 422

IPMT

Returns the interest payment for a given period for an investment based on periodic, constant payments and a constant interest rate.

Function syntax: rate,per,nper,pv,fv,type

Appears in topic: (page number) 432, 434

ISBLANK

Returns TRUE if Value refers to an empty cell.

Function syntax: value

Appears in topic: (page number) 39, 40, 41, 231

ISERROR

Returns TRUE if Value refers to any error value #N/A, #VALUE!, #REF!, #DIV/0!, #NUM!, #NAME?, or #NULL!.

Function syntax: value

Appears in topic: (page number) 58, 227, 234, 409

ISNA

Returns TRUE if Value refers to the #N/A (value not available) error value.

Function syntax: value

Appears in topic: (page number) 204, 237, 238

ISNUMBER

Returns TRUE if Value refers to a number.

Function syntax: value

Appears in topic: (page number) 41, 45, 55, 60, 61, 224, 230, 231, 299, 302, 410

ISTEXT

Returns TRUE if Value refers to text.

Function syntax: value

Appears in topic: (page number) 27, 41, 250

LARGE

Returns the k-th largest value in a data set.

Function syntax: array,k

Appears in topic: (page number) 170, 181, 327, 332, 336, 374, 385, 387

LCM

Returns the least common multiple of integers.

Function syntax: number1,number2, ..

Appears in topic: (page number) 383

LEFT

LEFT returns the first character or characters in a text string, based on the number of characters you specify.

Function syntax: text,num_chars

Appears in topic: (page number) 45, 47, 48, 49, 50, 53, 54, 55, 60, 63, 65, 72, 100, 102, 113, 128, 252, 299, 383, 386, 396

LEN

LEN returns the number of characters in a text string.

Function syntax: text

Appears in topic: (page number) 28, 48, 51, 61, 65, 113, 248, 255, 410

LOOKUP

Returns a value from an array.

Returns a value either from a one-row or one-column range.

Function syntax: lookup_value,array

Function syntax: lookup_value,lookup_vector,result_vector

Appears in topic: (page number) 168, 430

LOWER

Converts all uppercase letters in a text string to lowercase.

Function syntax: text

Appears in topic: (page number) 59

MATCH

Returns the relative position of an item in an array that matches a specified value in a specified order.

Function syntax: lookup_value,lookup_array,match_type

Appears in topic: (page number) 98, 132, 170, 172, 173, 179, 183, 184, 186, 194, 195, 196, 198, 199, 200, 201, 203, 206, 210, 211, 281, 319, 338, 356, 414, 421, 430

MAX

Returns the largest value in a set of values.

Function syntax: number1,number2,...

Appears in topic: (page number) 45, 66, 68, 83, 84, 136, 140, 147, 172, 177, 180, 184, 190, 203, 208, 210, 383, 386, 388, 411

MID

MID returns a specific number of characters from a text string, starting at the position you specify, based on the number of characters you specify.

Function syntax: text,start_num,num_chars

Appears in topic: (page number) 34, 45, 47, 50, 53, 54, 63, 64, 72, 113, 128, 396, 410

MIN

Returns the smallest number in a set of values.

Function syntax: number1,number2, ...

Appears in topic: (page number) 79, 84, 92, 147, 174, 184, 206, 207, 280, 376, 382, 383, 414, 419

MINUTE

Returns the minutes of a time value.

Function syntax: serial_number

Appears in topic: (page number) 114, 120

MMULT

Returns the matrix product of two arrays.

Function syntax: array1,array2

Appears in topic: (page number) 268, 283, 285

MOD

Returns the remainder after number is divided by divisor.

Function syntax: number,divisor

Appears in topic: (page number) 80, 33, 36, 95, 100, 130, 131, 161, 190, 222, 233, 261, 263, 275, 352, 377, 378, 380, 395, 420

MODE

Returns the most frequently occurring, or repetitive, value in an array or range of data.

Function syntax: number1,number2, ...

Appears in topic: (page number) 175, 333

MONTH

Returns the month of a date represented by a serial number.

Function syntax: serial_number

Appears in topic: (page number) 95, 72, 73, 92, 97, 98, 99, 231, 258, 273, 322, 413

NETWORKDAYS

Returns the number of whole working days between start_date and end_date.

Function syntax: start_date,end_date,holidays

Appears in topic: (page number) 77, 130

NOW

Returns the serial number of the current date and time.

Appears in topic: (page number) 125, 416

NPER

Returns the number of periods for an investment based on periodic, constant payments and a constant interest rate.

Function syntax: rate, pmt, pv, fv, type

Appears in topic: (page number) 432

OFFSET

Returns a reference to a range that is a specified number of rows and columns from a cell or range of cells.

Function syntax: reference,rows,cols,height,width

Appears in topic: (page number) 152, 178, 192, 211, 252, 280, 292, 319, 324, 326, 328, 335, 352, 355, 399, 421

OR

Returns TRUE if any argument is TRUE; returns FALSE if all arguments are FALSE.

Function syntax: logical1,logical2,...

Appears in topic: (page number) 218, 219, 221, 222, 347

PMT

Calculates the payment for a loan based on constant payments and a constant interest rate.

Function syntax: rate,nper,pv,fv,type

Appears in topic: (page number) 432, 433, 434, 435

PPMT

Returns the payment on the principal for a given period for an investment based on periodic, constant payments and a constant interest rate.

Function syntax: rate,per,nper,pv,fv,type

Appears in topic: (page number) 432, 434

PV

Returns the present value of an investment.

Function syntax: rate,nper,pmt,fv,type

Appears in topic: (page number) 432

RAND

Returns an evenly distributed random number greater than or equal to 0 and less than 1. A new random number is returned every time the worksheet is calculated.

Appears in topic: (page number) 36, 336, 402, 404, 406

RANDBETWEEN

Returns a random number between the numbers you specify. A new random number is returned every time the worksheet is calculated.

Function syntax: bottom,top

Appears in topic: (page number) 405, 416

RANK

Returns the rank of a number in a list of numbers.

Function syntax: number,ref,order

Appears in topic: (page number) 398, 399, 401, 402

RATE

Returns the interest rate per period of an annuity.

Function syntax: nper,pmt,pv,fv,type,guess

Appears in topic: (page number) 432

REPT

Repeats text a given number of times.

Function syntax: text,number_times

Appears in topic: (page number) 177

RIGHT

RIGHT returns the last character or characters in a text string, based on the number of characters you specify.

Function syntax: text,num_chars

Appears in topic: (page number) 47, 48, 51, 60, 65, 72, 102, 273

ROUND

Rounds a number to a specified number of digits.

Function syntax: number,num_digits

Appears in topic: (page number) 122, 235, 296, 390, 391, 393, 395, 396, 406

ROUNDDOWN

Rounds a number down, toward zero.

Function syntax: number,num_digits

Appears in topic: (page number) 119

ROUNDUP

Rounds a number up, away from 0 zero.

Function syntax: number,num_digits

ROW

Returns the row number of a reference.

Function syntax: reference

SEARCH

Returns the number of the character at which a specific character or text string is first found, beginning with start_num.

Function syntax: find_text,within_text,start_num

SMALL

Returns the k-th smallest value in a data set.

Function syntax: array,k

SQRT

Returns a positive square root.

Function syntax: number

SUBSTITUTE

Substitutes new_text for old_text in a text string.

Function syntax: text,old_text,new_text,instance_num

Appears in topic: (page number) 43, 45, 49, 51, 128, 248, 255, 256, 300, 301

SUBTOTAL

Returns a subtotal in a list or database.

Function syntax: function_num,ref1,ref2,...

Appears in topic: (page number) 187, 280, 294

SUM

Adds all the numbers in a range of cells.

Function syntax: number1,number2, ...

Appears in topic: (page number) 37, 66, 106, 106, 107, 135, 140, 143, 144, 156, 225, 244, 247, 252, 258, 264, 268, 277, 285, 290, 291, 292, 293, 294, 296, 299, 300, 301, 302, 305, 308, 314, 317, 319, 322, 324, 326, 327, 328, 366, 376, 391, 410, 411, 413, 434, 435, 436

SUMIF

Adds the cells specified by a given criteria.

Function syntax: range,criteria,sum_range

Appears in topic: (page number) 250, 298, 302, 304, 306, 310, 311, 312, 315, 320, 323, 371, 407

SUMPRODUCT

Multiplies corresponding components in the given arrays, and returns the sum of those products.

Function syntax: array1,array2,array3, ...

Appears in topic: (page number) 152, 208, 231, 244, 248, 256, 258, 261, 263, 265, 269, 271, 272, 273, 275, 276, 280, 283, 286, 295, 304, 306, 313, 314, 315, 348, 350

TEXT

Converts a value to text in a specific number format.

Function syntax: value,format_text

Appears in topic: (page number) 30, 31, 32, 35, 43, 94, 115, 132, 139, 165, 383, 386

TIME

Returns the decimal number for a particular time.

Function syntax: hour,minute,second

Appears in topic: (page number) 103, 107, 120, 126, 127, 149, 151

TIMEVALUE

Returns the decimal number of the time represented by a text string.

Function syntax: time_text

Appears in topic: (page number) 102, 106

TODAY

Returns the serial number of the current date.

Appears in topic: (page number) 72, 75, 80, 99, 156

TRANSPOSE

Returns a vertical range of cells as a horizontal range, or vice versa.

Function syntax: array

Appears in topic: (page number) 268, 285, 357

TRIM

Removes all spaces from text except for single spaces between words.

Function syntax: text

Appears in topic: (page number) 49, 43, 235

TRIMMEAN

Returns the mean of the interior of a data set.

Function syntax: array,percent

Appears in topic: (page number) 369

TRUNC

Truncates a number to an integer by removing the fractional part of the number.

Function syntax: number,num_digits

Appears in topic: (page number) 139

UPPER

Converts text to uppercase.

Function syntax: text

Appears in topic: (page number) 59

VALUE

Converts a text string that represents a number to a number.

Function syntax: text

Appears in topic: (page number) 44, 51, 235, 256, 299, 300, 301

VLOOKUP

Searches for a value in the leftmost column of a table, and then returns a value in the same row from a column you specify in the table.

Function syntax:
lookup_value,table_array,col_index_num,range_lookup

Appears in topic: (page number) 34, 118, 163, 167, 201, 204, 234, 235, 237, 238, 336, 402, 424

WEEKDAY

Returns the day of the week corresponding to a date.

Function syntax: serial_number,return_type

Appears in topic: (page number) 74, 81, 90, 147, 372

WEEKNUM

Returns a number that indicates where the week falls numerically within a year.

Function syntax: serial_num,return_type

Appears in topic: (page number) 87, 88

WORKDAY

Returns a number that represents a date that is the indicated number of working days before or after a date the starting date.

Function syntax: start_date,days,holidays

Appears in topic: (page number) 78

YEAR

Returns the year corresponding to a date.

Function syntax: serial_number

Appears in topic: (page number) 72, 73, 92, 97, 99, 413

Index

We'd Like to Hear from You!

Our goal is to publish a book that will help you to get the most out of Excel, upgrade your working level, and bring to your desk the best solutions needed for everyday tasks.

I would appreciate it if you could find a few moments and share with us your thoughts, comments, suggestions, ideas, tips, areas to cover, helpful solutions that other Excel users might need, and how we can improve and make this book better.

Looking forward to hear from you,

Joseph Rubin, CPA

Author

jrubin@exceltip.com

www.exceltip.com

Joseph Rubin's Excel books:

Φ *F1 Get the Most out of Excel! The Ultimate Excel Help Tip Guide (print & e-Book)*

Φ *Financial Statements.xls (print & e-Book)*

For more information and ordering: www.exceltip.com